DENALI

NATIONAL PARK

DENALI

NATIONAL PARK

**THE COMPLETE
VISITORS GUIDE**
TO THE MOUNTAIN, WILDLIFE, AND
YEAR-ROUND OUTDOOR ACTIVITIES

BILL SHERWONIT

THE MOUNTAINEERS BOOKS

THE MOUNTAINEERS BOOKS

*is the nonprofit publishing arm of The Mountaineers,
an organization founded in 1906 and dedicated to the exploration,
preservation, and enjoyment of outdoor and wilderness areas.*

1001 SW Klickitat Way, Suite 201, Seattle, WA 98134

© 2002, 2013 by Bill Sherwonit

All rights reserved

2nd Edition, 2013. First edition published in 2002 by Alaska Northwest Books
No part of this book may be reproduced in any form, or by any electronic, mechanical,
or other means, without permission in writing from the publisher.

Distributed in the United Kingdom by Cordee, www.cordee.co.uk

Manufactured in the United States of America

Copy Editor: Jane Crosen
Cover and Book Design: Peggy Egerdahl
Cartographer: Ani Rucki
Photographer: All photographs by the author unless otherwise noted
Cover photograph: *Adult Dall sheep ram resting near Savage River Valley in Denali National
    Park and Preserve* © Michael Jones/AlaskaStock.com
Back cover photographs: *A backpacker's tent sits beside an alpine lake on Kesugi Ridge, in
    Denali State Park. A grizzly bear in Denali National Park's prepares for winter's hibernation.*
Frontispiece: *A cow moose feeds in a tundra pond near Denali Park Road between Eielson Visitor
    Center and Wonder Lake, with McKinley River and Alaska Range (including lower slopes of
    Denali rising to the right) in background.*
The following photographs are used with permission from the National Park Service,
    Denali National Park and Preserve: Pg. 55 File # 16-1.7 DENA 22185; Pg. 57 File # 28.31
    DENA 1966; Pg. 63 File # 28.11 DENA 22782; Pg. 65 File # 39.1 DENA 23554; Pg. 80 File
    # 28.20 DENA 22793; Pg. 144 File # 11.3 DENA 21677; Pg. 145 File # 6.15 DENA 21370;
    Pg. 160 File # 38.49 DENA 23510; Pg. 251 File # 2.56 DENA 21122
Pg. 78 From Denali National Park Archives. Originally published in *The Ascent of Denali* by
    Hudson Stuck (public domain).

Library of Congress Cataloging-in-Publication Data
Sherwonit, Bill, 1950-
  Denali National Park : the complete visitors guide to the mountain, wildlife, and year-
round outdoor activities / Bill Sherwonit.—Second edition.
    pages cm
  Includes bibliographical references and index.
  ISBN 978-1-59485-713-3 (ppb)
  1. Denali National Park and Preserve (Alaska)—Guidebooks.
  2. McKinley,
Mount (Alaska)—Guidebooks. I. Title.
  F912.M23S54 2013
  917.98'3—dc23
                                        2013002163
ISBN (paperback): 978-1-59485-713-3
ISBN (ebook): 978-1-59485-714-0

SUSTAINABLE
FORESTRY
INITIATIVE

Certified Chain of Custody
Promoting Sustainable Forestry
www.sfiprogram.org
SFI-01268

SFI label applies to the text stock

For my daughter, Tiaré, and for Charlie Loeb,

whose passion and dedication made this book possible.

And also for Denali, both The Mountain and the region,

a place of immense wildness in many forms.

CONTENTS

LEGEND TO MAPS

——— road

------ featured trail

③ state highway

🟦 body of water

〰 river or stream

Ⓣ trailhead/start point

┼┼┼┼ railroad

—··— park/wilderness area boundary

Ⓟ parking

♿ access

• ■ building/point of interest

][bridge

)(pass

🔺 campground

▲ summit

⛱ rest area

● city/town

▨ Original Mount McKinley National Park

▧ Denali National Park

▨ Denali State Park

▨ Denali National Preserve

LIST OF MAPS

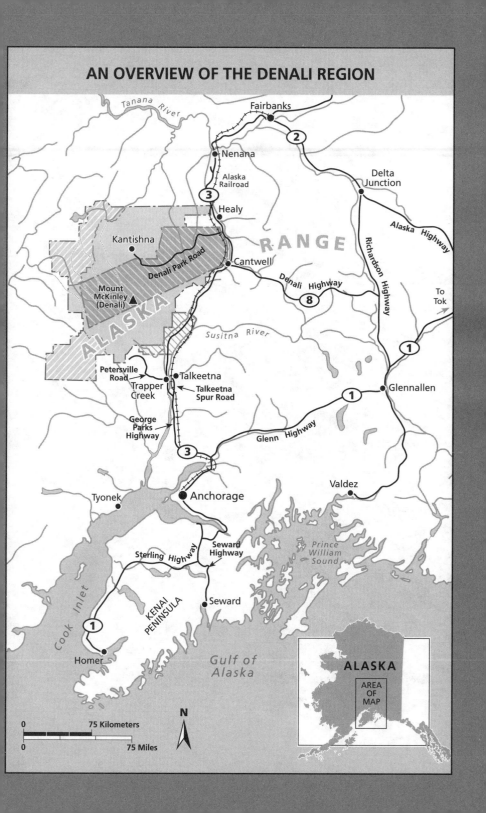

ACKNOWLEDGMENTS

I'm deeply grateful to all the people who have helped me with both editions of the Denali guidebook. Those who assisted in my Denali "field work" and other research for the first edition included Layne Adams, Chuck Bale, Phil Brease, Jane Bryant, Carrie Cahill, Clare Curtis, Wally and Jeri Cole, Chip Dennerlein, Sue Deyoe, Lisa Eckert, Kris Fister, Karl Frank, Dan Hall, Patrick Houlihan, Dave Johnston, Jeff Keay, Dennis Knuckles, Gary Koy, Justin Kramer, Carol McIntyre, Daryl Miller, Ed O'Connor, Gordon Olson, Bill Perhach, Dave Porter, Roger Robinson, Tracy Ross, Ken Stahlnecker, Jane and Mike Tranel, Vic Van Ballenberghe, Tom Walker, Bradford Washburn, and Jennifer Wolk. I'm especially indebted to Joe Van Horn and Steve Carwile, for their many conversations and insights into Denali's history and management.

Thanks to Denali National Park superintendent Steve Martin, former deputy superintendent Linda Buswell, and former chief ranger Ken Kehrer for logistical help, and to Denali Park Resorts and the Denali Outdoor Center for arranging trips by tour bus and raft, respectively. Thanks also to bus drivers Kate, Bobby, and Kevin, who enthusiastically shared their knowledge of Denali National Park and its wild residents with me and other passengers.

I used the works of many other writers and authors to learn more about Denali's human and natural history; chief among them were Thomas Ager, William Brown, Michael Collier, Sheri Forbes, Kim Heacox, Sandy Kogl, Richard Leo, Adolph Murie, Paul Matheus, Jon Nierenberg, E. C. Pielou, Charles Sheldon, and Tom Walker. Thanks to all.

I greatly appreciate the contributions made by the staff at Graphic Arts Center Publishing Company and its imprint Alaska Northwest Books, particularly those people most closely involved in the first edition project: Sara Juday, Ellen Wheat, Tricia Brown, and Susan Dupere. Project editor Kathy Matthews deserves special mention for shepherding the book to completion. Thanks also to designer Constance Bollen and copy editor Kathleen McCoy.

Special thank-yous go to Frankie Barker, who helped to get me started on this project; to Mary Anne Stewart, for her skilled editing of early drafts; and to the Alaska Natural History Association (ANHA)—now Alaska Geographic—for its support of the first edition. Above all, I am grateful to Charlie Loeb, former manager of ANHA's Denali branch, whose vision led to this book and

The immense granite faces of Mount Barrille rise precipitously above the Ruth Glacier, along the edges of the Alaska Range's Don Sheldon Amphitheater (also sometimes called the Ruth Amphitheater), an area popular with climbers and backcountry skiers.

whose countless hours of labor, while balancing other tasks, made it a reality. I applaud Charlie's passion, energy, persistence, and guidance and his hard work on the text. Spread over several years, his contributions to the book were immeasurable, and he deserves special recognition. I also applaud all those who've worked so hard to preserve Denali's wilderness spirit, from Charles Sheldon, Harry Karstens, and Adolph Murie to the present staff and park activists. And I thank Dulcy Boehle, who greatly supported my passion for writing about Denali and other wild places and who shared with me a couple of delightful journeys into Denali's wilderness during the making of the book's first edition.

For this new edition, I must first and foremost express my deep gratitude to Kate Rogers, editor in chief at The Mountaineers Books. Kate saw the value of this guidebook and recognized the need to again make it available to the public, and especially those planning trips to the Denali region or simply wishing to learn more about this special place. Thanks also to others at The Mountaineers who agreed with Kate that this is a book worth publishing.

Many thanks to those at Denali National Park who helped with this second edition, particularly Kris Fister, my main contact at the park. Others at the national park who assisted me along the way include Kirk Dietz, Maureen McLaughlin, Tom Meier, Dan Ostrowski, and Pam Sousanes. I also extend thanks to the Alaska State Parks staff who most helped with information about Denali State Park, Wayne Biessel and Justin Wholey

When it came to editing and producing this new edition, I had the good fortune to work with project editor Janet Kimball, who guided the second edition through its various stages of production; copy editor Jane Crosen; designer Peggy Egerdahl; and cartographer Ani Rucki. I extend my great appreciation to them all.

I also wish to extend my love and appreciation to three women who are central to my life: my beloved sweetheart, Helene Feiner, with whom I've shared many adventures in the Denali region and other wild places; my daughter, Tiaré Molina, who lives in far away Southern California but is always in my heart; and my dear mother, Torie Sherwonit, who was uprooted from her East Coast home to spend her final years in Anchorage.

Some of the best views of 20,320-foot Denali occur along the Parks Highway, within Denali State Park. Here, The High One and the peak's surrounding landscape are seen in late winter from the state park's Denali Viewpoint South, Milepost 135.2.

INTRODUCTION

A PLACE CALLED DENALI

In the far northwest corner of North America, in the heart of remote Alaska, is The Mountain. It is not just "a" mountain, or one of several mountains, but very clearly THE Mountain: an enormous massif of rock, ice, and snow that towers massively above its neighboring summits and river valleys. Next to The Mountain, a peak the size of Washington's Mount Rainier or California's Mount Whitney looks like a house cat next to a mountain lion.

"The Mississippi is not so truly the father of waters as McKinley is the father of mountains," wrote Hudson Stuck, leader of the first expedition to attain the 20,320-foot summit of North America's tallest mountain. Although he occasionally used the name given to The Mountain by American explorers—Mount McKinley—Stuck argued forcefully for the use of the more lyrical and more meaningful name given the peak by the Native Athabascan Indians: Denali, "The High One" (see sidebar "McKinley or Denali?"). Like Stuck and many other Alaskans, I choose the mountain name that best captures the essence of the peak and the region itself: Denali it shall be, through most of this book's pages.

Denali is the defining central point of the mountain range that stretches out from its massive base. Arcing southwest–northeast across the region, the Alaska Range's jagged and steep-walled spine harbors slow-flowing rivers of ice that sculpt the land below. Acting as a gigantic barrier, the range separates the coastal climate of Southcentral Alaska from the drier, colder climate of Interior Alaska, just as it separates the Susitna and Copper rivers, which flow south to the Gulf of Alaska, from the Yukon and Kuskokwim rivers, which drain into the Bering Sea. It partitions, too, the ancient homelands of the Ahtna and Dena'ina Athabascan Indians from those of their Interior relatives, the Koyukon, Tanana, and Upper Kuskokwim tribes. In the vicinity of Denali, only one significant gap provides easy access through the range: the Nenana River Valley, through which both the George Parks Highway (which Alaskans most often simply call the Parks Highway) and Alaska Railroad pass to connect Anchorage to Fairbanks, the state's two largest cities.

Along the range's northern edge, knife-ridged mountains descend to tundra-covered hills, and then to low-lying forest, lakes, and muskeg. To the south, the range drops steeply into forested valleys that hold murky rivers fed by enormous

A Dall sheep ram rests on a windswept ridge in Denali National Park's Outer Range.

glaciers. The land does not rise gradually to its ultimate heights so much as it ascends gently to the mountain's base and then suddenly soars upward, like a wall reaching from floor to ceiling. Denali's presence infuses the entire landscape with magic and majesty, whether the great peak is brooding behind gray clouds, bathed in the pink alpenglow of summer's midnight sun, or standing out impossibly high and crystal clear in bright daylight.

Over the years, the name Denali has come to represent much more than The Mountain. In 1917, members of the U.S. Congress established a park that encompassed the high, open valleys and mountains on the north side of the Alaska Range. Following the lead of early explorers, they named it Mount McKinley National Park. Sixty-three years later, in 1980, Congress greatly expanded Alaska's first national parkland and renamed it Denali. More than three times larger than the original park, Denali National Park and Preserve encompasses 6 million acres, an area larger than either Massachusetts or New Hampshire. Within its boundaries is the entire Denali massif, as well as all its nearby satellite peaks and the major glaciers that flow down the range's southern flanks. Also protected are the low-lying forests and hills that stretch north and west of the old park boundary to the myriad lakes and ponds that dot the landscape near Lake Minchumina, 65 miles northwest of Denali's summit.

Denali National Park and Preserve's landscape is breathtaking in its scale and wild riches. Because it is traversed by a single narrow road and has only a handful of trails and structures beyond the entrance area, travelers feel immersed in a vast wilderness, connected by only the thinnest trappings of civilization to the urban and cultivated world far away. Those who go deepest into these wildlands may, at least for a short while, leave behind any sense of that developed world.

The land possesses a liveliness that comes in part from the always-changing interplay of shadows and light, but even more so from the wanderings of the large northern animals this parkland protects. Denali National Park is one of the few places in the world where visitors can easily observe moose, caribou, Dall sheep, grizzly bears, and sometimes even wolves as they interact with each other and the many elements of their subarctic communities: other wildlife, shrubs, flowers, trees, berries, soil, rock, rivers and lakes, snow, ice, air, and weather.

Since the park's birth in 1917, a long line of rangers, managers, naturalists, and wilderness advocates have created a unique human community and culture inspired by the grandeur of Denali's wilderness, the unusual wholeness of its wild subarctic ecosystem, and the rigors of the far northern climate. In doing so, they have helped to make Denali unusual, even among national parklands. Rangers patrol the park by dog team during the long winter season, thus maintaining the traditions of early explorers, gold miners, and pioneer park rangers. In deference to the park's wilderness character, the backcountry has minimal maintained trails, and hikers and backpackers must rely on their own skills and devices to find routes, campsites, and the way home. Visitors traveling deep into the park by road must leave their personal vehicles and board a shuttle or tour bus, a practice that preserves opportunities to see wildlife and experience a primitive road that leads into the immense wilderness beyond the edge of North America's road system.

On the south side of the Alaska Range, the national park boundary hugs the base of mountains, great glaciers, and deep granite gorges. Even farther to the south are rolling hills topped by tundra and broad river valleys and expansive lowlands more densely forested than those to the north. There is another Denali here: Denali State Park. Spread across more than 325,000 acres, Denali State Park would be a large park almost anywhere else. In the vast Alaska landscape, it is dwarfed by its much larger federal neighbor. The state park is only one component of South Denali, a vast region that includes a patchwork of federal, state, local, and privately owned lands that lie in the shadow of The Mountain. Much younger than that of the national park, the vision for South Denali is still evolving, but it clearly is one that includes outstanding hiking and boating opportunities; a diverse natural wealth that ranges from rich salmon-spawning streams to glacially carved gorges; and an abundance of remarkable views that show The High One rising above lowlands and mountain neighbors.

ABOUT THIS BOOK

I've made almost-annual pilgrimages to the Denali region since the early 1980s. Every trip has been memorable, whether for wildlife encounters, the views of Denali, or backcountry adventures. But one summer was especially rewarding: In researching this book, I spent weeks in the Denali landscape, hiking and backpacking in places I'd previously only dreamed about. I've watched wildlife from tour and shuttle buses, gone on ranger-led walks and discovery hikes, rafted the Nenana River, ridden the rails north from Anchorage, shared a remote valley with grizzlies and caribou and golden eagles, been entertained by evening interpretive talks and slide shows, and overnighted in nearly all of the park's roadside campgrounds. And I've fallen even more deeply in love with this remarkable place. Now it's my privilege to share what I've learned.

During the past century, dozens of books have been written about Denali. Many have focused on the mountain and those who climb it; others have considered the park's human or natural history. Originally published in 2002, this book was the first to explore the entire "Denali experience," to provide an overview of the complete region and the adventures, encounters, sights, understanding, and inspiration that it offers to both residents and visitors. More than a decade later, now newly updated and reorganized for easier reference, it remains the only one to do so.

Unlike most guidebooks, this one emphasizes discovery over directions. It shows the possibilities that await Denali visitors, who can then choose the destinations and adventures that most appeal. It's possible, for instance, to explore parts of the Denali region by bus, car, train, bike, boat, or foot. It's possible to raft whitewater rapids, pick berries, climb the continent's highest mountain, backpack through forest and tundra, watch grizzlies dig for ground squirrels beside the park road, share a ridge top with Dall sheep, listen to howling wolves, attend sled dog demonstrations, go on ranger-guided hikes, or camp in solitude within glacially carved valleys. In winter it's possible to ski, snowshoe, or drive sled dog teams across the darkened, frozen landscape and stand beneath the dancing northern lights.

To help readers better understand Denali and prepare them for trips into the national park (and also the region that's called South Denali), this guidebook is divided into two main sections. Part I, "The Story of Denali," describes how both the landscape and the park came to be, from the geological processes shaping the region's landscape and the evolving nature of its plant and animal communities,

McKinley or Denali?

Indians living in Alaska's Interior traditionally called the great peak Deenaalee or Denali, while those on the mountain's south side called it a variety of names, including Doleyka, Traleika, or Dghelay Ka'a. The essence of the names' meaning is the same: "The High One" or "The Big Mountain."

European and American explorers had different rationales for giving the peak a name. British captain George Vancouver first spotted the mountain in 1784, but Princeton-educated prospector William A. Dickey is credited with giving it the name by which it's officially known today. Dickey's Alaska experiences were reported in the January 24, 1897, edition of a New York newspaper, *The Sun*. His most significant news was of a "great mountain...far in the interior from Cook's Inlet." Dickey estimated the mountain to rise more than 20,000 feet and named it Mount McKinley after Republican presidential candidate William McKinley of Ohio, champion of the gold standard. After its publication in *The Sun*, the name McKinley became widely used in references to the continent's tallest mountain and was soon accepted as its official name.

Over the years, many people have sought to have the mountain's name changed from McKinley to Denali. Among the most eloquent pleas was that made by Hudson Stuck, leader of the first expedition to reach The High One's summit and author of *The Ascent of Denali*. In Stuck's view, the use of the name McKinley was an affront to both the mountain and the region's Native peoples:

> There is, to the author's mind, a certain ruthless arrogance that grows more offensive to him as the years pass by, in the temper that comes to a "new" land and contemptuously ignores the native names of conspicuous natural objects, almost always appropriate and significant, and overlays them with names that are, commonly, neither the one nor the other.
>
> ...Should the reader ever be privileged...[to] see these mountains revealed as the clouds of a passing snowstorm [are] swept away, he would be overwhelmed by the majesty of the scene and at the same time deeply moved with the appropriateness of the simple native names; for simplicity is always a quality of true majesty.

Although Stuck recognized that there were many Native names for the mountain, he favored the name Denali because it was the most widely used.

More recently, the issue of officially renaming the mountain has flared several times since 1975, when the Alaska Legislature issued a joint resolution requesting Congress to change the peak and surrounding park's name from McKinley to Denali. Congress instead forged a compromise: Mount McKinley National Park became Denali National Park and Preserve in 1980, but the mountain stayed McKinley. Despite periodic appeals, that remains the great peak's name today, though a large and growing portion of Alaskans use Denali, a name that is more poetic and relevant, has a much longer history, and, as Stuck noted, was chosen by the region's original peoples.

to the human history of the region and the park—first inhabitants, explorers and prospectors, founders and park pioneers, climbers and mountaineers. Part II, "Exploring Denali," breaks the region into smaller areas and explains the experiences, natural features, and historical landmarks to be found in each. "Exploring the National Park Entrance" takes in the 15-mile-long corridor along the Denali Park Road that is a microcosm of the larger park and preserve; here is where interpretive activities and visitor facilities are concentrated, and most people seriously begin their Denali experience. "Traveling the Park Road" describes Denali's bus transportation system, highlighting outstanding opportunities for wildlife viewing, and, when the weather is right, mountain gazing. "Hiking the Backcountry" brings readers deeper into Denali's wilderness: millions of acres of wildlands untouched by human development, where hikers and backpackers follow their own instincts, make their own travel choices. "South Denali" explores the wild beauty of Denali State Park and the many Denali-viewing opportunities along the highway and railroad approaches from Anchorage to the national park. Part II ends with a chapter on the winter season and opportunities to explore the region during Denali's coldest, harshest months.

For all that guides (and guidebooks) and tours can contribute to a visitor's understanding and appreciation of a place like Denali, there is ultimately no substitute for the joyful—and often surprising—moments that come with a personal discovery, whether of an animal, a plant, or a place off the beaten path that offers some enchantment that will surely last a lifetime. Therefore readers are encouraged to use this book as a reference and starting point for more personal explorations of Denali, whether large or small.

HOW TO USE THIS BOOK

As noted earlier, this is a nontraditional guidebook in the sense that it places a premium on discovery, not directions to a specific trail, destination, or activity. Readers are encouraged to consider the many different ways they can have the "Denali experience." This experience can be enriched by learning about the region's natural and human history, told in Part I, "The Story of Denali." Of special note is Chapter 3's introduction to the park's varied ecosystems, followed by species descriptions of the mammals, birds, and common plants visitors are likely to encounter (with species checklists in Appendix A).

While Part II, "Exploring Denali" emphasizes broader discussions of the many ways to discover Denali's natural and cultural treasures, its chapters include specific park-resource information that will assist visitors in choosing what sort of experience best fits their desires, abilities, budget, and time frame. Readers are therefore encouraged to browse the "Resources and Information" at the beginning of each chapter, which expands on the general planning information provided in this opening section.

Though most of Denali is untrailed wilderness in which visitors are expected to choose their own routes and campsites, maintained hiking trails and designated campgrounds are found in Denali National Park's entrance area and within the park road corridor, as well as in Denali State Park (in South Denali). Detailed descriptions of trails and park campground facilities are in Chapters 4, 5, and 7. The following overview covers criteria used in the trail and campground listings along with information on park mileposts, buses, wildlife viewing, maps, and other topics of interest.

Maintained Hiking Trails

Where trails are described, they are listed in order of difficulty (from easy to strenuous/difficult), based on park staff's determinations. The two main criteria used to determine a trail's degree of difficulty are length and elevation gain; that is, the difference between a path's high and low points. Though subjective, the ratings are based on a reasonably fit (or "average") hiker. Trail descriptions also include information on each trail's location/route, including the type of surface; hiking distance (which may be given as either one way or round-trip, so be sure to check which it is); overall elevation change; the time it would take the average person to complete the hike; and highlights, such as wildlife-watching opportunities or panoramic views.

Park Campgrounds

Like maintained trails, developed campgrounds are available to visitors in Denali National Park's entrance area and along the park road, as well as in Denali State Park.

In the national park (Chapters 4 and 5), campgrounds are listed according to their distance from the park entrance. Visitors should note that the number of campgrounds is small (there are only six within Denali National Park's 6 million acres, all of them accessible from the park road) and plan accordingly; sites fill up quickly during the peak visitor season, June through August, and all sites must be reserved in advance (either before traveling to the park or upon arrival) at the Wilderness Access Center. Information is provided on the number of sites, when the campground is open, availability of potable water, whether recreational vehicles can be accommodated (a few sites are designated "walk-in" only), reservations and fees, emergency contacts, and campground regulations relating to fires, pets, quiet hours, cooking, and food storage.

Unlike the national park's campgrounds, those in Denali State Park (Chapter 7) are first-come, first-served. All are accessible by car, along the George Parks Highway, and they are listed in order from south to north, according to their location along the George Parks Highway. Each campground listing includes the number of sites, when they are most likely to be open, whether or not they have potable water, what facilities are present, the camping fee, and emergency contacts.

Three public-use cabins can be rented in Denali State Park, all of them at Byers Lake. Reservations must be made in advance, and, like campgrounds in the national park, they fill up fast during the summer season.

Mileposts

To assist visitors as they travel along both the George Parks Highway (the primary access through South Denali and to Denali National park entrance) and along the Denali Park Road, mileposts are provided. Along the Parks Highway, mileage is measured from Anchorage (green highway signs are placed at every mile); along the park road, mileage is measured from the park entrance. The park road's mileage signs may be difficult (or in some instances, impossible) to find, but bus drivers normally do an excellent job of keeping passengers apprised of their approximate location along the road.

Buses

The primary way most people explore Denali National Park is via the park road. And because the road is closed to most private vehicles beyond mile 15, visitors hoping to get deep into the park must use its bus system. Chapter 5 presents a detailed explanation of that system and the pros and cons of taking tour vs. shuttle buses. That chapter also describes landscape highlights and wildlife viewing opportunities along the various sections of the park road.

Backcountry Travel

For those who wish to leave developed areas behind, Chapter 6, "Hiking the Backcountry," discusses the types of hikes a backcountry explorer might consider, the primary challenges likely to be encountered, and the process backcountry travelers must follow in order to get a permit (all overnight camping in Denali National Park's backcountry requires a permit).

Winter in Denali

Though the great majority of people visit Denali between Memorial Day and Labor Day, some adventurous sorts choose to explore both the national and state parks during the "off season." Chapter 8 provides information on winter's recreational opportunities, highlights, and lodging.

Wildlife Viewing

Most people come to Denali to see The Mountain, and to observe the park's wildlife. Those who wish to know more about Denali's mammals and birds are encouraged to study Chapter 3 as well as this introductory section's "Wildlife

Viewing and Photography Guidelines" and "Safe Behavior in Bear Country." Sidebars on Denali's wildlife are scattered throughout Part II.

Maps

To give readers a better sense of Denali National Park and the South Denali region, the text is supplemented by eight maps of varying scales. An overview map presents the "big picture" of everything that's covered in this book, while other maps accompany the entrance area, park road, backcountry, and South Denali chapters. Where appropriate, these include park campgrounds, maintained trails, the park road, and other visitor facilities.

A detailed "Trails Illustrated" topographic map of Denali National Park and Preserve, at 1:225,000 scale, presents an excellent overview of the entire park; it is available from Alaska Geographic (www.alaskageographic.org) and is recommended as a resource. DeLorme's *Alaska Atlas & Gazetteer*, at 1:300,000 scale and also available from Alaska Geographic, is another good resource for exploring the area. For those seeking a backcountry experience, 15-minute USGS topos, at 1:62,500 (or 1 inch = 1 mile) scale, are even more detailed and highly recommended for route finding. They can be purchased at the park's Backcountry Information Center or the Alaska Geographic store while at Denali, or from the USGS online store (http://store.usgs.gov).

VISITING DENALI

This section includes information to help you organize and plan your trip to the Denali region (and especially the national park). Here you will find suggestions on when to go, how to get there, and where to stay. General hiking information is also provided here, along with leave-no-trace guidelines, and guidance for wildlife viewing and safe behavior in bear country. In addition to this more general information, Chapters 4 through 8 provide essential contacts and resources for transportation, hiking, camping, and other activities. Changes inevitably occur from year to year, so although this guide provides an outline of where to go for help, the most up-to-date information can be obtained by contacting Denali National Park and Denali State Park directly.

Denali National and State Park Contact Information

To learn more about the Denali experience and park facilities, visitors can contact Denali National Park or immerse themselves in the park's website:

Denali National Park and Preserve
P.O. Box 9
Denali Park, AK 99755
907-683-2294
907-683-9612 (fax)
www.nps.gov/dena

To find out more about Denali State Park, use the following contact information or see Chapter 7 for more resources:

Alaska State Parks
Mat-Su/Copper Basin Area Superintendent
HC 32, Box 6706
Wasilla, AK 99657
907-745-3975
907-745-0938 (fax)
www.alaskastateparks.org

A visitor to Denali State Park hikes on a boardwalk that protects moist, fragile woodland habitat on the Byers Lake Loop, one of the state park's most popular trails.

WHEN TO GO

The main visitor season for both Denali National Park and Denali State Park runs from late May through mid-September. This is when most visitor facilities are open, interpretive programs are presented, wildlife is most visible, temperatures are warmest, and buses travel the Denali Park Road. But the appropriate timing also depends on what a visitor desires.

March and early April are the optimal times for winter visits, as daylight hours increase and temperatures approach or rise above freezing. These months also boast some of the year's bluest skies and, therefore, optimal mountain and aurora viewing.

May and June are the prime months for climbing Denali and other Alaska Range mountains; May and June are also when flowers begin to bloom at lower elevations and migratory birds return. This time of year is special, too, because the long hours of daylight present expanded opportunities for exploration. The annual wildflower bloom—and mosquito explosion—reaches a crescendo from late June to mid-July. By the end of July or early August, berries begin to ripen. The peak for berries and the autumn color change is late August to mid-September, along with the only summertime opportunities to see the aurora.

Winter's first white usually arrives by mid- to late September (though snow is possible at any time of year, especially at higher elevations). Late summer and fall are also when resident mammals are most photogenic, as they've added winter's thick and lustrous coats of fur. There is, however, no single "best time" to see wildlife between May and September. The type and number of sightings may vary greatly from one day to the next—or even from hour to hour. In summer the chances of seeing 20,320-foot Denali are always less than 50–50: one good reason, among many, to linger a while.

Daylight Hours

Denali, like most of Alaska, is a summer land of the midnight sun. On June 21, the summer solstice, the sun remains in the sky for nearly 21 hours. And for the few remaining hours, the sun stays close enough to the horizon to keep stars and the northern lights hidden. By contrast, winter's days are cloaked in deep darkness: the sun shines less than 4.5 hours on December 21, the winter solstice. The following table summarizes daylight hours at Denali National Park's visitor center for the 21st day of each month.

DATE	SUNRISE	SUNSET	HOURS
1/21	10:06 AM	4:07 PM	6 hours, 1 minute
2/21	8:33 AM	5:46 PM	9 hours, 14 minutes
3/21	7:53 AM	8:13 PM	12 hours, 20 minutes
4/21	6:04 AM	9:44 PM	15 hours, 40 minutes
5/21	4:27 AM	11:18 PM	18 hours, 51 minutes
6/21	3:33 AM	12:22 AM	20 hours, 49 minutes
7/21	4:33 AM	12:31 AM	18 hours, 57 minutes
8/21	6:08 AM	9:50 PM	15 hours, 42 minutes
9/21	7:36 AM	8:01 PM	12 hours, 25 minutes
10/21	9:03 AM	6:18 PM	9 hours, 15 minutes
11/21	9:39 AM	3:44 PM	6 hours, 4 minutes
12/21	10:43 AM	3:04 PM	4 hours, 21 minutes

Temperature

Denali's range of temperatures, like its daylight hours, is extreme. Midsummer highs throughout much of the region average 60° to 70° Fahrenheit (16° to 21° Celsius) with extremes to 91°F (33°C), while deepest winter brings subzero weather for days on end, with lows to −54°F (−48°C). Yet the upper slopes of Alaska Range giants such as Denali and Mount Foraker may remain below freezing even in midsummer. The monthly temperatures given in the accompanying table were recorded at Denali National Park Headquarters.

Precipitation

Precipitation varies greatly throughout the Denali region. Areas north of the Alaska Range are relatively dry, despite the frequent overcast and extended periods of drizzle, while the range's south side has a wetter climate, with more abundant snowfall in winter and heavier rains in summer. The accompanying table gives month-by-month precipitation figures for Denali National Park Headquarters; numbers have been calculated combining both snowfall and rainfall.

MONTH	TEMPERATURE degrees Fahrenheit (Celsius)				PRECIPITATION inches	
	AVERAGE MAX.	AVERAGE MIN.	EXTREME MAX.	EXTREME MIN.	AVERAGE	EXTREME*
January	11 (−12)	−6 (−21)	51 (11)	−51 (−46)	0.72	4.77
February	17 (−8)	−3 (−19)	52 (11)	−54 (−48)	0.60	2.92
March	25 (−4)	1 (−17)	56 (13)	−47 (−44)	0.43	3.12
April	39 (4)	16 (−9)	67 (19)	−25 (−32)	0.44	7.15
May	53 (12)	30 (−1)	81 (27)	−14 (−26)	0.62	3.21
June	64 (18)	40 (4)	91 (33)	20 (−7)	2.19	5.83
July	67 (19)	44 (7)	88 (31)	23 (−5)	2.97	7.67
August	61 (16)	40 (4)	88 (31)	17 (−8)	2.70	6.84
September	51 (11)	31 (−1)	76 (24)	−6 (−21)	1.44	4.72
October	33 (1)	15 (−9)	69 (21)	−24 (−31)	0.95	4.26
November	18 (−8)	1 (−17)	56 (13)	−37 (−38)	0.76	5.19
December	12 (−11)	−5 (−21)	48 (9)	−52 (−47)	0.83	3.45

* "Extreme" is the highest or lowest temperature—or most precipitation—recorded at park headquarters since recordkeeping began in the 1920s. Conditions are widely variable across the park and the region.

HOW TO GET THERE

Most visitors begin their Denali trips in either Anchorage or Fairbanks. Travelers from out of state can fly into either city and then rent a vehicle, or take the train or one of several van services to Denali National Park's entrance area, at mile 237.3 of the Parks Highway. Another travel option is to drive to Alaska via the Alaska Highway. *The Milepost* is a handy reference for those doing the overland trip; this publication is available at many bookstores throughout the United States and may be ordered from Alaska Geographic, the nonprofit partner of Alaska's national parks (907-274-8440 or, from outside Alaska, 866-257-2757; www.alaskageographic.org). Another useful reference is DeLorme's *Alaska Atlas & Gazetteer,* (800-561-5105; www.delorme.com).

WHERE TO STAY

Both Denali National Park and Denali State Park maintain public campgrounds, and there are wilderness lodges at the former gold-boom town of Kantishna, within the heart of the park. In addition, there are many private campgrounds, cabins, hotels, and bed-and-breakfast-style accommodations along the Parks Highway. To learn more, visitors might contact the Greater Healy/Denali Chamber of Commerce (907-683-4636; www.denalichamber.com). Another option is to consult the *Denali Summer Times,* a visitor-oriented newspaper that's published annually and provides information on a wide array of visitor services; 800-478-8300; ncountry@gci.net; www.denali101.com.

The Milepost (see "How to Get There," immediately above) also includes some lodging options.

Detailed campground information for Denali National Park is provided in Chapters 4 and 5 and for Denali State Park in Chapter 7 (see the beginning sections of those chapters).

HIKING BASICS

Throughout the chapters of Part II, you'll find a variety of recommended hiking options, from easy day hikes in Denali National Park's entrance area and along the park road as well as in Denali State Park, to suggestions for more challenging backcountry adventures. Here are some hiking basics to keep in mind regardless of your interests and skill level.

Day Hikes

Day hikers do not need permits to enter the backcountry; they can venture into any of the national park's wilderness units as long as they stay out of designated wildlife closures. Day hikers ride the same shuttle buses that are used by nonhiking visitors to explore the park. Bus travel is the same as described in Chapter 5, "Traveling the Park Road," and it is possible to ride all the way to the turnaround destination (Toklat, Eielson, Wonder Lake, Kantishna) and get off to hike on the return trip. Steps for taking a day hike are as follows:

- Obtain shuttle bus tickets as described in Chapter 5.
- At the Backcountry Information Center, watch the park's backcountry safety video, talk with a ranger, and study maps of the park and preserve.
- Catch the shuttle bus into the park and look for good places to start your hike. If you are sure where you want to hike, mention to the bus driver the area you would like to get off. Or, when you see a likely starting point, ask the driver to let you off.
- Hike!

When you return to the road at the end of your hike, flag down a shuttle bus. Tour buses (tan buses) will not pick up day hikers. Shuttle buses (green) will not stop if they are full. You may have to wait for a few buses to find empty seats, particularly if your party is large.

Discovery Hikes

Presented daily in Denali National Park throughout the peak visitor season, these free ranger-guided backcountry hikes are moderate to strenuous and last 3 to 5 hours. Participants should expect uneven terrain, no trails, occasional dense vegetation, small stream crossings, and unpredictable weather; they also must wear sturdy hiking boots and carry raingear, food, and water. Rangers will check for required gear and will not allow inadequately equipped hikers to accompany them. Locations change daily. To participate in a Discovery Hike, do the following:

- Sign up for the hike one to two days in advance at the entrance area visitor center. Space is limited (no more than eleven people per hike), so early signups are best. Hikes may be reserved only in person, at the visitor center, and no earlier than two days in advance.
- After choosing a hike, reserve a spot on a "disco" bus at the Wilderness Access Center. Discovery buses leave the center at 8 AM; the bus ride may then last anywhere from 1 to 4 hours, depending on the hike's starting point. Take the appointed bus to meet a ranger at the starting point of the hike and then participate in a guided exploration of Denali's wilderness.
- When the hike is ended, the ranger will guide you back to the road to catch a returning bus.

Plan on taking a full day for a Discovery Hike, since return times vary widely and unpredictably.

Backpacking

Like day hikers, nearly all backpackers who travel into Denali National Park's wilderness do so from the park road. However, before starting their trips, they must first obtain the free permit required for any overnight backcountry trip. Permits are available at the entrance area's Backcountry Information Center (mile 0.75 of the park road). Permits are issued only at the park, immediately before a trip; advance reservations are not accepted. More details are included in Chapter 6, "Hiking the Backcountry."

Gear Essentials

On day hikes and overnight expeditions, all travelers should carry sufficient food, water, and gear to ensure their safety. These lists summarize the essential items to be taken on any journey into Denali's wilderness.

The Ten Essentials

1. Navigation (map and compass): Topographic maps are available at the Backcountry Information Center.
2. Sun protection (sunglasses and sunscreen)
3. Insulation (extra clothing): Prepare for cool, wet, and windy weather. Dress in layers that can be added or removed as needed. Wool, pile, fleece, or other nonabsorbent synthetic insulation is preferable to down or cotton, which don't retain warmth when wet. Blue jeans and other cotton clothes should be avoided. A warm hat and gloves or mittens are also advisable, along with sturdy raingear. Weather is unpredictable and changes rapidly. At higher elevations, snowstorms may occur at any time of year.
4. Illumination (headlamp or flashlight)
5. First-aid supplies
6. Fire (firestarter and matches/lighter)
7. Repair kit and tools (including knife): Also a signaling device such as a whistle, light or flare
8. Nutrition (extra food): Take more than you think you'll need, in case of emergency
9. Hydration (extra water)
10. Emergency shelter

Extras

- Water filter
- Sturdy hiking boots
- Toilet paper and trowel

- Insect repellent and head net or bug jacket
- Sitting pad
- Handkerchief
- Plastic bags, including one for garbage
- Trekking poles, for balance on uneven terrain or stream crossings

Leave No Trace Practices

Maintaining the wilderness spirit of Denali's backcountry depends on all hikers and backpackers minimizing their impact whether hiking trails, exploring the deep backcountry, or camping in park campgrounds. Following Leave No Trace principles and practices will help prevent damage to Denali's landscape, either visual or ecological.

- Plan ahead and prepare.
- Study the area, its regulations, and what to expect.
- Travel in small groups.
- Practice bear safety.
- Select appropriate equipment.
- Travel and camp on durable surfaces such as gravel bars whenever possible.
- In trail-less areas, disperse use.
- Avoid places where signs of human impact are beginning to show.
- Dispose of waste properly.
- Don't carry food or other items in packaging that becomes trash; repackage into reusable containers before starting travel.
- Carry out any garbage and dispose properly in a trash can.
- Use cat holes (shallow 6-inch holes) to bury human waste. Dig a small latrine hole up to 6 inches deep and at least 100 yards from the nearest water. Cover waste with soil and vegetation; double-wrap all toilet paper and used tampons in plastic, and carry out.
- Minimize soap and food residues in wastewater; avoid contaminating water sources.
- Leave what you find.
- Minimize site alterations.
- Avoid damaging live trees and plants.
- Avoid disturbing wildlife.
- If you fish, release what you catch.
- Leave natural objects and cultural artifacts.
- Minimize campfire impacts.
- Campfires are not permitted in the designated wilderness area. Use camp stoves.

- Carry extra clothing for warmth.
- Respect private land and subsistence users—Kantishna has private land inholdings and authorized subsistence hunting activities.
- Backcountry campers are also required to place their tents at least 0.5 mile (0.8 kilometer) from the park road and choose locations where tents aren't visible from either the road or other developed areas.

SAFE BEHAVIOR IN BEAR COUNTRY

Both grizzly and black bears inhabit the Denali region. The bears seen most commonly north of the Alaska Range are grizzlies, which mainly live on the open tundra; black bears are more common in South Denali's forested areas.

The chances of encountering a bear at close range are small, even in the most remote reaches of the Denali wilderness. The odds of being charged or injured are much, much smaller—as long as people know what actions to take. Only rarely in the park's recent history have bears attacked or hurt visitors. And only once, in 2012, has a hiker or backpacker been killed by a grizzly (in that instance the backpacker ignored park rules about keeping a safe distance from bears, venturing as close as 60 yards to an adult male grizzly while taking a series of photographs). Still, hikers and backpackers must always remember that bears are large predators capable of killing other large mammals. They deserve our respect and attention.

Backcountry travelers can take a number of precautions to minimize their chances of meeting bears. And if a bear is encountered, hikers and backpackers can take actions that diminish the likelihood of attack and serious injury.

Avoiding Encounters with Bears

For their own protection, as well as to keep the Denali bears healthy and wild, visitors are asked to carefully abide by the following rules (the National Park Service emphasizes that failure to do so can result in citations and fines):

Be alert at all times, in all places. Bears are active both day and night and can be found anywhere in the park. Watch for signs of their presence: tracks, scat, tundra diggings.

Avoid surprising bears. Travel where you have good visibility whenever possible. Bears may perceive you as a threat if you startle them. Never get between a sow and her cubs; grizzlies are notoriously protective of their young.

Sing, shout, talk, or make other loud noises as you walk, to warn bears of your presence. Be especially careful in dense brush, where visibility is low, and along rivers, where bears may not be able to hear you over the noise of the water, or when walking into wind (which would prevent a bear from catching your scent).

A grizzly cub stays close to its mom while traveling near the park road.

Never intentionally approach a bear. Denali's bears should live as free from human interference as possible, so give them space. It is illegal to approach within 300 yards (275 meters) of a bear.

If You Encounter a Bear

Do not run! Running may elicit a chase response from an otherwise non-aggressive bear. Bears can run faster than 30 miles per hour (50 km/hr), so you cannot outrun them. If the bear is unaware of you, detour quickly and quietly away. Give the bear plenty of room, allowing it to continue its activities undisturbed.

Back away slowly if the bear is aware of you but has not acted aggressively. Speak in a low, calm voice while waving your arms slowly above your head to identify yourself as human. Bears that stand up on their hind legs are not threatening you but are merely trying to identify you.

Should a bear approach or charge you, do not run—and do not drop your pack. Bears occasionally make bluff charges, sometimes coming within 10 feet (or even less) of a person before stopping or veering off. Dropping a pack may encourage the bear to approach people for food. Stand still until the bear moves away, then slowly back off.

If there is some way to increase your size, do it. As a rule, bigger is better with bears. With two or more people, it helps to stand side by side. In a forested area, it might be appropriate to climb a tree. But remember: Black bears and young grizzlies can climb.

If a bear makes contact with you, play dead. Curl up into a ball with your knees tucked into your stomach (the fetal position) and your hands laced around the back of your neck, and remain passive. Leave your pack on to protect your back. Once a bear feels there is no longer a threat, the attack will usually end. The one exception to this is when a bear shows predatory behavior. Instead of charging, a hunting bear will show intense interest while approaching at a walk or a run, or by circling. If you're certain that you're being treated as prey, fight back vigorously. Such instances are exceedingly rare and most often involve black bears, which are smaller animals and can, in most cases, be driven off.

Carry a gun only if you know how to use it, and only where firearms are allowed. As of February 2010, a new federal law permits visitors to carry firearms within Denali National Park and Preserve (though discharge of firearms remains illegal in Denali's wilderness core, and firearms remain banned in some park facilities). Firearms are allowed in Denali State Park.

Instead of firearms, consider bear spray as a deterrent. When used properly, bear spray can be an effective deterrent against bears, especially grizzlies. If you decide to carry it, be aware that wind, spray distance, rain, and product shelf life all influence its effectiveness. Do not let it serve as a false sense of security or as a substitute for recommended safety precautions while in bear country. Studies have shown that bear spray may actually attract grizzly bears if applied to gear, tents, or the ground around your campsite. Only use it to spray directly into a bear's face, when an attack seems imminent. Spray, like guns, should be a last resort. Because bear spray comes in aerosol cans that sometimes leak, it's best to store bear sprays in airtight containers. If traveling by air, notify the pilot; a leak could disable a pilot and lead to a crash.

For more information on human–bear encounters, read Stephen Herrero's highly acclaimed *Bear Attacks: Their Causes and Avoidance* or Dave Smith's *Backcountry Bear Basics: The Definitive Guide to Avoiding Unpleasant Encounters*. A detailed Park Service handout is available at the visitor center.

Food Storage and Garbage Disposal in Bear Country

Allowing a bear to obtain human food or garbage, even once, may cause it to seek out more human food. If the bear becomes a threat to human safety, it may be killed. For this reason, it is against the law to feed bears in Denali (or

Visitors seeking backcountry solitude camp on a gravel bar miles from the park road while exploring Denali National Park's vast and pristine wilderness.

anywhere in Alaska), either on purpose or by carelessly leaving food or garbage where bears can get to it. As visitors to this wildlife sanctuary, each of us has an obligation to respect bears and their habitat. The rules below are strictly enforced. Failure to observe them may result in citations and fines.

Campgrounds

All food, food containers, coolers, and dirty cooking utensils must be stored, whenever not in use, in a closed, hard-sided vehicle, or in campground food-storage lockers. This includes freeze-dried and canned foods, as well as beverages and odorous items such as soap, toothpaste, and sunscreen.

Keep a clean camp. Trash and garbage must be stored in the same manner as food or else deposited in a bear-resistant garbage can or Dumpster, located in park campgrounds (and at other visitor facilities). Scrape unwanted food from pots and plates into a bear-resistant garbage can. After using a Dumpster, make sure lids are closed and latched.

Never leave food, containers, or garbage unattended even for just a few minutes.

Backcountry

In most of Denali's backcountry units, all food and garbage belonging to backpackers must be stored in special bear-resistant food containers. Issued at the

Backcountry Information Center with a backcountry permit, these cylindrical canisters are designed to keep bears from obtaining food and garbage. Since the introduction of mandatory bear-resistant food-container use in 1984, there has been a 95 percent reduction in bears obtaining backpackers' food and 88 percent decrease in property damage.

All food, including freeze-dried and canned foods and beverages, as well as trash and other odorous items such as soap and sunscreen, must be kept in the bear-resistant food container when not in use.

Place tent, cooking, and food storage areas in a triangular pattern, each separated from the others by at least 100 yards (100 meters), in an area with good visibility in all directions. Cooking and storage areas should be downwind from your tent. Keep an eye out for approaching bears while eating, and be prepared to put food away in a hurry.

Avoid cooking greasy or odorous foods. Do not sleep in the same clothes you wore when cooking.

Keep a clean and tidy camp. Pack out all garbage; do not bury it. Store used toilet paper and tampons away from the campsite and pack out.

WILDLIFE VIEWING AND PHOTOGRAPHY GUIDELINES

Denali National Park has established a Code of Ethics for professional photographers and artists who travel into the park with special permits. The following guidelines are derived from that Code of Ethics; they apply to anyone who observes or photographs Denali's wildlife.

Intentional harassment or feeding of wildlife is prohibited. Visitors are cautioned not to pursue animals on foot or in vehicles despite the temptation to get a closer look. Harassment is defined as "any human action that causes unusual behavior, or significant change of behavior by an animal." While each individual encounter may seem inconsequential, the cumulative effects of repeated encounters may result in critical behavior change and affect the animal's ability to survive. Remember, the welfare of the wildlife is more important than any photograph.

- As a general rule, avoid any behaviors that might stress wildlife, which is engaged in a daily effort to find the necessary food, water, and/or shelter necessary to survive. Respect the animals and their home; remember that we humans are the visitors here.
- Be quiet when observing wildlife, to minimize disturbances to the animals.
- Park visitors may not intentionally approach, on foot or bike, within 300 yards (275 meters) of bears, or within 75 feet (23 meters, about two bus lengths) of wolves, caribou, moose, Dall sheep, and other animals, or their dens and nests. Photographers and wildlife watchers are urged

to always use sound judgment. Responsible visitors use binoculars, spotting scopes, or telephoto lenses to observe wildlife, rather than approach closely. And photographers should stop taking images and slowly back up if an animal approaches within the acceptable minimum viewing distance.

- Those driving the road in private vehicles (for instance to Teklanika Campground or within the entrance area) are requested to not interfere with other visitors' enjoyment of Denali wildlife. When buses are in the area, be as inconspicuous as possible. Avoid parking in places that congest or partially block the road. Parking or leaving any vehicle, whether attended or unattended, in a manner that interferes with the smooth flow of traffic or otherwise constitutes a hazard is prohibited. Be cognizant of the fact that visitors come to view animals in a natural setting, not with vehicles and people between themselves and wildlife.
- Visitors may not block or pursue moving animals while in vehicles or on foot.
- Visitors may not attract animals with food, calls, or scents, nor may they use blinds or alter vegetation around photographic subjects.
- Visitors may not disturb or chase bears, wolves, foxes, or other predators and scavengers from carcasses.
- Visitors may not disturb beaver dams and lodges; that includes walking or standing on the structures.
- Visitors must be aware of, and abide by, wildlife closures. Closed areas along the park road protect denning, nesting, or feeding wildlife; they vary from year to year and, in some cases, from day to day. Shuttle bus drivers will remind hikers not to enter closed areas when leaving the bus to explore the park.
- Visitors must obey the orders of park rangers, who are responsible for resource and visitor protection and often must make a judgment call when deciding what constitutes a problem situation.

A bull caribou with impressively large antlers feeds
on plants along one of the many ponds located near
the Denali Park Road in the Wonder Lake area.

PART I THE STORY OF
DENALI

Chapter 1

DENALI
PAST TO PRESENT

To fully understand the nature of Denali—from its landscape to its flora and fauna and its people—and the preservation of this special place's wilderness and culture in parklands, it's necessary to look at Denali's long and fascinating story. Divided into three parts—first a natural history, then human and park histories—that story begins with the forces that created The High One and other tall peaks, then moves through time and space to the region's habitation by changing communities of animals and plants and, eventually, people. And the story concludes with the circumstances that led to the creation of Mount McKinley National Park and its evolution into what today is one of the world's grandest wild treasures, Denali National Park and Preserve.

NATURAL HISTORY

The images of Alaska that attract people to the state are almost always natural images—grizzly bears feeding on the open tundra, eagles keeping a sharp lookout for prey, rushing rivers, blooming wildflowers, mountains capped with perpetual snow, and vast expanses of land that show no sign of human presence. The allure of experiencing a wild, undeveloped natural world is what brings people to Alaska, and to Denali.

Denali has an abundance of nature to offer. Denali, The Mountain, and its companion peaks Mount Foraker and Mount Hunter, rise above lesser mountains in the midst of the Alaska Range, arcing through Southcentral and Interior Alaska. Glaciers flow down the sides and valleys of the range's highest peaks, and rivers issue from the glacial snouts, flowing north to the Yukon River and then west to the Bering Sea or south to the Susitna River, and thence to Cook Inlet and the Gulf of Alaska. On their way, the northeastern rivers dissect the peaks of a smaller mountain range known as the Outer Range and wrap around the Kantishna Hills. On the south, the rivers are joined by streams flowing from the Talkeetna Mountains to the east.

Much of the land above 7000 feet is covered in perpetual snow and ice and is uninhabitable except to well-equipped mountaineers (and they stay only weeks or days). Below the line of permanent snow and down to approximately 2700 feet, the land is covered with tundra vegetation—small shrubs and other low-growing, durable plants that are able to persist in a harsh, windswept environment. Below 2700 feet on the north side of the Alaska Range is the taiga forest, a portion of the enormous boreal forest of northern North America that is dominated by spruce trees. On the south side of the range, where the climate is warmer and rainier, the taiga forest grades into the richer forests of Southcentral Alaska, which have a larger variety of species and a greater density of life. Wildlife adapted to each environment roams freely.

To the casual visitor, Denali appears timeless and unchanging. In reality, it is a landscape in constant motion. Some of the activity is detectable to the visitor—the flight of birds, the running caribou and rushing rivers, the fast-moving clouds, and the furious digging of a grizzly chasing a ground squirrel. It is also possible to detect other, slower movements: the sound of rocks clattering downstream in a swift-moving river, the young spruce tree growing just beyond the edge of tree line, and—more dramatically—the occasional tremor of an earthquake. Most sights, sounds, and smells raise questions that are not answerable without knowing the evolving story of the landscape. Why is Denali, The Mountain, so high? Why do nearly all the big glaciers flow south from the Alaska Range instead of north? Why are the rivers so gray and silty looking? Why is tree line so low? Why do we see bald eagles on the south side of the Alaska Range but golden eagles on the north?

The story that answers such questions spans tens of millions of years of geologic, climatic, evolutionary, and migratory history. Two essential features govern this story: first is the Denali region's location at the juncture of two enormous plates of the Earth's crust; second is the climate, determined by the region's position between 62 and 64 degrees north latitude, its center only 245 miles (395 kilometers) and 3 degrees of latitude south of the Arctic Circle. From these two basic features the natural history of Denali's landscape unfolds.

Mountains

One hundred million years ago, there was no Alaska Range or Outer Range. The Denali region's landscape was gentler and more subdued than it is today—and not nearly as far inland. Now more than 80 miles from the coast, the southern edges of present-day Denali National Park then lay along the shores of the North Pacific Ocean. Many of the rocks now high in the mountains, thousands of feet above sea level, were being deposited as mud and dirty sands in a large offshore basin bordered by low-lying coastal lands.

From that time until the present, the forces of plate tectonics have dramatically altered this gentle ancestral land.

A Giant Shake-Up

The many faults that run through the Denali region account for the dozens—and sometimes hundreds—of earthquakes that occur here each year, though most of these quakes are too small to register except on seismologists' sensitive recorders. Occasionally, however, gigantic earth tremors shake the region. In 2002, two major earthquakes occurred along the Denali fault system. On October 23, the "Nenana Mountain Event" was measured a magnitude of 6.7. Less than two weeks later, sudden slippage along the Denali fault system produced an even more spectacular magnitude 7.9 earthquake (to become known, appropriately enough, as the "Denali Fault Earthquake"). Alaska's largest inland quake in nearly 150 years had its epicenter about 40 miles southeast of Denali National Park's entrance area. Surface and subsurface ruptures occurred along a 210-mile (340-km) segment of the fault system. In places the land shifted more than 12 feet vertically; in other places there was lateral movement of nearly 30 feet. Most of this happened within the initial shaking, which seismologists determined to last about 100 seconds, but the ground continued to shift for many days afterward, accompanied by aftershocks. Despite severe shaking in the Denali region, most of the serious damage to human communities and industrial development (including the Trans-Alaska Pipeline) occurred far to the east.

A widely accepted geologic theory that explains how the Earth's surface is shaped, plate tectonics presumes that the planet's solid outer crust, along with the very top portion of the mantle—a layer of rock inside the Earth—is divided into fifteen to twenty major plates and many smaller ones. These plates more or less float on a layer of fluid, partially molten rock in the Earth's mantle. The plates come in two varieties: dense oceanic plates, which are formed when magma, hot molten rock from the Earth's interior, pours out of seafloor ridges; and continental plates, made of lighter rock types.

As oceanic plates spread away from the seafloor ridges, they eventually collide with the lighter continental plates and dive beneath them. Continental plates may also collide with each other, or move away from each other, and both types of plates can slide alongside each other. Plate boundaries, therefore, are often scenes of cataclysmic activity—of earthquakes along fault systems (deep cracks in the Earth's crust caused by plate movements), mountain building, and volcanic activity.

Most of the North American continent rides on one large tectonic plate, the North American plate, while the Pacific Ocean and small portions of the western United States ride on the Pacific plate. Along much of their adjoining boundaries, the Pacific plate is currently sliding northward along the North American plate on the order of millimeters to inches per year. But on large sections of Alaska's southern coast, the Pacific plate is diving beneath the continent. A portion of the seismically active boundary between these two plates has generally been known as the Denali fault system, which includes two major strands that run through the Denali region. The McKinley Fault runs along the southern base of the Alaska Range and crosses the mountains at Anderson Pass; movement along this fault may account for the dogleg in the Muldrow Glacier where it turns north below the pass. The Hines Creek Fault runs through the Hines Creek and Jenny Creek valleys north of the Alaska Range, just south of the park road in the entrance area.

As parts of the mainland are dragged down, others are being built up by the collision of the Pacific plate with Alaska. Much of the uplift occurs along faults between the plates, as one block of rock rides over another; some also happens as rocks are folded upward. Molten magma may ascend from the liquid mantle into the crust during these tectonic episodes. Where the magma reaches the Earth's surface, it erupts as lava and sometimes builds volcanoes. Where it cools below the ground, the molten material solidifies into solid masses of rock called plutons.

Around 56 million years ago, an upwelling of magma produced several layers of volcanic material now exposed in parts of the Alaska and Outer ranges as bright multicolored rocks of yellow, orange, lavender, purple, and brown. At about the same time and again 38 million years ago, upwellings of magma pushed up the light-colored granite plutons that today form the core of many high Alaska Range peaks, including Denali. Some geologists believe that the granite of Denali is less dense than surrounding rock, allowing it to float higher on the Earth's surface and accounting for its great height, but this theory is not universally accepted.

The uplift of the Alaska Range began during or soon after the first upwelling of magma, as the crush of plates began to lift Denali's terrain ever higher. Geologists estimate that the range has been gradually rising for the past 55 to 60 million years, though most of its uplift has occurred within the last 5 to 6 million years. This long period of uplift, combined with erosion of surrounding softer rocks, has exposed the region's plutons—collectively called the McKinley granites—as giant spires and huge Yosemite-like walls. The most recent buckling of land (within the last 6 million years) has also formed Denali's Outer Range. Though younger than the Alaska Range, much of the Outer Range consists of the oldest rocks in the Denali region, rocks that were formed 500 million years ago and were part of the coastline of ancestral Alaska. These gray-green rocks may still be seen in the park, on Outer Range mountains such as Mount Healy, Primrose Ridge, and Mount Wright.

Still considered a young mountain chain by geologic standards, the Alaska Range continues to gain height at a rate of about 1 millimeter a year. This may seem like miniscule growth to humans, but over the millennia it has elevated some rocks—deposited 100 to 140 million years ago as sediments in ocean basins—more than 18,000 feet (5500 meters) above sea level. It has also produced the highest massif in North America and one of the greatest vertical reliefs on Earth: when measured from base to top, Denali rises almost 18,000 feet above the surrounding landscape, more than nearly all Himalayan mountains, which are otherwise the tallest in the world (because they stand upon a high mountain plateau).

To complicate the matter of plate tectonics, oceanic plates like the Pacific plate sometimes carry land masses from one part of the world to another as they float along the mantle. Geologists believe that over the course of hundreds of millions of years, the Pacific plate has carried large numbers of such transplanted landmasses—called "suspect" or "exotic" terranes—thousands of miles from their original point of origin. Then, as the Pacific plate dived beneath the continent, it scraped these traveling terranes onto Alaska's southern edge. Geologists have identified several such terranes within the Denali region, intermingled in a complex and confusing mosaic of rock types. A particularly large exotic mass collided with Alaska's coast 70 million years ago or more, pushing other large pieces of land ahead as it rode over the mainland. By the time this collision ground to a stop (an estimated 55 to 65 million years ago), considerable new land had been added to Alaska's mainland. This collision and others after it eventually separated Denali from the coast even as they added to the height of the Alaska Range.

Glacial Sculpting

The forces that form rocks and build mountains are counterbalanced by others that tear rocks apart, grind mountains down, and carve out valleys and basins. In Denali, as elsewhere, water in its many forms is chief among erosive agents. The landscape in much of the accessible part of the Denali region is distinct, however, in that it has been shaped by glaciers.

Glaciers begin to form when more snow accumulates annually than melts, so they require both moisture and the cold climates of high altitude or high latitude. As snow piles up in the high mountains and is buried, pressures from the increasing weight cause the snow to recrystallize into granular ice grains. Given enough time and pressure, these crystals combine to form the dense, pale to deep blue ice of glaciers. In places this ice may be hundreds or even thousands of

In places, the Ruth Glacier's surface is deeply furrowed by crevasses. These cracks in the ice may be tens of feet wide and hundreds of feet deep.

feet thick. Pulled by gravity, glaciers slowly move downhill, usually on the order of an inch to a couple of feet per day; occasionally, however, glaciers will surge or "gallop" several miles within a period of months or even weeks. For the most part, these rivers of ice exhibit plastic behavior and flow around obstacles. But when the terrain is steep or corners too tight, they will crack and break, forming fractures called crevasses. Breaks in the ice may be anywhere from an inch to several tens of feet wide and several hundred feet deep. Many are narrow at the surface but broaden into huge chambers below. From winter through early summer, such crevasses may be hidden by heavy snowfall, slowly appearing as summer's warmth melts the overlying snow.

When snow accumulation exceeds melting, a glacier advances. When melting is greater, the glacier recedes. When a glacier does move forward, it gouges and grinds the rock through which it passes. High in the mountains, as it begins its passage through the landscape, the glacier may sculpt knife-edged ridges, called aretes. Then, while flowing downward, it carves the channels and basins through which it moves into rounded, U-shaped forms characteristic of the large valleys north of the Alaska Range and crossed by the Denali Park Road. (Stream erosion, by contrast, forms V-shaped valleys like those that penetrate the Outer Range north of the park road.)

Rock chunks big and small, from boulder to silt sized, are incorporated into the glacier as it flows through the landscape. Some are carried along the side, some are pushed in front, and many are carried on the surface. In some instances—the Muldrow Glacier on the Alaska Range's north side is a prime example—the glacier's icy surface may eventually be covered with several feet of rock and soil, allowing hardy plants like alder and willow to take root. Rock deposits pushed ahead by a glacier's advance and left at its snout are known as terminal moraines; those deposited along its flanks, as lateral moraines. Visible from the park road as it approaches its end near Wonder Lake, the Muldrow Glacier shows both. When two or more glaciers merge, their lateral moraines join to become medial moraines, which appear as dark streaks on the glacier's surface. Depending on the extent of a glacier's advance—in both time and distance—morainal deposits may measure a few feet to several hundred feet high. Some of the medial moraines on Denali's largest glaciers have been forming for thousands of years; they can be seen from both the Parks Highway and Denali Park Road.

Glacial Leftovers: Erratics and Kettle Ponds

Glaciers also drop debris as they retreat across the landscape, including boulders that may be larger than a house. Called "erratics," such huge rocks are scattered across lowland areas north and south of the Alaska Range. Many of the largest are visible from the Denali Park Road near Polychrome Pass. Receding glaciers may also leave large blocks of ice behind; as the ice melts, it forms depressions in the ground that eventually fill to form "kettle ponds." Such ponds dot the landscape in the Polychrome Pass and Wonder Lake areas of the park.

Denali's Glaciers

Most of what we today call the Denali region was periodically covered by glaciers during the Pleistocene Ice Age, 2 million to 9500 years ago. The Alaska
Range—still in the midst of its uplift—and lands to the south were blanketed
in ice for nearly all of that period, while the Outer Range and lowlands farther
north remained ice-free because of a drier climate. Geologists have identified
between five and seven major glacial advances and retreats during the Ice Age.
The earliest and most extensive glaciation took place about 2 million years ago;
the most recent episode occurred as a series of smaller glacial advances between
25,000 and 9500 years ago.

Climate Change and Denali

Denali, like arctic and subarctic regions around the world, has proven to
be especially susceptible to climate change. Since the mid-1900s, average temperatures here and throughout much of Alaska have risen 4° to
7° Fahrenheit (2° to 4° Celsius). The local effects of global warming have
included reduced snowfall in late winter and spring, earlier snowmelt and
"green-up" of the park's landscape, thawing permafrost, receding glaciers, shifts in the plant communities (for instance, forests encroaching
on tundra), and changed breeding times for some of the region's wildlife.
Not only will such changes directly affect the animals, plants, and landscape, but they are also likely to change the nature of the visitor experience; for instance, as forested areas expand into tundra, people traveling
the park road will have less open ground to scan when looking for the
park's wildlife.

Because Denali presents a special opportunity to study a large, intact,
and naturally functioning ecosystem, scientists have begun a number
of climate-change studies to determine how global warming is affecting
various elements of that ecosystem. In monitoring both short- and long-
term changes, they are tracking such things as shifts in snow cover;
the retreat of glaciers; the advance of the tree line into open tundra; the
melting of permafrost and resulting "thermokarst" terrain (slumping and
depressions that result from the melting of subsurface ice); the shrinking
of lakes and ponds; changes in the landscape's phenology (the timing of
seasonal changes, such as the start of green-up, maximum "greenness"
of the landscape, the shift to fall colors, first snowfall, and freeze-up);
changes in the distribution of wildlife and their use of different habitats, and
predator-prey relationships; and the frequency and intensity of wildfires.

Nowadays we are between glacial episodes. Most of Denali's glaciers, like those elsewhere in Alaska, are in the process of retreat, accelerated in recent times by global warming. In 2007, researchers reported that all the Denali glaciers they studied were retreating, at an average rate of about 66 feet (20 m) annually; many are also thinning dramatically. Still, there is plenty of frozen water to be found: about 17 percent of Denali National Park and Preserve's 6 million acres is covered by ice or perennial snow. Glaciers flow both north and south out of the Alaska Range, some of them 40 to 50 miles long, and hundreds of smaller glaciers dot its higher slopes. With the notable exception of the Muldrow Glacier, all of the large glaciers are found on the range's south side. This is because moisture-rich coastal storms blow inland from the Gulf of Alaska on the south, hit the high mountains, and release their moisture as year-round snows. Blocked by the mountain barrier, Denali's north side, like the rest of Interior Alaska, has drier weather, and therefore less snow to accumulate and begin the transformation into glacial ice.

Denali's glaciers feed large, braided streams, whose milky- to gravy-colored waters are filled with huge quantities of glacier-ground sediment. Normally this sediment is fine grained and flourlike, but at flood stage the rivers may carry sand, cobbles, and boulder-sized rocks. These glacially fed streams rarely run bank-to-bank, but migrate back and forth across their wide, ice-carved, U-shaped valleys as they fill in old channels with gravel deposits and scour new channels nearby.

Ancient Plant and Animal Communities

Even as tectonic forces shaped the landforms of today's Denali region, varying assemblies of plants and animals have inhabited the landscape for tens of millions of years, the nature of those communities shaped and reshaped both by evolution and ever-changing climatic conditions.

Until recently, little was known about the region's flora and fauna prior to the Pleistocene Ice Age. That changed in June 2005. While on a field trip, geology graduate student Susi Tomsich discovered the track of a three-toed dinosaur near Igloo Creek, some 35 miles from the park entrance. The track was later linked to what scientists call a theropod, a meat-eating dinosaur that walked on its hind legs and roamed the ancient Denali landscape during the Late Cretaceous Period, 65 to 70 million years ago.

In the years since then, scientists have discovered dozens of other dinosaur tracks at Denali, left by several different species, including four different-sized theropods, a hadrosaur (duck-billed plant eater) and its young, and ceratopsians (beaked plant eaters). Other Cretaceous fossil finds include worm burrows, fish fins, bird tracks, snail traces, possible claw marks, and even some suspected small-mammal tracks. Fossil plants have included ferns, horsetails, the leaves and stems of deciduous shrubs or trees, and spruce cones. This remarkable fossil record suggests the landscape ranged from riparian and floodplain habitats to drier upland areas. Researchers still have a long way to go before they can more fully reconstruct the ancient ecosystems, but they say that Denali's fossil-rich areas are a national treasure, perhaps second in importance only to Dinosaur National Monument among the nation's parklands.

Before the Denali dinosaur discoveries, the region's oldest fossils had been found near the town of Healy (outside Denali National Park's northeast corner), in rocks dated back to what's called the Miocene Epoch, about 20 million years ago. That fossil assemblage suggests a woodland ecosystem, much like the mixed hardwood forests of today's northern Great Lakes region. Trees included spruce, pine, hemlock, fir, redwood, elm, oak, birch, maple, and willow. For such species to grow, temperatures must have been 12 to 18 degrees warmer than those of today, with warmer summers and milder winters. The climate eventually turned against these species, however, and extended periods of cooler temperatures killed them off.

Ice Age Steppe

Despite the recent Cretaceous fossil finds, little remains known about Denali's ancient plants and animals until about 2 million years ago, at the start of the Pleistocene Ice Age. The Ice Age's fluctuating climates—periods of extreme cold mixed with warmer interglacial spans—dramatically influenced plant communities. Some fossil evidence suggests that treeless plant communities similar to today's tundra began to develop in northern Alaska with the Ice Age cooling. Tundra has a uniform matlike appearance from a distance, almost like a lawn, but on closer look it is a complex community of wildflowers, grasses, tussock-forming sedges, woody plants, mosses, and lichens. There is also evidence that forests vanished from Alaska during the most severe glacial periods. If any trees did survive, they were probably small and scarce communities of the hardiest species: balsam poplar, aspen, and shrub willow.

The Ice Age produced two phenomena that influenced the Denali landscape north of the Alaska Range: First, even during the periods of greatest glacial cover, about half of Alaska remained ice-free. Scientists reason that the Alaska Range—now far along in its uplift—and other mountains prevented large amounts of moisture from reaching Interior Alaska and Denali's northern lowlands, much as they do today. With little snowfall, there was no way for glaciers to form. So while most of present-day Denali remained ice-covered throughout the Pleistocene, the Outer Range and much of the region's northern lowlands stayed ice-free.

Second, because so much of the world's water was locked up in ice during the major glaciations, sea level dropped hundreds of feet and a land bridge connecting northern Alaska and Siberia was periodically exposed during the Ice Age. Consequently, unglaciated Interior lands stretched from Canada's present-day Yukon Territory through Alaska and west across the Bering Land Bridge to Siberia. Scientists call this large, ice-free landmass Beringia.

Fossil pollens suggest that plant communities of sage, aster, sedge, wildflowers, willow shrubs, and berry plants extended across parts of Beringia, including portions of the Denali region north of the Alaska Range. Some of this vegetation likely resembled present-day tundra communities. On the other hand, from the evidence of fossil records that show an abundance of large grazing mammals, some paleontologists argue that much of the Beringian landscape—and northern Denali—must have been covered by high-quality grasses and sedges not typical of tundra plant communities.

If not tundra, then what? The Interior dryness that prevented glaciers from forming north of the Alaska Range may also have produced a cold, arid, and treeless grassland called a steppe. Extending through the northern Denali region and other parts of Beringia during peak glacial times, these steppe environments were characterized by abundant grasses and sedges and lesser amounts of willows, sagebrush, and forbs. Intermixed with these steppes were tundra-like plant communities and patches of bare, silty soils.

Although it was cold, dry, and treeless, the Ice Age steppe supported a remarkably diverse collection of large grazing mammals and carnivores. Paleontologists call this assemblage of Ice Age mammals the Mammoth Fauna, in honor of the steppe's most famous inhabitant, the woolly mammoth (a large, hairy elephant that stood up to 14 feet tall at the shoulder and had curled tusks up to 13 feet long). The ecosystem these animals inhabited is similarly called the Mammoth Steppe. In all, scientists have identified nearly fifty Beringian mammal species. By comparison, thirty-nine species of mammals inhabit Denali National Park today.

Fossil evidence suggests that the steppe's three most abundant large mammals were the mammoth, bison, and horse. Other Mammoth Steppe residents included musk oxen, camels, antelope, caribou, Dall sheep, moose, lemmings, voles, hares, badgers, ferrets, and arctic ground squirrels. Preying on those grazers, browsers, and smaller mammals were a wide variety of carnivores: lions, saber-toothed cats, giant short-faced bears, grizzlies, lynx, wolverines, and wolves.

Forest and Tundra

During the Ice Age's occasional warmings and glacial retreats, trees recolonized parts of Alaska and provided habitat for woodland creatures: mastodons (another type of hairy elephant), giant ground sloths, giant beavers, elk, and black bears.

*Though it appears to be a uniform carpet from a distance, much of Denali's
subarctic tundra is diverse and hummocky in nature.*

About 9500 years ago, temperatures began warming again, and glaciers
began a slow retreat. In response, new plant communities moved into northern
Denali's treeless plains. First shrub-birch tundra, then willow thickets and poplar and aspen groves replaced the steppe. Eventually, white and black spruce
also returned to Interior Alaska, spreading there from northwestern Canada. At
the same time, the retreat of glaciers on the Alaska Range's south side enabled
forests to gradually move north from the Lower 48, across southern Alaska, and
into the South Denali region. Both north and south of the Alaska Range, tundra
plant communities found niches where trees could not survive, as in high alpine
environments.

The most recent climate change also meant the demise of many large mammals that once inhabited Alaska's steppe. Without extensive grasslands to support them, most of the grazers died out. And as herbivore numbers dwindled, so
too did the number and types of carnivores. Species like the saber-toothed cat,
lions, and short-faced bears were too specialized or strict in their all-meat diet
to survive. Predators like wolves, grizzlies, and black bears that could subsist
on other foods—small mammals, berries, roots, insects—and adapt to changing
environments were the ones that survived this great wave of extinctions. Across
North America, between thirty-five and forty large mammal species died out as
the climate warmed.

As the steppe disappeared and glaciers retreated into the uppermost reaches
of the Alaska Range, mammals and birds that were adapted to tundra and

A Possible Beringian Scene

"Imagine the Mammoth Steppe on a cool, breezy midsummer day. A few bison might be lying on a green hillside, ruminating cud and scanning for predators stalking through sparse short grasses. Below in broad valleys where most of the grasses were already brown, herds of anxious little horses might be grazing and on the move, an occasional head popping up to make sure the two lions in the draw have not crept any closer. If the lions moved in, the fleet ponies would be off in an instant, running to safety before taking up their grazing again without much more than a nervous blink. Across the valley, an old mammoth matriarch would be leading her sisters, aunts, and their young on a twice-daily trek to the watering hole. Cacophonous trumpeting from their suitors and brothers would rattle the evening's approach in long shadows under the still-bright midnight sun."

— *Paleobiologist Paul Matheus*

forest environments repopulated the Denali region. Slowly, the living landscape evolved into the plant and animal communities that visitors see today. Scientists have traditionally deemed the retreat of the ice 9500 years ago as the end of the Ice Age and the Pleistocene Epoch. However, more recently some experts have suggested that the Earth is merely in the midst of another interglacial period within a longer Ice Age that is not yet over. Someday, the glaciers and the steppe may return, they argue, though this seems less and less likely as global warming accelerates.

A Moving Picture

Visitors to Denali receive a snapshot in time of its grizzlies, taiga, and enormous mountains. Knowledge of the region's ancient past and some understanding of the natural processes that led to today's wilderness ecosystems adds motion to this snapshot. With an animated view to the distant past, it is remarkable to see how the basic forces of plate tectonics and the northern climate—albeit a highly variable climate—shape everything at Denali, from the mountains to the vegetation to the wildlife. Even more remarkable is that, unlike so many places in the world today, the influence of human development has not yet become a major player in defining the environment. More than just the opportunity to see wildlife and mountains, the opportunity to see an intact natural ecosystem is the most valuable resource that Denali preserves for the world.

THE PEOPLE OF DENALI

Geologic and evolutionary forces have largely shaped the landscape seen at Denali today, but another important force must still be addressed: people. The roots of human inhabitation here are deep, stretching back to the earliest peopling of North America some 14,000 years ago. However, much of this ancient history is largely invisible without a significant amount of digging. On the surface, a visitor encounters only the bloom of twentieth-century exploration and development—sled dog kennels, mining towns, pioneer cabins, railroad tracks, and park visitor facilities. Paradoxically, the most vibrant part of Denali's human history is the legacy of a few determined individuals who sought to preserve undisturbed the place's wilderness character and natural ecological relationships. Their success means that the cultural landscape is largely a natural landscape.

First People

The earliest people to occupy the Denali region were hunters who migrated from Asia to Alaska via the Bering Land Bridge during the Pleistocene Ice Age. When they arrived, the dry grasslands of Beringia's Mammoth Steppe north of the Alaska Range and immense ice fields on the range's south side had begun their retreat, gradually replaced by tundra and boreal forest more typical of today's Denali landscape. Most of the Pleistocene's large mammals had disappeared, though small populations of elk and bison continued to share the landscape with caribou, moose, Dall sheep, black and grizzly bears, and wolves.

Archaeologists and anthropologists once believed that these early people were almost exclusively big-game hunters, but their views were changed by a well-preserved prehistoric campsite east of Denali National Park, known as Broken Mammoth. Artifacts from the site show that hunters who lived in the region 10,000 to 12,000 years ago depended on a variety of animals: big game (bison, elk, caribou), small game (snowshoe hares, ground squirrels, foxes), birds (ducks, geese, swans), and fish.

While Broken Mammoth has provided key insights into the diets and hunting strategies of prehistoric settlers in the Denali region, two archaeological digs inside the park have helped researchers better understand when humans first inhabited the landscape. The first of those sits atop a granitic bedrock bluff above the Teklanika River; for this reason it's been named the "Teklanika West" site. First discovered in 1960, the dig has yielded more than 1500 artifacts, including stone tools, charcoal fragments (from campfires) and the bones of various animals, including bison, caribou, and sheep. For many years, researchers estimated the age of oldest occupation to be somewhere between 8000 and 10,000 years old. But only during a 2009 re-excavation of the site did researchers find clear evidence (animal bones that could be dated using radiocarbon methods) that humans occupied this bluff at least 10,000 years ago and perhaps long before that. Artifacts from other layers at the Teklanika West site indicated later use by humans at several other times. Scientists have noted that the site provides excellent views both up and down the Teklanika, so it's no surprise that early Alaskans used the site repeatedly across the millennia, while scouting for the animals they hunted.

The second major discovery occurred in 2007, when a team of archaeologists found a remote upland site at a place called Bull River. Though there is still much to be learned from the dig, early findings have included fragments of stone spear points, a scraping tool, and flakes of flint that were chipped off the rocks being shaped into tools. Along with the tools, the team found bits of charcoal, which were dated to between 12,180 and 12,460 years ago. That would make Bull River the oldest human-occupied site yet found inside Denali National Park and Preserve. It also provides additional compelling evidence that prehistoric hunters inhabited the Denali region at the very end of the last Ice Age, a period that scientists describe as "a time of drastic global warming and environmental change."

Other ancient bluff-top sites have been discovered near the park's northeastern corner, at places named Panguingue Creek, Dry Creek, Walker Road, Owl Ridge, and Moose Creek. Those too were most likely occupied by hunting bands, possibly groups of extended families, which camped there for weeks at a time while keeping watch for wildlife in the valleys below. Once killed and butchered, game would be taken back to the hunters' main village in the valley bottoms.

Adapting well to the boreal forest, Denali's early people evolved into the modern group of Alaska Natives known as the Athabascan Indian people (sometimes also spelled Athabaskan or Athapaskan). Spread throughout the vast Interior, Athabascans are one of Alaska's six main Native groups, separated from the others by geography and cultural traditions. Nomadic people for most of their history, they depended on the land and its wildlife and plants to provide food, clothing, tools, and shelter.

Five different Athabascan tribes have historically inhabited parts of the Denali region: the Ahtna, Tanana, Dena'ina, Upper Kuskokwim, and Koyukon Indians. These tribes are distinguished by their respective dialects of the Athabascan language and also by location, which in turn dictated distinct lifestyles. For example, the Dena'ina lived on the south side of the Alaska Range between the mountains and Cook Inlet and had access to ocean resources in addition to freshwater fish and game animals, while "highland" tribes in the foothills on the north side of the range depended most heavily on big-game animals, especially caribou.

Athabascans belonging to at least three tribes—the Koyukon, Lower Tanana, and Upper Kuskokwim peoples—inhabited the Lake Minchumina area, just beyond what is now the northwest corner of Denali National Park and Preserve. An important Native crossroads for thousands of years, Lake Minchumina was a place of trade and cultural exchange. Ancient cultural sites reveal the day-to-day realities of Athabascans who resided there before contact with European and American explorers. Taking into account some local variations (such as available foods), their lifestyles were probably typical of Athabascans throughout the Denali region.

Life for these peoples revolved around hunting. Family members from two to five households joined into local bands that ranged through large areas, averaging 2500 square miles. Led by a family patriarch, they would stay together year-round unless resources were scarce, in which case they would break into households to search for game. Strong kinship ties led to mutual cooperation and a sharing of food and other resources.

In winter the bands usually stayed in permanent dwellings along rivers or lakes and hunted a variety of animals: caribou, beaver, bear, ptarmigan, hare, moose, fish. In late March they would abandon winter settlements and follow a nomadic lifestyle for the next five to six months; dome-shaped or conical tepee-like frames with caribou skins for walls served as their mobile shelters. In spring and fall, two or more bands often joined to hunt caribou; in summer the bands would split and wander the Alaska Range foothills in search of caribou, Dall sheep, and bear.

The Denali region's Minchumina–Upper Kantishna River area was among the last to be explored by white pioneers. Consequently, its Athabascan residents were able to maintain their traditional ways into the early 1900s—far longer than most Alaska Native groups. As elsewhere in Alaska and the Lower 48, when explorers, miners, missionaries, and settlers did arrive, they brought drastic changes. Diseases like smallpox, measles, influenza, and tuberculosis devastated Native populations while commercial and trophy hunters competed for animals. At the same time, missionaries and government schools imposed new values, often in direct conflict with Native ones. Assimilation was emphasized at the expense of cultural traditions. Many Athabascans relocated to fixed villages outside the Denali region. The result has been a reduced and acculturated Native population. Gone forever are the self-sufficient nomadic bands that once traveled throughout Alaska's Interior.

Most of the region's Native residents now live in towns along Alaska's highway system and navigable rivers, but some continue to inhabit rural areas and follow lifestyles heavily dependent on subsistence harvests of fish and wildlife. No Athabascan communities now exist in the park and preserve, but some Natives do own land within its boundaries and return seasonally to hunt and trap in areas where these activities are permitted.

Explorers

European exploration of Alaska began a century and a half before the Minchu-mina Indians encountered the new immigrants. In 1741, Danish explorer Vitus Bering discovered and claimed their lands for Russia, whose government ruled Alaska until the territory was sold to the United States in 1867. While the Russians actively managed and exploited both natural resources and the Native peoples whom they encountered along the coast, they never explored Alaska's Interior. Likewise, Hudson's Bay Company traders encroaching from British territory to the east never approached the Denali region. American fur traders and prospectors occasionally passed through the region's fringes during the 1870s and 1880s, but the area immediately surrounding Denali remained unexplored by non-Natives until the late 1890s, when gold stampeders and American survey expeditions began filling in the last blank spaces of maps.

Public interest in Alaska surged in the late 1890s, particularly after gold strikes in Canada's Klondike. In 1898, directed by Congress to learn more about Alaska's Interior goldfields, the U.S. Geological Survey (USGS) sent two expeditions to map the Denali region. One expedition made the first recorded crossing of the Alaska Range in the vicinity of Denali. The other, led by geologists George Eldridge and Robert Muldrow, mapped the Susitna River south of the Alaska Range. Before returning to the coast, they reached the Nenana River, which borders the present-day national park's eastern boundary. Muldrow measured Denali's position and altitude, determining the mountain's height to be more than 20,000 feet. Eldridge, meanwhile, was happy to report the discovery of a pathway from the Gulf of Alaska to the Interior, suitable for train or wagon route (and now followed by Parks Highway and Alaska Railroad travelers). Large glaciers in Denali National Park are named for both men. Between 1898 and 1902, several other reconnaissance expeditions explored the Denali region, including some sent by the U.S. Army to find all-American overland routes through the Alaska Range to known goldfields, thus avoiding passage through Canada.

Among the most notable reconnaissance parties was a USGS expedition led by geologist Alfred H. Brooks, which in 1902 produced maps and reports that served as standard references on the Denali region for half a century. Brooks also was apparently the first modern-day person to walk on Denali's lower slopes and to suggest a route for climbing the mountain. Only a year later, two mountaineering parties came seeking a path to Denali's summit.

Gold Seekers

Neither of Denali's first two climbing expeditions came close to reaching the mountain's top, but one group, led by Judge James Wickersham, found traces of gold in the Kantishna Hills, 50 miles to the north of Mount McKinley. Among the most influential Alaskans of his time, Wickersham had been assigned to the

This undated photo shows a group of Kantishna gold miners near one of the sluicing operations; an arrow points to one of the miners, identified as Johnny Busia, a Croatian immigrant who came to the region in the early 1900s.

territory in 1900 as a U.S. District judge; later he would serve in the Territorial Legislature and become Alaska's delegate to Congress. Although Wickersham's gold claims never paid out, news of his discovery lured other prospectors to the Kantishna Hills. Miners Joe Quigley and Jack Horn found paying quantities of gold along Glacier Creek in the spring of 1905, and, as word spread, the first large wave of stampeders appeared in July. Within weeks, they had staked most of the creeks flowing out of the Kantishna Hills from headwaters to mouth, and established several camps. Winter settlements included Diamond, Glacier City, Roosevelt, and Square Deal; the primary summer camp was Eureka, later renamed Kantishna. During that first summer, Eureka was home to about 2000 people.

Miners lucky enough to stake land along Glacier and Eureka creeks found well-paying deposits, but little gold was discovered elsewhere. By the summer of 1906, only fifty miners remained; most resided in Eureka in summer and in winter moved north to camps where game and timber were more readily available. But a few began living in Eureka/Kantishna year-round. Among the best known were Joe and Fannie Quigley, whose hospitality and wilderness skill are legendary. Joe was one of the two prospectors whose discoveries on Glacier

Creek had sparked the Kantishna gold rush. Fannie came to the Kantishna Hills as a prospector, and proved a match for Joe in her ability to live off the land. Despite her rough speech, many distinguished visitors were charmed by Fannie's famous meals, concocted from wild game she hunted herself, produce harvested from a large garden, and a small amount of staples such as flour and butter hauled 100 miles from Nenana. Caribou stew, mashed potatoes, cabbage, hot rolls, currant jelly, and pie with crust made from bear lard were among the delicacies available at Fannie's table.

Originally from a Bohemian community in Nebraska, Fannie had moved north to the Klondike during the gold rush of 1898. Following gold strikes across the north, she moved from one camp to another until finally arriving in Kantishna, where she was known in the district's early days as Mother McKenzie. At Kantishna she met and married Joe Quigley, who'd been lured north by gold in 1891. A small woman, Fannie was strong and tough, able to do a man's share of packing and as comfortable with a rifle as any miner. But she also kept a clean home filled with books and magazines and tended a garden rich in flowers and vegetables.

The Quigleys and other dedicated miners formed the heart of the Kantishna community, people who subsisted on a combination of placer mining, hunting, trapping, gardening, and hope. The hopes never panned out for most. Miners shifted from placer to hard-rock mining, and they found minerals besides gold. Antimony was particularly abundant, and the Stampede Mine in the eastern Kantishna Hills became Alaska's largest producer of the ore. But the region's isolation, combined with fluctuating prices for metals and the eventual park expansion in 1980, ultimately conspired against the miners. Still, the Kantishna District produced nearly 100,000 ounces of gold between 1905 and 1985, when a lawsuit filed by environmentalists forced the federal government to shut down any existing mining operations inside what had become Denali National Park. Known production of other metals from the Kantishna Hills were 309,000 ounces of silver, 5 million pounds of antimony, and about 1.5 million pounds of combined lead-zinc. The total value of the metals has been estimated at nearly $24 million during the life of the mines. Today, only ghostly ruins and tailing piles remain from Kantishna's mining era.

Two other goldfields were discovered in the Denali region between 1903 and 1907: the Bonnifield District to the northeast; and deposits south of the Alaska Range, within the Susitna River drainage in the Dutch and Peters hills, the upper Chulitna River valley, and the Valdez Creek area east of Cantwell. The latter southern fields were remote, with high transportation costs. Like Kantishna, they typically were worked by small operators at a subsistence level. However, the mines produced enough revenue to spur the development of supply centers to service them, such as the town of Talkeetna, which grew up alongside the new railroad in the 1920s to supply the Cache Creek miners in the Dutch and Peters hills.

Though gold and its associated minerals were the primary lures for prospectors and miners, the landscape also hosts large coal deposits. Scattered throughout much of the region, shallow beds of coal were used locally for decades early in the century; only when the Alaska Railroad was pushed through from Anchorage to Fairbanks in the early 1920s were expanded coal-mine operations possible. While gold's importance has faded since the early 1900s, coal's has increased greatly. Nowadays, the Usibelli Coal Company extracts about 1.5 million tons per year of low-sulfur, sub-bituminous coal from Alaska's only commercial coal mine, located near the town of Healy, 10 miles from Denali National Park's entrance area.

Founders

Three men, more than any others, have become associated with the creation of a wilderness park in the Denali region. Each recognized that such a park should not only preserve the magnificent landscape but, just as importantly, provide a refuge for Denali's remarkable community of subarctic wildlife. Here then, are the stories of Charles Sheldon, Harry Karstens, and Adolph Murie.

Charles Sheldon

In 1906—three years after the first mountaineers were lured into the region by the hope of reaching Denali's summit, and a year after gold stampeders invaded the Kantishna Hills—a Vermont-born, Yale-educated hunter-naturalist named Charles Sheldon traveled to the Alaska Range in search of other treasures: Dall sheep, the wild white sheep of the far north. He would leave the territory with something far more valuable than any trophy animal: the idea for a park-refuge unlike any other in the nation.

A successful businessman, gifted writer, first-class hunter, enthusiastic naturalist, devout conservationist, and

Easterner Charles Sheldon worked hard to preserve Denali's wilderness as a park refuge.

astute political lobbyist, Sheldon was passionate about all species of wild sheep, which he believed were the noblest of wild animals. He had studied and hunted them throughout their North American range, finally pursuing his passion to the most remote mountains of the continent. For a guide he chose Harry Karstens, a transplanted midwesterner who'd been lured north by the Klondike gold rush at age nineteen. Known to be a first-rate explorer and woodsman, Karstens would later become the first superintendent of Mount McKinley National Park.

Accompanied by a horse packer, Sheldon and Karstens lived off the land as they explored the Alaska Range's northern slopes and searched for sheep during the summer of 1906. The trio began their survey in late July, but not until August 5 did they spot any sheep: a band of a dozen ewes and lambs. Over the next eleven days, Sheldon saw hundreds more, in groups of up to sixty or seventy, but all were ewes, lambs, or young rams. Finally, on August 17, while making a solo reconnaissance of Cathedral Mountain in the Outer Range, Sheldon spotted a group of mature rams, including nine with "strikingly big horns."

As recounted in his book *The Wilderness of Denali*, Sheldon painstakingly stalked the rams, killing seven. He butchered the sheep; hauled the meat, skins, and skulls down Cathedral Mountain; treated them for preservation; took measurements; and studied the stomach contents. Then, reunited with his companions, he packed his specimens out and returned east, satisfied that the trip had been a great success.

Sheldon's main work was now complete. The sheep he'd killed and collected would be studied by scientists and displayed in the American Museum of Natural History. But Sheldon also realized the need for a longer stay to better understand the sheep's life history, so before leaving he found a spot along the Toklat River and built a cabin suitable for overwintering.

On August 1, 1907, Sheldon returned to that cabin for a ten-month visit. Besides studying sheep, he gathered facts on other species large and small: caribou, bear, moose, foxes, birds, even voles. He paid close attention to the landscape, the wildlife habitat, and the changing weather and seasons, and he made friends with the area's year-round residents. He was astounded by the abundance of wildlife on the north side of the Alaska Range, but also fearful of the damage done by the market hunters who supplied wild meat to the region's mining camps and towns, hunters who, if uncontrolled, would someday threaten Denali's wildlife populations.

Sheldon fell in love with the Denali region and began to envision a plan for its preservation as a park and game preserve. In a journal entry dated January 12, 1908, he even named this park-refuge: Denali National Park. Though he never again returned to Denali country, it remained an inspiration for this dream.

Back in New York, Sheldon shared his Denali vision with fellow members of the Boone and Crockett Club, a politically influential group of big-game trophy hunters and conservationists. His colleagues responded with enthusiasm; but momentum for the park did not develop until after Congress in 1914 mandated construction of a railroad from the port town of Seward to the Interior town of Fairbanks, a project that surely would bring increased people and development to the Denali region.

In December 1915 Sheldon wrote a letter to Stephen Mather, soon to become the National Park Service's first director, explaining his McKinley park and game-reservation idea. It ended with a plea for urgency: delaying action could lead to destruction of the region's wildlife, the key reason to establish such a park in the remote Alaska wilderness.

Once appointed director, Mather quickly endorsed the proposal. Along with the Park Service's approval, Sheldon gained the support of prominent artist, explorer, hunter, and mountaineer Belmore Browne and the American Game Protective and Propagation Association. Although better known for his Denali mountaineering accomplishments, Browne independently formulated a preservation plan similar to Sheldon's and, with Sheldon and others, helped draft the legislation to create Mount McKinley National Park.

Sheldon also won the backing of Alaska's delegate to Congress, James Wickersham, who recognized that a park could be a major visitor attraction and a boost to Alaska's economy. With everything now moving quickly, bills to establish the park were introduced into the Senate and House of Representatives in 1916, and passed the following February.

In recognition of his years-long effort, Sheldon personally delivered the legislation to President Woodrow Wilson, who signed it into law on February 26, 1917. Mount McKinley National Park thus became the first new park admitted to the recently formed national park system.

Shaped roughly like a parallelogram and running northeast–southwest, McKinley Park was nearly 100 miles long and 25 miles wide on average and protected 2200 square miles (1.4 million acres) of wildlife habitat, primarily on the Alaska Range's northern side. Its boundaries intentionally excluded the Kantishna mining district and forested country to the northwest, where many miners hunted. In Sheldon's own words, the new park was a place

...mostly above timberline, and yet with tongues of timber extending up the rivers. Outside of the rough ranges are gently rolling hills, hundreds of little straggling lakes, a region which, when roads are once established there, and conveniences for tourists, you can ride all over it with horses. It is accessible in every part, and the game of the region will be constantly in sight, a thing which is not true of most of the regions of our other national parks.

Harry Karstens

Once established, Alaska's first park suffered from several years of neglect, without funding, staff, or any form of protection. The Alaska Railroad, as Sheldon had predicted, brought increased development pressures to the region. And market hunters continued to kill wildlife as they pleased. Finally, in 1921, Congress appropriated $8000 for the park's management. That same year, Sheldon's former guide, Harry Karstens, was appointed McKinley's first superintendent. His mandate was clear and simple (though not easy): protect the park's wildlife. Visitor facilities and recreation would have to wait, but Karstens recognized the need for a base camp accessible to both the park and the railroad; it would serve as his supply line and link to the outside world. Begun in 1915, the Alaska Railroad line connecting Anchorage and Fairbanks had nearly been completed by late 1921. Conveniently, it came within a few miles of the park entrance. (See Chapter 7 for a look at the railroad today.)

Using materials from abandoned railroad camps, Karstens spent most of his first year setting up shop along Riley Creek, near the railroad and a small settlement known as McKinley Park Station. With one assistant ranger, he constructed a superintendent's home and office, barn, storehouse, and workshop. For transportation he obtained two sled dog teams, three horses, a bobsled, a wagon, and the materials necessary to do horseshoeing, blacksmithing, and harness repair. (The Riley Creek site proved less than ideal for making contact with visitors and enduring Denali's bitterly cold winters; in 1925 Karstens constructed a new headquarters in its present location on a forested bench, at mile 3.4 of the park road.)

Besides his camp construction, Karstens supervised the surveying and marking of the park boundary. And, as a necessary step to establishing a presence within the park, he and his assistant built a wagon road along Hines and Jenny creeks to the Savage River. At its end they cached a ton of supplies for trips into the park's interior.

With all this to do, little time remained for ranger patrols. The plan to protect wildlife first had already begun to unravel, simply because Karstens was besieged by too many demands. In addition to everything else, developers, politicians, tourism promoters, and potential concessionaires pressured him with grand schemes for hotels, access routes, and other visitor amenities along a proposed road into the heart of the park.

Plans for a road through Mount McKinley National Park were in the works even before Karstens became superintendent. The Alaska Engineering Commission, the Alaska Road Commission, and the National Park Service had agreed to collaborate on a wagon route that would connect the railroad with Kantishna and benefit both miners and park visitors. In 1920, the Alaska Road Commission tested two routes through the park. Ultimately the higher route was chosen because of drier land, narrower river crossings, better timber for bridges, and better road grades. Coincidentally, this route also offered the best opportunities for viewing the park's wildlife. Workers began construction of the 90-mile park road in 1923 and completed it to Kantishna in 1938. It is largely this same road that park visitors travel today.

The combination of railway access and road construction inevitably brought the first visitors to McKinley. By 1923, horse packer Dan Kennedy had built a tourist tent camp at Savage River. That same year, a series of VIP tours—including one with President Warren Harding—traveled the newly completed Alaska Railroad and made ceremonial stops at McKinley Station. By the following summer, the park road's first 12 miles were passable for buses and touring cars. In 1925, more than 200 visitors entered the park, most brought in by the newly formed Mt. McKinley Tourist and Transportation Company, which had taken over Kennedy's tent-camp operation.

Though these early tourism developments complicated his mission, Karstens kept sight of his number one priority: wildlife protection. However, the congressional legislation that created Mount McKinley National Park also protected valid preexisting mining claims within the park's boundaries and gave miners the right to "take and kill therein so much game or birds as may be needed for their actual necessities when short of food."

As might be expected, such a hunting regulation proved difficult, if not impossible, to enforce. Although the legislation also stipulated that "in no case shall animals or birds be killed for sale or removal therefrom, or wantonly," continued evidence of illegal market hunting and wasteful killing by miners and renegade trappers outraged conservationists, biologists, and park officials. In 1924, respected biologist Olaus Murie reported the park's big-game animals to be endangered. To close all loopholes for abuse, Karstens recommended the entire park be closed to hunting because "as long as prospectors are allowed to kill game, just as surely will the object of this park be defeated. Any townie can take a pick and pan and go into the park and call himself a prospector. This is often the case."

Despite the hunting loophole and their limited resources, Karstens and his growing ranger staff managed to gradually slow the park's wildlife slaughter. From fall through winter and into spring—when most illegal hunting occurred—Karstens and his rangers roamed through the park on sled dog patrols, talking with locals, citing violators, and generally making their presence felt. Aided by a system of patrol cabins, they would spend days or weeks deep in the park or along its boundaries. By the end of Karstens's seven-year term, all but the park's most remote corners were regularly patrolled and the widespread poaching of earlier years had ended. That same year, in response to the mounting protestations of Karstens, Murie, Sheldon, and other conservationists, Congress repealed McKinley Park's hunting provision.

The final years of Karstens's superintendency were difficult ones. He grew increasingly frustrated by the administrative demands of his job, mounting tensions with park neighbors and employees, and conflicts with his superiors in Washington, D.C. At the same time, a growing number of Alaskans accused Karstens of arrogant and even violent behavior and criticized his combative style of leadership. Disgusted and under pressure, Karstens resigned in October 1928, his legacy ensured. As historian William Brown recounts:

> By 1928 the park road extended 40 miles into the park. Appropriations were up to $22,000. The much enhanced concession operation hosted close to 1,000 visitors with facilities and activities that combined comfort, entertainment, and challenge in balances attuned to visitor tastes. The park headquarters and supporting administrative facilities made possible reasonable park operations. A small but barely adequate ranger staff patrolled and protected the park from all but the most remote incursions. Much work remained to be done. But much had already been done. This accomplishment had been wrought largely by the fallible but dedicated man who entered the park alone on a borrowed horse in 1921.

Adolph Murie

The wildlife-preservation ideal that figured so strongly in the creation of McKinley National Park would, ironically, lead during the 1930s and 1940s to one of the park's earliest crises, predator-prey relationships. That conflict would be resolved—and a more clearly defined wildlife-management philosophy established—largely because of the work done by Adolph Murie, a naturalist described by historian William Brown as "the single most influential person in shaping the geography and the wildlife-wilderness policies of the modern park."

Adolph Murie joined his older brother Olaus at McKinley in the early 1920s to help with caribou studies. Over the next half-century he wrote scores of reports and several books about McKinley's mammals, birds, and general ecology. Those writings, combined with his studies of wolf-sheep relationships, his many letters and commentaries in opposition to unnecessary park development, and his loud and prolonged call for the preservation of Denali's "wilderness spirit," exerted a powerful influence on the park's direction. For decades he served as the conscience of Mount McKinley National Park.

Adolph Murie's influence in shaping park policies was first manifested in his wolf-sheep studies. A series of hard winters from 1927 through 1932 caused McKinley's Dall sheep population to crash. Many starved; others, weakened by winter's hardships, succumbed to disease and predators. Dall sheep, more than any other animal, symbolized McKinley National Park's raison d'être, for they had sparked Charles Sheldon's interest in the region and the original movement to establish a game preserve. Reports that wolves had killed as many as a

*Biologist Adolph Murie came to then Mount McKinley National Park in the early
1920s and served as its "conscience" over the next half century.*

thousand sheep in a single winter created a stir, and in 1931 some eastern sportsmen's groups began to pressure the National Park Service for predator control.

The growing clamor forced the Park Service to consider a critical question: In
managing America's national parks, should it favor one species over another?
Or should it apply an ecosystem approach in which all native species had "equal

rights" to exist? Although it had already begun a limited wolf-control program at McKinley in 1929, the agency initially declared its position as "preserving all forms of wildlife in their natural relationship" within the park. That stance only served to inflame the debate, sparking angry protests by both sportsmen's groups and local Alaskans. Critics claimed that the agency's romantic attitude toward McKinley's predators led to the destruction of preferred game animals, like sheep and caribou. The same sportsmen's and wildlife-protection groups that had lambasted Alaska's hunters as "wanton killers of game" now found themselves siding with local residents against the Park Service.

Widely respected, Adolph Murie was sent by the Park Service to McKinley in 1939 to study wolf-sheep interactions and, it was hoped, offer a solution acceptable to all parties. His conclusion after conducting research from 1939 through 1941 was that the park's sheep population had not yet recovered from the severe winters of 1927–32; however, McKinley's wolves and sheep had apparently reached a place of equilibrium. Wolves, in fact, might actually benefit the sheep population by eliminating weak and sick animals—a radical idea at the time.

Based on Murie's conclusions, the Park Service decided in 1943 to terminate its limited wolf-control program. That, in turn, caused a severe backlash. Supported by a broad coalition of local organizations, both public and private, the Alaska legislature petitioned the president and Congress, demanding that wolves be exterminated in McKinley and any other national parks that might serve as wolf sanctuaries.

The timing of that petition coincided with a disconcerting follow-up report by Murie. In 1945, he counted only 500 Dall sheep in McKinley National Park, down from 3000 a decade earlier. Facing renewed pressures and an alarmingly small number of sheep, the Park Service had little choice but to reinstate limited wolf-control. Initially headed by Murie, the control program lasted until 1952, when the park's rebounding sheep population made it unnecessary. In all, a total of seventy wolves had been destroyed since 1929. None would ever again be killed in Mount McKinley (later to become Denali) National Park through Park Service control programs. Thanks in large part to Murie's studies, interpretations, and philosophies, the sheep crisis—and the species' eventual recovery—ultimately led to a strengthening of ecosystem rather than "favored game" management in McKinley National Park. It also spurred Murie's now-famous book, *The Wolves of Mount McKinley*.

PARK HISTORY

Despite great pressures to develop the park and provide ever-greater amenities and facilities for its visitors, wilderness and wildlife advocates both within and outside the National Park Service have over the decades managed to protect the park's wild values, while also expanding its reach far beyond the original

Visitors driving into Mount McKinley National Park in June 1939 pass beneath the park's entrance arch.

1.4-million-acre wilderness core, so that the modern Denali National Park and Preserve is deservedly known as one of America's greatest wild treasures.

Development

Almost from its birth, Alaska's political and business leaders had exerted pressures on the National Park Service to make Mount McKinley National Park a more visitor-friendly place, one that would serve as a visitor destination and help the territory's economy. The first steps in that direction had been taken during Karstens's reign, with the early stages of road construction and the start-up of a tent camp and tour company. The year after his departure, the Park Service proposed an ambitious development plan that included an entrance-area hotel near McKinley Station; an improved visitor facility at Savage River; a hotel deep inside the park; and an airfield for plane tours. All but the remote hotel eventually became reality.

The agency also urged an expansion of McKinley Park east to the Nenana River, which would serve as a natural boundary, while Territorial Governor George Parks campaigned for the addition of Wonder Lake, at the end of today's Denali Park Road, because of its potential as a tourist destination. Congress satisfied both desires in 1932, when it expanded Mount McKinley National Park to nearly 2 million acres. Both Governor Parks and Park Service director Horace

Albright envisioned major visitor facilities—including a hotel—at Wonder Lake, which in Albright's words, "would afford a finer view of Mount McKinley than any now had in the park."

By the mid-1930s, the Alaska Railroad schedule had been adjusted to give visitors at least 24 hours in the park, and the Savage River camp had been expanded to a hundred "tent houses." Savage also served as the jumping-off point for horseback trips, unrestricted auto tours along the park road—now approaching completion—and "flightseeing" tours.

The late 1930s brought more changes. The 92-mile park road to Kantishna was finally finished in 1938, and the McKinley Park Hotel—the only one ever to be built within the park—was completed in June 1939. A short walk from the railroad station near the park's entrance, it had room for up to 200 guests. To avoid competition with the new hotel, the Park Service ordered the Mt. McKinley Tourist and Transportation Company to move its tent camp from Savage River to a site near the present-day Eielson Visitor Center, 66 road miles into the park. That same year, 2200 people visited McKinley, a number not matched until after World War II. (The park's development as a visitor attraction was put on hold during the war, during which it was converted into an army recreational camp.)

Besides expanding McKinley's visitor accommodations, the Park Service completed a number of other projects, thanks in large part to the Civilian Conservation Corps (CCC). In 1938–39, a 200-man CCC crew built employee housing, garages, a forty-dog kennel and equipment house, and a machine shop at park headquarters, plus a ranger station–residence at Wonder Lake. It also installed utility lines and cleaned up debris along the park road.

The 1957 completion of the Denali Highway from Paxson to the park entrance by way of Cantwell (30 miles south of the park entrance) gave motorists their first direct access to Mount McKinley National Park, though the rough condition of this 150-mile east–west gravel road initially produced more of a trickle than a flood of auto traffic into the park. This new link with Alaska's highway system naturally increased pressures for even more park development. As part of a national program to upgrade park facilities across the United States during the 1950s and 1960s, the Park Service proposed to build an interpretive center deep in the park (at the site of the present-day Eielson Visitor Center), to improve campground and headquarters facilities, and to upgrade the park road to meet the needs of increased traffic. The reconstructed road would be paved for its first 30 miles, and the 36-mile section beyond that would be both widened and straightened, with future paving likely. Only the 19-mile section from Eielson to Wonder Lake would stay in a "primitive" state.

The road plans riled conservationists, including Adolph Murie, who insisted that the park road should remain primitive and contribute to visitors' sense of adventure: "Because McKinley is a wilderness within a vast northern

wilderness," he wrote, "the ill effect of any intrusion will here be proportion-
ately greater; and any 'dressing up' will be more incongruous, will clash more
with the wilderness spirit...." For similar reasons he advocated a ban on hotels
within the park, a prohibition against airplane tours, and an expansion of park
boundaries to protect additional wildlife ranges and prevent helter-skelter
development in the Kantishna area.

The appeals of Murie and other conservationists for less development influenced park planners and nudged McKinley's management toward a turning
point. The Park Service ceased road reconstruction in the mid-1960s after paving
only the first 15 miles and widening and straightening the roadbed to mile 30.
The remaining 63 miles would indeed retain their primitive essence. Instead of
allowing unlimited vehicle access, the Park Service in the 1970s would substitute
buses for private vehicles to limit visitor impacts on McKinley's wildlife and wilderness values. And to further minimize development at the expense of wildness,
the Park Service finally quashed its decades-old plan for a hotel at Wonder Lake.

The pressing need for a new park-road policy became clear after the 1972
completion of the Parks Highway, connecting Anchorage and Fairbanks, by
way of the McKinley Park entrance. Anticipating a greatly increased flow of
private-vehicle traffic, the Park Service quickly established a dual mandatory
bus system, in which free government-operated shuttle buses would comple-
ment concession-run tours. Park officials correctly figured that limiting traffic to
buses would minimize impacts on the road's wild setting and on wildlife that
inhabited the landscape along the road.

This new bus system culminated a significant shift in park policy. The
emphasis on park development and visitor amenities, so pronounced from the
late 1920s through the early 1960s, had—thanks largely to the efforts of brothers
Adolph and Olaus Murie and other prominent conservationists—given way to
a philosophy that emphasized wilderness and wildlife preservation over visitor
conveniences. Mount McKinley National Park would largely remain as it had in
the time of Sheldon and Karstens: above all, a place of immense wildness.

Expansion

The bus system was the first step taken to ease visitor pressures on McKinley's
wilderness core. A second step would be park expansion. Proponents had long
argued that further additions were necessary to better protect the park's wildlife
and keep intact an entire ecosystem north of the Alaska Range. Naturalist Sigurd
Olson had reported after a 1963 survey that park boundaries cut across normal
game habitats without regard for migration routes or breeding patterns. Both
in winter and in spring, many resident mammals strayed beyond the park into
unprotected areas. From an ecological perspective, Mount McKinley National
Park was simply too small.

An adult, female grizzly crosses the Denali Park Road behind a shuttle bus near Sable Pass, an area frequented by bears.

Park planners also looked to expand the park south of the Alaska Range as well as north. This expansion would protect additional lands and wildlife and join the national park with Denali State Park, established in 1970. State officials envisioned Denali State Park—less than a 3-hour drive from Anchorage—as a major year-round destination, complete with luxurious hotel, visitor center, hiking and snowmobile trails, and scenic ridge-top drive. If McKinley Park were expanded toward the more highly developed state park, visitor pressures at the national park's northern entrance and along the park road would likely be lessened.

Momentum to expand McKinley Park continued to build through the 1970s, despite widespread local opposition. Fearing added restrictions on their use of federal land, many Alaskans fought any park expansion. But the Fairbanks branch of the Pioneers of Alaska—an association of old-time Alaskans—unanimously recommended a doubling of McKinley Park's area to protect wildlife wintering range, prime sheep habitat, and the Alaska Range's southern slopes and glaciers. Among the Alaska conservationists who supported McKinley's

Human History Timeline of the Denali Region

15,000–30,000 years ago Humans first come to Alaska over the Bering Land Bridge.

12,000+ years ago Hunter-gatherers settle in the Denali region.

1898 The U.S. Geological Survey sends two mapping expeditions into the Denali region.

1902 Geologist Alfred Brooks explores Denali's north side, becomes the first person known to walk upon the slopes of North America's highest peak.

1903 Judge James Wickersham's party finds traces of gold and stakes claims in the Kantishna Hills.

1905 Gold stampeders populate the Kantishna Mining District.

1906 Hunter-naturalist Charles Sheldon visits the Denali region to study Dall sheep, accompanied by Harry Karstens. Sheldon returns in 1907–8.

1917 Mount McKinley National Park is established.

1921 Harry Karstens begins work as McKinley Park's first superintendent.

1923 The Alaska Railroad is completed between Anchorage and Fairbanks, and a visitor camp is established at Savage River. Work begins on the park road.

1924–38 The park road is constructed from Savage River to Kantishna.

1939 The McKinley Park Hotel is completed.

1939–41 Adolph Murie conducts a groundbreaking study of McKinley National Park's wolf and sheep populations.

1957 The Denali Highway is completed, providing the first road access to Mount McKinley National Park.

1959 Alaska becomes the forty-ninth state; the Eielson Visitor Center is opened.

1970 Denali State Park is established.

1972 The George Parks Highway from Anchorage to Fairbanks is completed, with access to McKinley Park. The National Park Service restricts road access and institutes a bus transportation system. The McKinley Park Hotel burns down and is replaced by a temporary structure.

1980 The Alaska National Interest Lands Conservation Act (ANILCA) passes Congress, enlarging Mount McKinley National Park from 2 million to 6 million acres and renaming it Denali National Park and Preserve. A court order stops mining at Kantishna.

1992 Denali is selected to participate in a Long-Term Ecological Monitoring Program, to help detect and better understand changes in the park's varied ecosystems.

2000–Present New visitor facilities and trails are added to the park's entrance area and along the park road corridor, and several studies are initiated to learn the impact of climate change on the Denali ecosystem.

growth, Camp Denali founders Ginny Wood and Celia Hunter proposed additional buffers in the Wonder Lake area to protect it from development (Wood and Hunter had built their wilderness camp just outside the original park in the early 1950s). Such calls for McKinley's enlargement became part of a greater movement, pushed by the Park Service and a coalition of national and local conservation groups, to increase the number and size of Alaska's national parklands.

Other forces were at work as well. Giant oil-field discoveries had been made in 1968 at Prudhoe Bay, which led developers and public officials to call for an 800-mile pipeline to be built across the state. In 1971, to settle long-standing demands by the state's indigenous peoples, Congress enacted the Alaska Native Claims Settlement Act (ANCSA), which gave Alaska's Natives nearly $1 billion and the right to select 44 million acres of land. As a compromise with conservationists, the act also required federal agencies to recommend certain public lands to Congress for inclusion in parks, wildlife refuges, wild-and-scenic rivers, and national forests. The state of Alaska, meanwhile, wanted the 104 million acres it had been promised by the statehood act of 1959, so it could begin developing those lands. In short, says historian William Brown, Alaska was beset by "storms of development vs. preservation conflict."

In 1980, Congress resolved many outstanding Alaska lands issues through the Alaska National Interest Lands Conservation Act. Through ANILCA, as the act is commonly known, Congress set aside 106 million acres of conservation lands in Alaska, including nearly 44 million acres of new and expanded parklands. Close to 4 million acres were added to Mount McKinley National Park, both north and south of the Alaska Range. Tripled in size, the expanded parkland was renamed Denali National Park and Preserve.

Now legally designated wilderness by Congress, the 2-million-acre former Mount McKinley National Park forms the core of this unit, with special protections for the land and its wildlife. The "old park," as it is sometimes called, is managed under the Wilderness Act so that no new human developments are allowed except along the existing road corridor. Backcountry use is regulated, and most usual national park restrictions apply: no campfires, pets, aircraft access, snowmobile access, or sport hunting is allowed. Subsistence hunting, fishing, and trapping are also prohibited. The old park, in turn, is surrounded by 2.4 million acres of new parkland and 1.6 million acres of national preserve. The national park additions (familiarly known as "new park") are managed in the same way as other national parks, except that ANILCA allows traditional subsistence activities by local residents who have a personal or family tradition of such use, thus recognizing their longstanding dependence on local wildlife, fish, and plants. The preserve, meanwhile, allows traditional subsistence uses as well as sport hunting, trapping, and fishing, as permitted by Alaska's state fish and game regulations.

The expansions have helped to make the park ecologically whole. As Adolph Murie, Sigurd Olson, and other conservationists had long desired, the northern additions completed an entire natural ecosystem that encompasses ice-capped mountains, alpine tundra, lowland forests, and river valleys, and which offers increased protections to wide-ranging animals like caribou and wolves. The southern addition, meanwhile, ensures that the Alaska Range's entire north–south expanse is now wholly within the park's boundaries.

Preservation

In the three decades since Mount McKinley National Park was expanded and renamed, visitor numbers have increased greatly and the bus transportation system has expanded; more than 225,000 people now take either shuttle or tour buses into the park each summer. At the same time, development has boomed along the Parks Highway, and both the Park Service and the state of Alaska have targeted Denali's south side for new visitor access and amenities. Inside the national park, several new visitor facilities and trails have been added to the entrance area (and the hotel removed), the Eielson Visitor Center at mile 66 has been rebuilt and modernized, and new trails and refurbished rest stops have been constructed in the park road corridor. At the end of the road, the park's expansion led to mining-claim conflicts in the Kantishna district; and since the end of mining in the 1980s, Camp Denali has been joined by other wilderness lodges built on private Kantishna holdings or nearby lands, making the end of the road a destination for increasing numbers of both day and overnight travelers.

For all the pressures, conflicts, and changes, Denali National Park and Preserve continues to serve its original purpose of a wildlife preserve, while providing recreational opportunities for hundreds of thousands of visitors each year, protecting the subsistence traditions of local residents, and maintaining a sense of the region's natural and human history. The wilderness visions and values of Charles Sheldon, Harry Karstens, and Adolph Murie remain intact, available to anyone who explores Denali's wildlands. And the preservation of "wilderness spirit" advocated by Murie remains a guiding principle of today's park.

Chapter 2

CLIMBING
DENALI

The history of climbing Denali, The Mountain, stands alone. Although it is interwoven with the mapping of Interior Alaska, the Kantishna gold rush, and the national park's pioneer history, Denali's mountaineering history is distinct from the rest. It's as if the intensity of the story requires as much focus as the climbers who seek the mountain's summit.

Denali presents one of the world's greatest climbing challenges. With a 20,320-foot summit that rises 18,000 feet (5490 meters) above surrounding lowlands, it is among the world's tallest mountains when measured from base to top, and its great height, combined with its subarctic location, makes it one of the coldest mountains on Earth, if not the coldest. Halfway to the summit, Denali's climate equals that of the North Pole in severity. Even in June, nighttime temperatures on its upper slopes may reach –30° to –40°F (–34° to –40° C). In winter, temperatures to –75°F (–60°C) have been documented, with wind chills to below –150°F (–100°C).

Denali is so massive it creates its own weather systems. Some storms have produced hurricane-force winds exceeding 150 miles per hour. The mountain is also frequently battered by gales originating in the North Pacific. Long periods of clear and calm weather are rare, particularly on the peak's upper slopes. Because of Denali's northerly location, scientists estimate the available oxygen at its summit is equal to that of Himalayan mountains 2000 to 3000 feet (600 to 915 meters) higher. To reach the summit, climbers must avoid immense avalanches, icefalls from hanging glaciers, and deep, sometimes hidden crevasses in glacial ice. They must also endure severe cold, thinning air that may cause high-altitude illnesses, and mountain storms that may last for days, dropping several feet of snow and creating whiteouts in which visibility is almost zero.

Despite all the hazards, as of 2012, 20,062 people had stood upon Denali's summit since The High One was first attempted in 1903; that's slightly more than half of the 38,529 climbers who'd tried. And more than a thousand attempt to reach the top every year.

Clouds drape the West Buttress of 20,320-foot Denali, seen here from an elevation of about 7500 feet along the Kahiltna Glacier.

EARLY CLIMBS

Though Denali is enormously popular and easily accessible today, at the turn of the twentieth century it was terra incognita. A foreboding and mysterious mountain, it remained unclimbed, unexplored, and unknown to most Americans. It wasn't unknown to Alaska's Native peoples, however. Generations of Indians regarded the mountain as a holy place, treating it with a distant reverence and using it as a point of reference. Only after non-Native pioneers—with their passion for discovery, exploration, and conquest—learned of the mountain's existence did people attempt to unravel its secrets. In doing so, it was only natural that they would seek a route to its top.

The first to record his steps on Denali's slopes was Alfred Brooks, who approached the mountain from the north while exploring the Alaska Range for the USGS in 1902:

> *My objective point was a shoulder of the mountain about 10,000 feet [3,500 meters] high; but at three in the afternoon, I found my route blocked by a smooth expanse of ice. With the aid of my geologic pick I managed to cut steps in the slippery surface, and thus climbed a hundred feet higher.... Convinced at length that it would be utterly foolhardy, alone as I was, to attempt to reach the shoulder for*

which I was headed, at 7,500 feet [2,300 meters] I turned and cautiously retraced my steps....

I gazed along the precipitous slopes of the mountain and tried again to realize its great altitude, with a thrill of satisfaction at being the first man to approach the summit, which was only nine miles from where I smoked my pipe.

In his "Plan for Climbing Mount McKinley," published in *National Geographic* in 1903, Brooks suggested a northern approach, explaining that any attempt from Cook Inlet, to the south, would require too much time and effort for the difficult 100- to 200-mile trek through largely unexplored wilds to the mountain's base. Brooks proved to have remarkable foresight. Of the nine Denali expeditions staged over the next decade, those approaching from the south exhausted themselves, their time, or their supplies before making any summit try. Teams attacking from the north side would reach the North Peak in 1910 and then pioneer a route to the mountain's top in 1913.

The first attempts to reach Denali's summit took place in 1903. Led by James Wickersham, U.S. district judge for the Alaska Territory, a five-man party left Fairbanks on May 16 and, approaching from the northeast, established a 4000-foot (1200-meter) base camp in the upper McKinley River drainage on June 18. Two days later, four team members headed up the Peters Glacier, which flows off Denali's north side, then turned up a smaller spur that seemed to offer a more direct route to the summit. It proved to be a dead end, hemmed in by a "tremendous precipice" of vertical rock. Frustrated by their blocked path and worried that warm weather was making the mountain's snowpack prone to avalanches, the climbers reluctantly turned back. The enormous face that stopped the Wickersham party was later appropriately named the Wickersham Wall; it wouldn't be climbed until 1963, when it was conquered twice.

Less than two months after Wickersham's departure from Denali, an expedition led by explorer Dr. Frederick Cook came upon the earlier group's abandoned base camp. Cook's six-man, fourteen-horse expedition had come from the south, traveling "450 miles through trail-less forests and over tundra, under the curse of mosquitoes and bulldog flies," as team member and journalist Robert Dunn recounted in *The Shameless Diary of an Explorer*. The nine-week trek left the team low on both supplies and time. After reaching an estimated elevation of 11,300 feet (3450 meters), the party was thwarted by what Cook called "an insurmountable wall" (though different from the one that stopped Wickersham). Although it failed in its primary mission, the Cook expedition completed the first circumnavigation of Denali, a remarkable feat in itself.

Looking upon Denali as a stepping-stone to an even grander adventure—a North Pole expedition—Cook returned to the mountain in June 1906 with a team that included two other talented mountaineers, Herschel Parker and Belmore

Browne. After two months on Denali's southern flanks, the party returned to the coast, convinced the mountain couldn't be climbed from the south. However, just as the group was breaking up, Cook decided to make "a last desperate attempt on Mount McKinley," as he telegraphed to a New York sponsor. Accompanied only by horsepacker Ed Barrill, Cook returned to the Alaska Range, reappearing a few weeks later with the announcement that he had reached the summit. The news was quickly relayed to the media, whereupon it made major national headlines.

Browne and Parker were unconvinced. As Browne later explained:

> *I knew the character of the country that guarded the southern face of the big mountain, had traveled in that country, and knew that the time that Dr. Cook had been absent was too short to allow his even reaching the mountain. I knew that Dr. Cook had not climbed Mount McKinley.*

In response to such doubts, Cook offered visual proof: a map purporting to show his route and a photograph supposedly showing Barrill on the summit. Before the claims and counterclaims could be settled, Cook headed north again—this time to the North Pole. On September 1, 1909, he announced that he'd reached the pole—and within days was embroiled in yet another controversy, this time with Robert Peary, who challenged Cook's story and claimed the pole for himself. By the end of 1909, Cook's once highly regarded reputation had taken a severe beating. The Explorer's Club, of which he'd once been president, organized an expedition led by Parker and Browne to investigate Cook's Denali claims.

Using Cook's own map and photos, the team traced his route, as Browne put it, "peak by peak and snowfield by snowfield, to within a foot of the spot where he had exposed his negatives." The painstaking detective work paid off on June 22, 1910, when team members found Cook's summit: nearly 20 miles from Denali's top, it stood at less than 10,000 feet (3050 meters) elevation.

TOM LLOYD AND THE SOURDOUGH EXPEDITION

The most legendary of all Denali climbs also took place in 1910. A group of four gold miners challenged the mountain with the most rudimentary gear and no technical climbing experience, simply to disprove Frederick Cook's summit claim and to demonstrate that Alaskans could outdo the exploits—whether real or imagined—of any "Easterners."

The Sourdough Expedition began with barroom braggadocio. The expedition's leader and instigator was Tom Lloyd, who'd come north during the Klondike gold rush and settled in the Kantishna Hills. In the fall of 1909, during a debate about Cook, a Fairbanks bar owner asserted that no one alive could climb the mountain. Lloyd bet that "for two cents" he'd show it could be done. Eventually, $1500 was put up. In December, Lloyd and six others left Fairbanks for the mountain. Their send-off included an editorial in the *Fairbanks Daily Times* that promised, "Our boys will succeed...and they'll show up Dr. Cook and the other 'Outside' doctors and expeditions."

Three team members eventually quit the expedition, leaving Lloyd, Billy Taylor, Pete Anderson, and Charles McGonagall, all of them miners in the Kantishna district. Approaching from the north, the Sourdoughs reached the Muldrow Glacier in early March 1910. Despite the dangers of glacial crevasses and precipitous slopes, the climbers ascended unroped, a practice most Denali mountaineers would consider foolhardy today. With the notable exception of a 14-foot spruce flagpole—which they planned to leave on the summit—the team traveled light. Their climbing gear consisted of the bare essentials: snowshoes, homemade crampons they called "creepers," and crude ice axes. To endure the subzero cold they simply wore bib overalls, long underwear, shirts, parkas, mittens, Indian moccasins, and shoepacs (insulated rubber boots).

The Sourdoughs established a final camp March 17 at the head of the Muldrow Glacier, at 11,000 feet (3355 meters) elevation. They made their first try for the summit April 1 but were stopped by stormy weather. Two days later, they tried again. Outfitted with a bag of doughnuts, three thermos bottles of hot chocolate (and caribou meat, by some accounts), plus their flagpole, Taylor, Anderson, and McGonagall headed up. Lloyd apparently had descended to a lower camp; exactly why isn't clear, but he may have been suffering from altitude sickness.

McGonagall stopped a few hundred feet below the top, but Taylor and Anderson continued on, still hauling the spruce pole. Sometime in the late afternoon of April 3, they stood atop Denali's 19,470-foot (5940-meter) North Peak, widely recognized as a more difficult ascent than the mountain's higher—and ultimately more prestigious—20,320-foot (6200-meter) South Peak. The Sourdoughs' reason for choosing the North Peak seemed quite logical at the time: the miners hoped their 14-foot pole, complete with 6-by-12-foot American flag, would be seen from Kantishna and Fairbanks in the north and serve as proof of their conquest. They made no attempt to reach the South Peak, which from the north is blocked from view.

In an interview twenty-seven years later, Taylor said he and Anderson spent two-and-a-half hours on top, though "it was colder than hell. Mitts and everything was all ice." The trio returned to high camp late that day, completing their 8000-foot (2450-meter) ascent and the descent in 18 hours. By comparison, most present-day Denali expeditions climb no more than 3000 to 4000 vertical feet (915 to 1200 meters) on summit day, which typically lasts 10 to 15 hours.

Mission accomplished, Taylor, Anderson, and McGonagall returned to Kantishna. Lloyd, meanwhile, went to Fairbanks with the news. Given a hero's welcome, he unfortunately chose to mix fact with fantasy, proclaiming that the entire party had reached the summits of both the North and South peaks and had found no evidence to support Cook's claims.

Word of the success spread quickly. But challenges to Lloyd's account soon mounted. Before long, his story was regarded as simply another Alaska tall tale. (The other Sourdoughs, who'd remained in Kantishna, didn't know about Lloyd's false claims; perhaps out of misguided loyalty, none publicly challenged his story until years later.)

A final blow to the Sourdoughs' credibility was struck in 1912, when Belmore Browne and Herschel Parker made their third—and last—attempt to climb Denali, this time following the Sourdoughs' Muldrow Glacier route. On two separate days, team members came within a short distance of the South Peak, only to be turned back by extreme winds, cold, and near-zero visibility.

Browne and Parker said they'd found no evidence of the Sourdoughs' flagpole. And because they'd so carefully documented their own ascent, great credibility was given to their point of view that the Sourdoughs' claims were false.

HUDSON STUCK AND THE SOUTH PEAK

The first decade of Denali mountaineering had left North America's highest peak shrouded in controversy and confusion. The triumphs asserted by Cook and Lloyd, once applauded, had been largely discredited. There was so much uncertainty as to who had really done what that Denali became known in some quarters as the "Mountain of Mystery."

Into this picture stepped Hudson Stuck. An Episcopal missionary and amateur climber who'd ascended several mountains, including 14,410-foot (4375-meter) Mount Rainier, Stuck by his own admission was more concerned with men than mountains. Arriving in Alaska in 1904 as archdeacon of the Yukon region, he focused his attentions on the Native people of Alaska's Interior. However, in 1906 Stuck's passion for mountaineering was rekindled by a view of Denali: "What a glorious, broad, massive uplift that mountain is!" he wrote. "The Mississippi is not so truly the father of waters as McKinley is the father of mountains.... I would rather climb that mountain than discover the richest goldmine in Alaska."

In 1913, he did. Putting together a summit expedition, Stuck first recruited Harry Karstens—the same Harry Karstens who had guided Charles Sheldon and would later become Mount McKinley National Park's first superintendent—a first-rate explorer, woodsman, and backcountry traveler. The expedition's two other climbing members were Robert Tatum and Walter Harper. Tatum worked at the Episcopal mission in Nenana, while Harper, part Native, served as Stuck's attendant, interpreter, and dog-team driver. Two Native teenagers helped on the approach.

*Members of the 1913 Stuck Expedition. From left: Robert Tatum, a teenager
known only as Esais, Harry Karstens, Johnny Fredson, and Walter Harper.*

In preparation for the climb, during the summer of 1912 Stuck had food, fuel,
and equipment shipped into the Denali region and cached as close as possible to
the mountain. Then, in late winter, Stuck's dog teams transported these supplies
onto the Muldrow Glacier. The expedition left the town of Nenana, 100 miles
northeast of Denali, on March 17, 1913, and reached Denali's Muldrow Glacier—
"the highway of desire," as Stuck put it—in mid-April. By June 6, the climbers had established their high camp at 18,000 feet (5500 meters). The following
morning, on a windy but clear day, they headed for the top. Led by twenty-
one-year-old Walter Harper, they reached the South Peak's summit in early
afternoon of June 7. Only after prayers and some scientific work did the climbers allow themselves to enjoy the surrounding landscape. The most impressive
views, Stuck later wrote, were those to the south and east, where an "infinite
tangle of mountain ranges filled the whole scene, until gray sky, gray mountain
and gray sea merged in the ultimate distance."

In addition to their own success on the South Peak, the Stuck party also confirmed the Sourdoughs' success on the North Peak. In his expedition account,
The Ascent of Denali, Stuck recalled that during a rest break,

> . . . *we fell to talking about the pioneer climbers of this mountain who claimed
> to have set a flagstaff near the summit of the North Peak—as to which feat a great*

deal of incredulity existed in Alaska.... All at once, Walter cried out: "I see the flagstaff!"...Karstens, looking where he pointed, saw it also and, whipping out the field glasses, one by one we all looked, and saw it distinctly standing out against the sky.

Nine different teams had attempted to reach Denali's summit between 1903 and 1913, but following its "conquest," nearly two decades would pass before another party walked its slopes. In 1932, two different teams attempted ascents in what proved to be another milestone year. Among other firsts, these were the first expeditions to visit Denali since the national park was formed in 1917; they were also the first to need approval from park managers to ascend the mountain.

In April 1932, a four-man party led by park superintendent Harry Liek and Minnesotan Alfred Lindley made the first attempted ski ascent, via the Muldrow Glacier. Icy conditions kept the Lindley-Liek expedition from reaching the top on skis, but its four members—who included park ranger and future superintendent Grant Pearson—became the first to scale both the North and South peaks.

Led by well-known mountaineer and scientist Allen Carpé, the second 1932 expedition also recorded several firsts. Flown by Fairbanks pilot Joe Crosson, its members made the first-ever glacier landing anywhere, on the Muldrow. They were also the first to receive air-dropped supplies. And, sadly, two members of the team became the first mountaineering deaths on Denali: Carpé and Theodore Koven were killed by crevasse falls while traveling the Muldrow Glacier unroped. Another member of the team, apparently suffering from food poisoning, was the first to be rescued from the mountain, by Fairbanks pilot Jerry Jones.

BRADFORD WASHBURN AND THE WEST BUTTRESS

From his vantage point atop Denali in 1913, Hudson Stuck felt certain the mountain would never be climbed by any route other than the Muldrow Glacier. Stuck's view remained the conventional wisdom for nearly four decades: every expedition between 1932 and 1950—eight in all—followed his and the Sourdoughs' footsteps up the Muldrow. Not until 1951 did a party attempt another avenue to the top. Leading that expedition was a New Englander whose name has become intimately linked with the mountain: Bradford Washburn.

A highly successful mountaineer, photographer, author, lecturer, cartographer, explorer, and scientist, Washburn was widely recognized as the world's leading authority on Denali until his death in 2007. Starting with his first photographic and aerial mapping flights in 1936, he devoted much of his life to the peak's study and exploration. In 1960, he produced his highly acclaimed Mount McKinley map, still considered a cartographic work of art. His photographic record of the mountain is unmatched.

Two Denali legends: "Mr. McKinley" Bradford Washburn, left, talks with Grant Pearson, who climbed Denali in 1932 and later became park superintendent.

Washburn also acted as Denali's visionary, recommending several new routes to its summit. He first climbed the mountain in 1942, via the Muldrow Glacier route, and again reached the summit in 1947 with his wife, Barbara, the first woman to stand on the roof of North America. That same year, he proposed a new path to the summit—which he called the West Buttress Route—and

Beyond Denali

Climbers wishing to escape the mountaineering crowds needn't look far beyond Denali. Several of Denali's satellite peaks are among the most beautiful and challenging mountains in North America. Yet most years these other peaks are attempted by few, if any, expeditions. The 17,400-foot Mount Foraker is North America's sixth-highest mountain and third-highest in Alaska, but it is only rarely climbed despite alluring route names such as the Pink Panther, Infinite Spur, and Highway of Diamonds. The 14,570-foot (4440-meter) Mount Hunter, the third member of Denali's family, was called by mountaineering author Jon Waterman "the most difficult 14,000-foot mountain in North America." The list of famous and obscure peaks within the boundaries of the park and preserve is endless—Mount Huntington, Mooses Tooth, Kichatna Spires, Little Switzerland, Mount Silverthrone, Mount Russell, Mount Brooks, Mount Dickey, Mount Barrille, Kahiltna Dome, Peters Dome, and Mount Deception, to name a few. Each has its own story, its history of ascents, its still unmet challenges. Climbers who do their research—who read Denali literature and The American Alpine Journal, talk with park rangers, and contact mountain guide services—will get a sense of what's possible. Besides these named and storied landscape features, dozens of other anonymous ridges and walls remain unclimbed and unexplored, still hidden in the shadow of The High One.

predicted that it, not the Muldrow, would be the safest, easiest, and quickest way up Denali, if an expedition received aerial support.

Despite the climbing community's unsupportive response to his proposed route, Washburn returned to Denali's slopes for a third time in June 1951 with a team from Colorado. Half the party approached from the north, while the other four, Washburn among them, were dropped by pilot Terris Moore at 7700 feet (2350 meters) on the previously unexplored Kahiltna Glacier. Landing on the Kahiltna gave Washburn's team an enormous advantage over early-twentieth-century explorers because it eliminated an extremely long and arduous approach hike from the coast. And it set the stage for Denali's climbing future.

The climb was largely uneventful, except for one fierce blizzard, and at 5:45 PM on July 10, Washburn, Jim Gale, and Bill Hackett gained the summit (eventually all eight team members would reach the top). Afterward, Washburn reflected with considerable pride, "Our new route up McKinley's 'impregnable' western face…was proved to be an ideal avenue for future scientific work atop the roof of North America."

The West Buttress has also proved to be an ideal avenue for the climbing public. Eighty to 90 percent of those attempting to reach Denali's summit nowadays follow the West Buttress route. Its popularity is easy to understand: as Washburn predicted a half century ago, it is the easiest, safest way to the top. Not that an easy way up Denali is *that* easy—even among well-conditioned and trained climbers, success rates are comparatively low. Most years, nearly half of West Buttress climbers fail to reach the summit, and more than fifty people—including some expert mountaineers—have died along this route because of crevasse falls, climbing falls, altitude sickness, and hypothermia.

OTHER MILESTONE EXPEDITIONS

Even as the mountaineering masses have been drawn in growing numbers to the West Buttress, others have sought new and different paths to the top. Since Washburn's historic expedition in 1951, nearly every major ridge and face has been climbed, and the mountain has been ascended in winter. Among those ascents are several mountaineering milestones. Here's a sampling:

Cassin Ridge. After his success on the West Buttress, Brad Washburn proposed several new routes to the summit, including "the great central bulge on the fabulous 10,000-foot [3050-meter] South Face of the mountain." In 1961, an Italian team led by legendary alpinist Riccardo Cassin took on the challenge. Cassin and five teammates reached the summit shortly before midnight on July 19 and then survived a harrowing descent in severe weather and returned to Italy as heroes. Bradford Washburn called their ascent of the South Face's "central bulge" (later named the Cassin Ridge) "without question, the greatest climb in North American mountaineering history" up to that time.

First Winter Ascent. By the mid-1960s, Denali was no longer a mysterious place to climb—except in winter. In 1967, a team of six Americans, one Frenchman, and one Japanese made the first winter attempt on the summit via the West Buttress. Despite bitterly cold and often stormy weather, Art Davidson, Ray Genet, and Dave Johnston made it to the top at 7 PM on February 28. But the greatest challenge lay ahead: On the descent the trio got caught in a ferocious storm just above 18,200-foot (5500-meter) Denali Pass. Forced to dig a shelter, they spent six days in a tiny snow cave with little food, water, or warmth. All three managed to survive, and their riveting story is told in Davidson's *Minus 148°: First Winter Ascent of Mount McKinley*.

First Solo Ascent. One of mountaineering's extreme challenges is to solo: to climb alone, without the security and support—both physical and emotional—of teammates. The first climber to go one-on-one with Denali was Japanese adventurer Naomi Uemura in August 1970. Then twenty-nine, Uemura had already proven himself one of the world's outstanding mountaineers. Traveling light and fast—his pack weighed only 55 pounds—and subsisting on a diet of salmon,

salmon eggs, and bread, Uemura ascended the West Buttress in only eight days, two to three times faster than the average expedition.

In 1984, Uemura also became the first person to attempt a winter solo ascent of Denali. He reached the summit on February 12 (his forty-third birthday), but disappeared while descending the mountain. How he died remains a mystery, because Uemura's body has never been found.

Four years later, in March 1988, Alaskan mountaineer Vern Tejas became the first climber to reach Denali's summit in winter and survive his solo effort.

Denali Mountaineering Firsts

1903	First expedition to attempt Denali's summit, James Wickersham expedition.
May–September 1903	First circumnavigation, Frederick Cook Expedition.
April 3, 1910	First ascent (North Peak), Pete Anderson and Billy Taylor.
June 7, 1913	First ascent (South Peak), Hudson Stuck, Walter Harper, Harry Karstens, Robert Tatum.
June 6, 1947	First female ascent, Barbara Polk Washburn.
July 10, 1951	First ascent (West Buttress), Bradford Washburn, Jim Gale, Bill Hackett.
June 1961	First guided ascent, Richard McGown and five clients.
February 1967	First winter ascent, Dave Johnston, Art Davidson, Ray Genet.
August 1970	First solo ascent (West Buttress), Naomi Uemura.
May 28, 1979	First dog-team ascent, Susan Butcher, Joe Redington Sr., Rob Stapleton, Ray Genet, Brian Okonek.
July 21, 1982	First female solo ascent, Miri Ercolani.
February 12, 1984	First winter solo ascent (West Buttress), Naomi Uemura (died on descent).
May 1985	First ascent by full-leg amputee (no artificial limb), Sarah Doherty.
March 7, 1988	First successful winter solo ascent (West Buttress), Vern Tejas.
May 30, 1993	First ascent by a blind climber, Joan Phelps.
February 17–April 2, 1995	First winter circumnavigation, Mark Stasik and Daryl Miller.
June 2011	First person to complete fifty ascents of Denali, climbing guide Vern Tejas.

Mountaineers work their way along Denali's popular West Buttress Route, on their way to establishing a camp at 14,200 feet.

CONTEMPORARY CLIMBS

Brad Washburn's vision, combined with the increased availability of bush pilots, mountain guides, and high-tech climbing equipment, eventually opened up the mountain to a new breed of Denali mountaineer: the adventure traveler. Through

Climbing the Mountain Today

Mountaineers must preregister at least sixty days in advance for expeditions to Denali and nearby Mount Foraker and pay a $350 special-use climbing fee (as of 2013) for attempts on those two peaks (the cost is $250 for climbers twenty-four or younger). The Park Service emphasizes that this is not a rescue fee. Rangers recommend that climbers planning any expeditions into Denali National Park contact the mountaineering center ahead of time for the most up-to-date information and advice on trips into the Alaska Range. Park staff can also provide lists of guide services permitted to operate on McKinley and Foraker, as well as air-taxi companies that transport climbers from Talkeetna to the Alaska Range. Contact:

Denali National Park and Preserve
Talkeetna Mountaineering Center and Ranger Station
P.O. Box 588
Talkeetna, AK 99676
907-733-2231
www.nps.gov/dena/planyourvisit/mountaineering.htm

the first five decades of Denali mountaineering, from 1903 through 1953, only 114 people tried to climb the peak. Over the next half-century (through 2003), 27,320 climbers would make attempts, the large majority along the West Buttress Route. As noted above, more than 38,500 people tried to scale the great peak through the 2012 climbing season (the most recent year for which such statistics are available at this writing), with more than 20,000 of them successful.

Interest in the mountain began growing dramatically in the mid-1970s as the Park Service loosened its mountaineering restrictions (for instance, in regard to preregistration, group size, medical certificates, gear inspection, and trip itineraries) and as professional guides began to escort climbers up Denali. And there's no sign of it letting up. More than 1100 people have attempted Denali every year since 1993, with the number often exceeding 1200 people since 2000 and an all-time high of 1340 in 2005. Many have had little or no prior high-altitude experience and have relied on the expertise of guides.

Adding to the mountain's allure are its high visibility and, since the advent of commercial bush-pilot services in the 1950s, its remarkable accessibility. Denali can be seen from Alaska's two largest cities as well as from the Parks Highway south of the Alaska Range, which has countless splendid views. For those desiring a closer look, the mountain is only a 30-minute plane ride from the town of Talkeetna, which has justifiably earned a reputation as the "Gateway to Denali."

Talkeetna's air-taxi services provide both sightseeing opportunities and transportation to the Kahiltna Glacier, which since the late 1960s has served as base camp for the great majority of Denali's mountaineering expeditions. From the 7200-foot (3100-meter) base camp, it's about 16 miles and 13,000 vertical feet (4000 meters) to the summit.

Though it's been proven that climbers with little or no previous high-altitude climbing experience can reach the mountain's top when benefited by expert guidance and state-of-the-art equipment, a mastery of basic mountaineering skills, excellent physical conditioning, good judgment, and a willingness to endure pain are required. Those who underestimate Denali's dangers suffer the consequences: altitude sickness, broken bones, hypothermia, frostbite, or even death. Especially risky are solo ascents. The dangers of traveling alone on Denali's glaciers—or unroped, even if with partners—are well documented. In the eight decades since Denali's first climbing deaths in 1932, ten climbers died in crevasse falls. Others, never found, may have shared similar fates.

In all, 120 people died on Denali's slopes from the earliest expeditions in 1903 through 2012. More than sixty have been killed in falls; others by avalanches, falling ice, high-altitude illnesses, or the cold. Hundreds more have been seriously injured. Eleven deaths occurred in one calamitous season, 1992; the single worst disaster took place in 1967, when seven members of a twelve-person expedition died during a severe midsummer storm.

On Denali's Most Popular Route

Back in the mid-1980s I, like thousands of others, came under Denali's spell. Because of my limited climbing experience, I joined a guided climb on the West Buttress. Following in the footsteps of Bradford Washburn and other West Buttress pioneers, I learned firsthand that Denali's most popular route is indeed achievable by someone who is not a hard-core mountaineer. At the same time, the West Buttress proved itself far more challenging than the "walk-up" some climbers claim it to be.

DAY 1. I lie in my sleeping bag trying to nap, but sleep is impossible. It's late afternoon on May 31, and the tent is too bright, too hot. And I have too much nervous energy. Just a few hours ago I flew by ski-equipped air taxi to the Kahiltna Glacier Base Camp, with seven teammates. Our chief guide, Vern Tejas, has reached the summit ten previous times. Less than a year from now he will become the first person to complete a solo winter ascent of Denali.

Outside the tent, the glacier broils in summertime heat. Temperatures in the shade read only 50°F (10°C). But in direct sunlight, with afternoon glare reflected off ice and snow, the mercury rises much higher—it's like being

A team of climbers ascends 20,320-foot Denali while following the West Buttress Route, taken by the great majority of mountaineers who seek to reach the summit.

tossed in a frying pan. At 7200 feet (2200 meters), under clear blue skies, the primary dangers are heatstroke and sunburn rather than hypothermia and frostbite.

Because of the heat, we temporarily move to a night-shift operation: we'll travel during the cool of evening and early morning. After we set up camp, the guides suggest we rest. Sleep doesn't come, so I listen to the rumble of avalanches.

DAY 2. Our first night in the Alaska Range is one of the worst. The food-and-fuel carry begins at midnight and lasts until eight in the morning. We travel 5 miles up the Kahiltna Glacier to Camp I, at 7500 feet (2300 meters), while carrying 50-pound packs and pulling plastic sleds loaded with supplies. A new storm arrives, bringing wet snow and whiteout conditions, and we return to base camp soggy and exhausted. Like most expeditions, we'll make double carries between camps to reduce the weight we have to haul on each trip.

(continued)

On Denali's Most Popular Route (continued)

DAY 4. We make our first carry to Camp II, at 9500 feet (2900 meters). At midnight, Denali's summit ridge is bathed in a golden alpenglow, while a bright quarter-moon slowly sinks behind neighboring Kahiltna Dome. Except for a solitary skier, our team is alone on the trail. The only sounds are the sleds dragging in soft snow, our steady breathing, and the occasional rush of wind. Pink, then orange, and finally yellow bands of light on surrounding peaks signal morning's arrival as we return to camp.

DAY 6. It's no longer too hot for day travel, so we nightcrawlers become day-trippers. Reaching 11,000 feet (3355 meters) in late afternoon, we establish Camp III. Like most climbers, we guard against Denali's often-ferocious winds by constructing snow-block walls around our tents; others prefer snow caves or igloos.

After getting settled, we practice crevasse-rescue techniques. Breaks in the glacier ice, crevasses may be hundreds of feet deep. Many are narrow at the surface but broaden into huge chambers below. Sometimes hidden, they are among the chief dangers facing mountaineers on Denali.

DAY 8. We break Camp III at midday and ascend into a full-blown blizzard. Standing on an exposed ridge, we are blasted by 50-mile-an-hour gusts. Wind-driven snow stings our faces and reduces visibility to a few feet. The air temperature is 20°F (–7°C), but gales drive the wind chill far below zero.

Vern calls for a rest stop, and although my mind screams, "Let's move, let's move!" his decision makes sense. Conditions may be even worse up ahead; we need food and water to guard against exhaustion and dehydration. Pulling the water bottle out of my pack is an excruciating task. To work the zipper, I remove my overmitts and wool mittens. My hands grow numb in seconds.

After a short break we resume our ascent, wind-driven snow now beating directly into our faces. We hit a stretch of trail heavily drifted by soft, fresh powder. I struggle, my miseries compounded by glacier sunglasses that fog so badly I can barely see. Breathing hard and fast, I fight off panic and, for the first time, think of death. Fortunately the clouds break, the snow stops, the wind eases, and we stumble into Camp IV, 14,200 feet (4330 meters), at nine in the evening.

DAY 10. Early in the afternoon we carry supplies from 14,200 feet to our next campsite, Camp V, at 16,400 feet (5000 meters) along the crest of the West Buttress ridge. To get there we must climb a snow- and ice-covered wall 2000 feet (610 meters) high, strapping sharp-spiked crampons to our climbing boots to grip the slick slopes. The upper 1000 feet crosses hard-packed crusted snow and ice at angles of 45 to 60 degrees. Across that section a fixed-line rope is bolted into the snow to assist us as we move up or down, digging in our sharp-pointed ice axes for added safety.

Upon reaching the ridgeline I feel exhausted, light-headed. We cache our gear, take a rest break, then go back down the fixed line. I know I'm not too sharp, so I try to concentrate harder. Descending, I stumble or lose my balance several times, but the combination of my roped teammates and the fixed line prevents any serious falls. Back at Camp IV I feel sharper, more in control, more relaxed. Vern believes my exhaustion was complicated by altitude problems, that I'd suffered a loss of coordination caused by a lack of oxygen.

DAY 14. We've ascended to our high camp, Camp VI, at 17,200 feet (5250 meters) without any significant delays, putting ourselves in position for a shot at the summit—but not today. Winds gusting to 40 miles an hour rattle our tents and push the wind chill far below 0°F (–18°C), driving us into the security of sleeping bags.

DAYS 18–19. June 17 starts out just like the previous four days: cold and windy. Late in the afternoon, the wind dies and the clouds break. Suddenly it is sunny and calm. There's no telling how long this window might last, so Vern announces, "Start getting your things together. We're going up." My legs feel like lead weights as we set out at 5:30 PM, thanks to four days of inactivity. But as we ascend the ramplike trail to 18,200-foot (5550-meter) Denali Pass, they gradually lighten. What bothers me more is the subzero cold.

Led by Vern, only four of us are making this final ascent; the altitude or exhaustion has stopped others on the team. Continuing upward, I have breathing problems. No matter how deeply I inhale, I can't seem to get enough oxygen into my lungs. And with 1000 vertical feet still to climb, my feet are painfully cold. Despite the physical problems, my determination has grown. If one of us is unable to continue, the entire summit party will be forced to retreat. Knowing that, it becomes easier to put up with the pain.

(continued)

On Denali's Most Popular Route (continued)

We take a break near a landmark named the Archdeacon's Tower. It's now well after midnight. Leaving our packs at the tower, we cross a shallow bowl. Then, in what seems like slow motion, we ascend the 800-foot-high wall leading to the summit ridge, which is covered with fresh, trackless snow.

Nearing Denali's summit I feel no elation or sense of victory, only relief that the ordeal is ending. We reach the top at 3:54 AM on June 18 after more than 10 hours on the trail. Our stay is painfully short, no more than 10 minutes. We let loose with a couple of "Yee-hahs!" and link hands in tribute to our success. It's very cold, −30°F (−34°C). A gentle breeze skims the summit, driving the chill even deeper. I try taking some summit photos to document our success, but my coordination is poor and I snap only a couple of blurred pictures. The sun has just risen above a layer of low-lying clouds into an immense azure sky, bathing Denali and surrounding peaks in a rosy glow, but I'm too exhausted to appreciate the beauty.

Heading down, we carefully watch our steps; a high percentage of mountaineering accidents occur on the descent, when climbers often lose their focus. We reach camp at eight in the morning. Despite worries about my feet, the only damage to my skin is one tiny frostnip blister on my right hand, which I got from foolishly holding my camera barehanded on the summit.

DAYS 20–21.   We quickly descend under clear, calm skies and make camp at 11,000 feet. During the night another storm moves in, and we awaken to 3 feet of new snow, strong winds, and whiteout. The trail is obliterated, so the route down-glacier is defined only by the wands placed every couple of hundred feet to mark it. Progress is slow as we trudge forward surrounded by flat gray nothingness. Within a few miles of Kahiltna Base Camp the cloud ceiling lifts and the snowfall ends. We're home free.

Chapter 3

DENALI'S
WILDLIFE AND PLANTS

Two things, above all, bring people to Denali National Park: the continent's highest mountain and large northern mammals. While it's an exaggeration to call Denali—or any part of Alaska—a "northern Serengeti," this park, more than any other, gives visitors the best chance to see a variety of Alaska's large land mammals without spending days or weeks in the backcountry. But in looking for grizzlies, wolves, Dall sheep, caribou, and moose, visitors are encouraged to also pay attention to the smaller animals and the multitude of plants that make up Denali's still-intact ecosystem. Without them, there would be no large mammals to gaze upon. What follows is a natural history guide to Denali's plant and animal communities, with a discussion of the "bigger picture" followed by more detailed descriptions of several of the park's better-known animals—big and small—and some of its more recognizable plants.

A SUBARCTIC ECOSYSTEM

Denali National Park and Preserve's 6 million acres encompass an entire subarctic ecosystem. What this means, in part, is that the park protects a full range of interconnected and undeveloped habitats, from high mountain glaciers to alpine tundra, wooded lowlands, and river basins. It also means that the park's wildlife residents can meet all of their basic needs—food, water, cover, mating, birthing—within Denali's boundaries. It doesn't mean that animals never leave the park. Many birds, for example, reside here seasonally and spend their winters in warmer climates—a long-distance migration that is naturally part of their annual cycle. Far-ranging mammals like caribou and wolves occupy ranges or territories that include lands outside the park.

North of the Alaska Range, Denali's three primary plant associations are northern Interior forest, also known as the boreal forest or taiga; the treeless plant assemblages collectively called tundra; and the transitional zone between the two. These are the plant communities seen by visitors as they travel the Denali Park Road or explore the national park's backcountry. To inhabit this subarctic climate, all of the plants found here—from the tallest spruce and cottonwood

Early bloomers in Denali National Park's alpine tundra, mountain avens prefer rocky slopes. These mountain avens had gone to seed by the end of July.

trees to the tiniest wildflowers and shrubs—must be able to endure long, harsh winters, short growing seasons, and a low annual precipitation equivalent to 12 to 15 inches of rainfall. For seven to nine months of every year the ground is snow-covered and frozen, temperatures are subfreezing, and many plants are dormant.

Permafrost

Permafrost, or permanently frozen ground, underlies much of the northern Denali region, though its depth beneath the surface varies considerably, from several inches to several feet (the permafrost layer, in turn, may range from a few feet to thousands of feet thick). This distance from ground surface to permafrost strongly influences plant distribution because roots are confined to the "active" layer above the year-round ice.

Some species, particularly trees, cannot survive where permafrost is too close to the surface, because it doesn't leave room for their roots. Permafrost also hinders the ability of soils to absorb water in summer when snowmelt and rainfall occur; areas underlain by permafrost are therefore often boggy and saturated with acidic waters. Some of these bogs, called muskegs, form thick layers of peat from undecayed plant materials.

Permafrost, then, is one factor that determines the tree line—the line beyond which trees can't survive. Others factors include: the extent of summer warming, which places limits on photosynthesis; poorly developed soils; and exposure to winter's severe and desiccating winds. The term tree "line" is misleading, however, because the start of the north side's treeless tundra habitat ranges from 2700 feet on wind-blasted hillsides to 3800 feet on sunny, protected slopes. Rarely, if ever, is there a sharp demarcation between taiga and tundra. One grades into the other—hence the transitional zone.

Taiga

Denali's taiga is well represented in the national park's entrance area and along much of the park road to Igloo Creek (mile 34), and again in the Wonder Lake area, at road's end. White and black spruce trees dominate most of this northern forest. Of the two, the more scraggly looking black spruce has the shallower root system and tolerates acidic waters, so it can more easily grow in bogs above permafrost. The straighter, taller, and more conical white spruce prefers well-drained soils. Heights vary greatly: in protected valleys, white spruce may grow to 80 feet or more; on exposed ridges, a tree several decades old may be no higher than a yardstick.

In some parts of the taiga, spruces intermingle with a variety of deciduous hardwood trees: quaking aspen, paper birch, balsam poplar, and cottonwood. The age of a forest can be approximated by the relative abundance of these

A beaver feeds on willow along the shores of Horseshoe Lake, in Denali National Park's entrance area. Beavers inhabit many of Denali's lakes and ponds.

leafy trees. A young boreal forest—for example, one that's recovering from a fire—is rich in hardwoods. As the forest matures, spruce trees increase in number and gradually take over. A sampling of Denali's other taiga plants includes willow, alder, prickly rose, Labrador tea, several berry plants—soapberry, crowberry, blueberry, high- and lowbush cranberry, red bearberry—and numerous wildflowers, such as tall fireweed, tall Jacob's ladder, bluebells, northern green orchid, dwarf dogwood, shy maiden, larkspur, and monkshood.

These plants, in turn, provide food and shelter for numerous animals adapted to forest life. In the taiga, the red squirrel can be heard chattering loudly as it harvests spruce cones. Snowshoe hares eating grasses and plant buds freeze in place to avoid detection by their primary predator, the graceful lynx. Beavers and muskrats make their homes in woodland ponds, moose forage on willow and aspen, and black bears move like shadows among the spruce as they search for grasses, catkins, insects, carrion, small mammals, and berries. Up in the treetops, boreal and black-capped chickadees feed on seeds and insects, ravens squawk loudly, and American kestrels hover above the ground or wait in perches while seeking out insects, voles, and small songbirds like the yellow warbler or common redpoll. Other mammals that inhabit the taiga include shrews, northern flying squirrels, porcupines, coyotes, wolves, red foxes, martens, weasels, and wolverines. Grizzlies too sometimes pass through the forest, but over the millennia they've adapted more closely to life on the open tundra. Among the taiga's birds are goshawks and merlins, great horned and hawk owls, common flickers, gray jays, magpies, American robins, three species of thrush, ruby-crowned kinglets, and a variety of warblers, finches, and sparrows.

Ecotone

The vaguely defined transitional zone between taiga and tundra is called an "ecotone." Observable along stretches of the park road, it is a place of dense willow and alder thickets, widely spaced spruce trees, and a variety of smaller shrubs and berry plants. Some taiga animals—moose, foxes, and some songbirds, for example—have adapted to this transitional zone, but other wildlife changes occur because of food, shelter, and nesting requirements. Instead of chattering red squirrels, the ecotone is home to yelping arctic ground squirrels. The hoots of great horned owls give way to those of short-eared owls, and the fluid melodies of thrushes are replaced by the cackles of ptarmigan.

Tundra

Beyond the ecotone is Denali's vast tundra landscape, a complex community of low-growing plants that supports a similarly diverse assemblage of insects, birds, and mammals adapted to this treeless environment. Two main types of tundra occur within Denali: wet and dry (or alpine). Both tundra varieties may be underlain by permafrost, and in many places they grade into one another over short distances. Near Wonder Lake, for example, many of the hillsides are patchworks of intermingled wet and dry tundra communities.

Wet tundra is characterized by moisture-loving plants: knee- to chest-high thickets of willow, alder, and dwarf birch, intermixed with lush berry patches, hummocks of grasses and sedges, and wildflower gardens. Among the most common plants are felt-leaf and diamond-leafed willow, blueberries and lowbush cranberries, Labrador tea, white heather, mountain alder, wild geraniums, monkshood, tall Jacob's ladder, frigid shooting stars, pink plumes, and Richardson's saxifrage.

Dry tundra is more likely to be found where temperatures are cooler, winds more severe, and soils poorer, thinner, and drier; in other words, in more mountainous terrain. Curiously, despite what seems to be harsher conditions, tundra assemblages at higher elevations tend to be the most diverse of all Denali's plant communities.

*The braided channels of the East Fork Toklat River are accentuated by Sep-
tember snow. The East Fork is one of several glacially fed braided streams that
flow north out of the Alaska Range.*

Alpine tundra plants rarely grow more than ankle high. Instead of reaching for the sky, woody plants like the arctic willow and blueberry are more likely to sprout only an inch or two or to send their limbs sprawling horizontally in ground-hugging fashion, while many wildflowers grow as mats and mounds. Though delicate in appearance, alpine tundra wildflowers are among the hardiest of flowering plants. Some manage to gain a foothold on the barest and rockiest of soils. Among the most common and colorful are pink moss campion, alpine azalea, and woolly lousewort; yellow spotted saxifrage and arctic poppy; white mountain avens; sky-blue mountain forget-me-not; violet-blue mountain harebell; purple mountain saxifrage; green to teal blue glaucous gentian; and magenta Lapland rosebay.

What's noticeable about these and other Denali flowers is the paucity of reds. This is because Denali's wildflowers are primarily pollinated by insects—flies, bumblebees, butterflies, and mosquitoes—and insects don't see red well. Yellows, blues, violets, and whites are what most attract them. If anyone ever asks, "What good are mosquitoes?" remember this: They're important pollinators of blueberries.

Whether wildflowers or willow, almost all wet and dry tundra plants are perennials that use a die-back strategy. To survive the winter, they either die back to their roots or to their limbs. They put more energy into flowers or fruits than into size, because bigness doesn't help plants survive subarctic winters. The result is low-growing plants with big leaves, flowers, or fruits. The tundra is famous for its berries: blueberries, lowbush cranberries, crowberries. Their seeds are dispersed by a variety of birds and mammals, but the best-known disperser, by far, is the grizzly, which leaves piles of berry-rich scat across Denali's open landscape.

A remarkably adaptable animal, the grizzly developed the tools necessary for tundra life as it evolved: long claws and powerful neck and back muscles to make it easier to dig plant roots and rodents from the earth, plus a large body and aggressive nature to defend itself—or, for a female, its young—in open spaces. Other large open-ground mammals of the Denali region to survive the end of the Pleistocene Ice Age and the Mammoth Steppe environment were the Dall sheep, caribou, and wolf.

A wide variety of smaller mammals and birds have adapted to life on the tundra and in its many ponds. A sampling includes arctic ground squirrels, hoary marmots, collared pikas, beavers, voles and lemmings, shrews, foxes, wolverines, golden eagles, northern harriers, gyrfalcons, long-tailed jaegers, ptarmigan, short-eared owls, sandpipers, ducks, swans, loons, gulls, horned larks, and snow buntings. Most of the birds are seasonal residents that migrate south for the long, bitterly cold winter, while a few of the mammals spend their winters in the deep sleep of hibernation.

The large glacial rivers that pass through Denali's tundra and forests north of the Alaska Range are mostly barren of fish because of the streams' braided nature and the heavy sediment load they carry. Some of the smaller clearwater creeks have populations of grayling, while lake trout and freshwater sculpin live in Wonder Lake.

South Denali

Plant communities south of the Alaska Range are distinctive from those of the north, as determined by the wetter and more moderate climate. Deeper snowfall means that snowfields remain on alpine slopes much later in the summer than on the north, favoring tundra species that thrive in a very short growing season. The species resemble those in Southcentral Alaska's coastal mountains, and the subalpine areas have very lush meadow vegetation that is much taller and greener than the dry, grassy areas on similar slopes north of the range. The southern slopes also lack the endemic plants of Asian origin, like alpine forget-me-nots, which are Beringian remnants.

Likewise, the forest of the south side begins to resemble the coastal forests of Southcentral Alaska. Many of the dominant species are the same as on the north—spruce, aspen, and birch, for example—but the density of life is greater, the size of the trees and plants grander. Grasses and fireweed may grow head-high or taller; cottonwoods soar above 100 feet. In places, thickets of alder and willow are so dense as to be impenetrable. There are thick ferns and shrubs on the forest floor, unlike the northern forests, and coastal species such as devil's club appear, an appropriately named large, leafy plant that has stalks lined with a host of tiny, painful needles.

Fed by abundant moisture (in the form of rainfall, snow, and glacial melt), the Susitna River is the southern region's largest stream and one of South Denali's central features. Huge runs of five Pacific salmon species—chinooks, cohos, sockeyes, chums, and humpbacks—spawn in the many clearwater tributaries to the "Big Su." Rainbow trout, arctic grayling, northern pike, and char also inhabit many rivers and lakes. Here too on Denali's south side are increased numbers of black bears, trumpeter swans, and bald eagles. Rarely seen on the Alaska Range's northern flanks, the fish-eating bald eagles are drawn to spawned-out salmon carcasses along the Susitna and other large streams.

MAMMALS

Though most people come to Denali to see the park's larger and more charismatic animals, the landscape is home to thirty-nine species of mammals, including some that are rarely if ever seen by visitors. Besides the species described below, Denali is inhabited by weasels, river otters, mink, martens, pikas, flying squirrels, porcupines, muskrats, mice, shrews, and bats. All of the mammals are

Dall sheep rams graze on alpine plants, with snow-covered peaks of the Alaska Range rising in the background.

listed in the checklist at the back of the book. For those seeking additional natural history information, Adolph Murie's *Mammals of Denali* includes descriptions of thirty-five species. Both Murie's book *A Naturalist in Alaska* and Tom Walker's *Denali Journal* include many wonderful accounts of wildlife behavior and encounters.

Dall Sheep (*Ovis dalli*)

It can be argued that Dall sheep, as much as 20,320-foot Mount McKinley, grizzly bears, or vast tundra expanses, are perfect symbols of what Adolph Murie called Denali's "wilderness spirit." Dall sheep drew naturalist-hunter-author Charles Sheldon to the Denali region in 1906. And their preservation, as much as anything, inspired him to seek park status for this wildlife-rich part of Alaska. Later in the park's history, severe Dall sheep declines in the 1930s and '40s caused great alarm and forced park managers and politicians to confront wildlife-management policies that favored one species (sheep) over another (wolves). Thanks largely to Murie, the sheep crisis—and the species' eventual recovery—ultimately led to a strengthening of ecosystem rather than favored game management in Denali National Park. It also led to Murie's now famous book, *The Wolves of Mount McKinley*.

Snow-white in color, these are the only wild sheep to reside in Alaska. Nowadays, an estimated 2500 of them inhabit Denali National Park and Preserve's alpine heights; based on 2008–9 surveys and those done in the mid-1990s, park biologists believe sheep numbers throughout most of the park to be "fairly stable" entering the 2010s. The large majority live on the Alaska Range's northern side, in both the Alaska and Outer ranges, between the Nenana River on the east and the Muldrow Glacier on the west.

The Denali Park Road borders some of the sheep's prime habitat, which means that visitors have an excellent chance of seeing these animals—though usually from a distance of several hundred yards to a half mile or more. They are most often seen as tiny white dots on the upper flanks of tundra-covered hills, though occasionally they can be spotted near or even on the road, especially in the Igloo Mountain, Polychrome Pass, and Eielson Visitor Center areas. Hill climbers are also likely to find sheep—or at least their hoofed tracks—in the Primrose Ridge and Mount Healy areas of the Outer Range and in the Alaska Range foothills that border large glacial valleys south of the park road.

A small percentage of Denali's Dall sheep actually cross the park road on seasonal migrations between the park's two mountain ranges. These migratory sheep spend their winters in the Outer Range, where snowfall is light and high winds often keep exposed ridges free of snow. In May or June they form groups of up to sixty or seventy animals and cross wide lowlands to reach the Alaska Range's northern foothills for summer's green-up. There the sheep remain until late August or September, when they retrace their steps. Biologists since Adolph Murie have known that a portion of Denali's sheep migrate, but it remains a mystery why some do and others don't.

Male and female sheep live apart except during the early winter rut, which occurs in November and December. Ewes give birth to a single lamb in late May or early June; as the birth approaches, a pregnant ewe will go off by itself and head for steep, extremely rugged terrain where predators are less likely to be. Lambs usually do fine their first summer, when food is abundant, but up to half die their first winter, depending on the season's severity. Sheep that survive their first couple of winters may live to between twelve and fifteen years. Older mature rams may weigh up to 160 pounds, ewes 110 to 130 pounds.

Both sexes of adult sheep have horns, though only males grow the large, sweeping, and outward-curling horns so often seen in Denali photos. As rams mature, their horns gradually form a circle when viewed from the side and reach a full circle or "curl" in seven to eight years. The amber-colored horns are male status symbols; large mature rams can sometimes be seen displaying their horns to other sheep as a sign of their dominance. Those of females are shorter, slender spikes that resemble the horns of mountain goats, which sometimes causes people to confuse the two species. For reference, goat horns are shiny black and sharper than sheep horns; goats also have more massive chests. Such confusion is unlikely in Denali, where only a couple confirmed sightings of mountain goats have been made since the park was founded in 1917; no mountain goats have been sighted here in recent years, and as of 2012 the species isn't included on the park's mammal checklist. If you see a horned, white mammal along the park road or in the backcountry, it's almost certainly a sheep.

Unlike the antlers of moose and caribou, sheep horns are never shed; they continue to grow throughout a sheep's life. Horn growth occurs only during the summer; winters are marked by a narrow groove or ridge. So, much like a tree, the age of sheep can be determined by reading their "annual rings."

Dall sheep are grazing animals that feed on grasses, sedges, willows, herbaceous plants, and, in winter, lichens. They prefer to stay up high because their hill-climbing skills make it easier to escape predators in steep, rugged, mountainous terrain. Wolves are the most efficient predators of Denali's sheep, but grizzlies, lynx, and wolverines sometimes successfully hunt the species and golden eagles now and then take a lamb.

Because Denali's sheep are unhunted, they've become highly tolerant of humans. Away from the road, they often can be closely approached, though park rules require that people remain at least 75 feet away to minimize harassment, even if unintentional. It's a special treat to share a hillside or alpine ridge with Dall sheep. As Murie has written, "Mountain sheep have a high esthetic appeal. In part this may be due to their setting, for we associate them with their beautiful haunts, the precipitous cliffs and ledges intermingled with green slopes and spangled with flowers. This is idyllic country in which to hike and climb."

Grizzly Bear (*Ursus arctos*)

Grizzly bears, by their nature, demand vast expanses of wild, undeveloped land to survive. Yet in Denali they are frequently seen near the park's lone road, by visitors traveling in large, noisy buses. A couple of circumstances help to explain this apparent paradox. First, much of Denali Park Road passes through the tundra habitat that grizzly bears prefer; at the same time, the open tundra makes it easier to spot wildlife—especially large, blond to chocolate brown mammals weighing up to 600 pounds. Second, Denali's grizzlies have grown habituated to people and bus traffic. Humans and their vehicles aren't a threat, nor a source of food. Busloads of people come and go and the bears simply go about their business, which mostly is the business of food gathering.

Grizzlies, it's been said, are "eating machines." This is especially true in the subarctic reaches of Denali National Park, where they must survive an entire year on the food they eat during their five- to seven-month waking period. An adult bear that weighs 450 pounds in May (about average for a male Denali grizzly) is likely to weigh 550 or 600 pounds when it enters its den in October. Females are considerably smaller, on the average weighing 250 pounds in spring and 350 in fall.

The grizzly's diet varies with the season: roots, emerging plants, winter-killed animals, and moose or caribou calves are favorite foods in spring and early summer, while from mid-July into fall and early winter the bear's number one choice is berries, especially blueberries and soapberries. As den-up approaches, grizzlies may consume hundreds of thousands of berries a day. They do this by taking as many as a hundred bites per minute for up to 12 hours a day. They also like to munch on ground squirrels, particularly in late summer and fall when the squirrels have more body fat and there's an abundance of less-savvy juveniles. Only rarely do grizzlies prey on adult moose, caribou, or wild sheep, and the ones they do kill are usually older, injured, or sick individuals.

By late fall, a high percentage of the grizzly's body weight will be fat. Once fat reserves reach a certain level, an internal mechanism shuts off the bear's appetite and its body chemistry begins adjusting to the long winter sleep ahead. The timing of den-up varies from bear to bear, but generally pregnant females are the first to enter their dens and, accompanied by their newborn cubs, the last to leave in spring. Adult males, meanwhile, are the last to den and the first to reappear from winter's sleep. On average, females spend up to seven months (from late September or early October to May) in hibernation, males about five months.

During their five- to seven-month waking period, Denali's grizzlies are among the park's most visible residents. If you see a bear, it's almost certain to be griz; black bears are much more shy and tend to stay hidden in forested areas. To be certain, look for these features: Grizzlies have large shoulder humps and a concave, dish-shaped facial profile. Many are blond or cream colored, but they may also be light brown, chocolate, or even black. You probably won't get close enough for a good look, but grizzlies also have long, rather straight claws adapted for digging in the tundra.

Some biologists suspect that certain bears—most notably mothers with cubs—frequent the road corridor because it acts as something of a "safe zone." Mature male grizzlies, which sometimes prey on cubs, appear to be less tolerant of humans and their traffic than younger bears and females; that is, they're more likely to shy away from the road corridor. Either by instinct or learned behavior, some female bears may have discovered this fact. And so they tolerate road traffic, because it helps to keep danger away.

This is good news for bear watchers, because it means that family groups— moms with cubs—are among the grizzlies most commonly seen by Denali visitors. Cubs can sometimes be observed as they nurse, though it's more likely you'll see them grazing, napping, or playing—with each other, mom, or objects they find on the tundra. Cubs learn by example, so often they'll mimic whatever mom is doing. That may mean digging for roots or squirrels, scratching themselves on spruce trees or road signs, or sliding down a snowbank.

Researchers estimate that 300 to 350 grizzlies inhabit Denali National Park on the north side of the Alaska Range; grizzlies also inhabit the foothills and lowlands of South Denali and though their number is uncertain, the presence of abundant food—especially salmon—suggests a higher density of bears. On occasion, a grizzly will even travel up a glacier into the park's high mountain country.

On Denali's north side (where most visitors travel), bear-viewing is consistently best in the alpine tundra west of Igloo Creek; those who travel as far as Eielson are especially likely to see grizzlies (more than four out of five shuttle bus passengers did so between 1999 and 2011). This is where the country opens up and becomes prime grizzly habitat. Sable and Highway passes, the East Fork and Toklat rivers, Stony Hill, and even the Eielson Visitor Center are likely places to see grizzlies in action. To prevent harm to either humans or bears, visitors outside of vehicles are required to stay at least 300 yards from grizzlies. See the introductory section "Safe Behavior in Bear Country" for other guidelines.

Though it may not seem so when viewing bears as they feast on berries, Denali's grizzlies lead a tough life, on the edge of survival. This is especially true of cubs. Since the early 1990s, nearly two-thirds of Denali's grizzly cubs have failed to survive their first year, and 40 percent of those survivors died their second year. That means cubs have about a one-in-seven chance of reaching their second birthday. Some are killed by other grizzlies, though it's uncertain how much of the mortality is from such infanticide. Male grizzlies are usually blamed, but researchers admit they don't know for sure. In some other parts of Alaska, female bears as well as males have been seen killing the cubs of another family. Other possible causes of death are starvation, accidents (for instance, drowning), or predation by wolves. If they reach maturity—which for Denali bears means four-and-a-half to five-and-a-half years old—grizzlies tend to be long-lived. Among the park's bears are several individuals twenty years or older.

Those who would like to learn more about Denali's grizzly population are advised to read Adolph Murie's *The Grizzlies of Mount McKinley*, which contemporary researchers say is just as relevant today as when Murie wrote it.

Black Bear (*Ursus americanus*)

Black bears are infrequently seen on Denali's north side, either along the park road or in the tundra backcountry; on occasion they are spotted in the Wonder Lake area. They're considerably more common in the South Denali region, particularly in the Byers Lake, Troublesome Creek, and Kesugi Ridge areas of Denali State Park.

A creature of forest and shadow, the black bear is more shy and secretive than the grizzly—except when it has learned to associate people with food. Then it can become a nuisance or "problem bear," as we humans put it. Black bears can be distinguished from grizzlies by the absence of a shoulder hump and a straight, "Roman-nose" facial profile. They also have shorter, more curved claws, which produce a different track. Though black is their most common color, they may also be brown, cinnamon, blond, blue-gray, or even white (though white and blue-gray varieties don't occur in the Denali region). Even bears with black coats aren't entirely black; most have brownish muzzles and many have white to cream-colored patches on their chest or throat.

Considerably smaller than grizzlies, black bear females usually weigh 120 to 175 pounds in Alaska, while males range from 200 to 400 pounds. Like grizzlies, black bears are omnivores whose diet is primarily plants. They'll eat grasses, sedges, horsetails, insects, berries, snowshoe hares, mice, birds, and carrion. Some will also prey on moose calves. Again, like grizzlies, Alaska's black bears spend much of their year in hibernation: between 190 and 230 days, on average.

Caribou (*Rangifer tarandus*)

Sometimes called the "nomads of the north," caribou are long-distance travelers that may cover hundreds of miles during their annual migrations between wintering ranges, calving grounds, summer feeding spots, and fall rutting areas. As they travel, they feed on lichens—their most important food—plus shrubs, grasses, sedges, and mushrooms.

Members of the deer family, caribou are unique in that both sexes have antlers. Female antlers are small and spiked, while those of bulls, as Adolph Murie put it, are "towering and picturesque." Measuring up to 5.5 feet long and 3 feet wide, male antlers also have a forward-facing "shovel" that extends over the nose, which may offer protection during rutting battles. Bulls use their antlers to intimidate competitors and attract cows; they are dropped in mid-October, soon after the rut. Pregnant cows, meanwhile, keep their antlers until the following spring; biologists suspect this helps them to defend feeding sites during the winter. Considerably smaller than their cousins the moose, caribou bulls weigh 450 to 600 pounds, females 200 to 250. Mostly dark brown, they have white underbellies. Males also have a white cape and mane around the shoulders and neck.

Caribou are gregarious creatures that form herds ranging in size from a few hundred animals to 200,000 or more. Approximately two dozen herds roam through Alaska; one of those—appropriately named the Denali Caribou Herd—inhabits Denali National Park and Preserve. Its members are commonly seen along the road corridor and in the backcountry north of the Alaska Range; in fact a study conducted between 1999 and 2011 showed them to be the large mammal most frequently observed on shuttle bus trips, seen by 91 percent of passengers during that period. Only rarely, however, do park visitors see large groups of caribou; most often they're observed singly, in pairs, or groups of less than ten. They can be found from the entrance area all the way to Wonder Lake, though they are naturally most easily seen where the landscape opens up. Caribou belonging to other herds can sometimes be seen along the Parks and Denali highways, on the Alaska Range's south side.

In the early 1900s, the Denali Caribou Herd numbered 20,000 or more animals, and naturalist Adolph Murie reported that he once watched a single group of 5000 caribou as it migrated through the park. A series of bad winters caused the herd to decline, and by the 1960s its numbers had fallen by more than half. Another series of severe, high-snow winters in the early 1970s continued the crash. By the mid-1970s, only a thousand remained. The herd then began a gradual recovery; in 1989, researchers estimated its size to be 3200 animals. Yet another series of high-snow years caused additional losses, and in the first decade of the twenty-first century the herd varied between 1800 and 2150 members, with a most current estimate of 2070 caribou in 2010. Such up-and-down cycles are typical of caribou throughout the north. The circumstances that lead to population swings are not fully understood, but winter weather and predation by wolves and bears (especially on calves) are clearly important factors. In some parts of Alaska, human hunting also plays a role, but the Denali Caribou Herd is protected from human harvest. Because this is the only unhunted barren-ground caribou herd in North America of this size (or larger), biologists place great value on what they can learn from it.

The relationships among caribou and their two prime predators, wolves and bears, are complex. Only since the mid-1980s have Denali researchers begun detailed predator–prey studies among these species. One thing they've learned is that deep-snow winters greatly favor wolves at the expense of caribou, while winters with little snow have the opposite effect. Not only are caribou easier to hunt when the snowpack is deep, but pregnant cows suffer nutritionally. As a consequence, calves born the following spring are more susceptible to predation and a much smaller percentage survive their first year. The end result: a caribou decline. For example: between 1989 and 1993—a period of snowy winters—Denali's caribou population dropped from 3210 to 1960, a decline of nearly 40 percent. Over that same period, estimated wolf numbers fluctuated between 143 and 169, nearly double what they were before the string of high-snow winters.

Though they belong to a single herd, Denali's caribou are usually widely scattered. Most remain on the Alaska Range's northern flanks throughout the year, but some occasionally travel to the park's south side. Males and females generally remain separated except for the annual rut, which occurs from late September into October. Caribou ruts are similar in many ways to those of moose (see below), with one complication: caribou breeding occurs while groups of the animals are on the move.

Calves are born between early May and early June, with nearly three-quarters born during a two-week span in mid-May. Biologists believe this "synchronous production" increases their odds of surviving. Some years, about half the Denali herd's pregnant cows will gather in alpine calving grounds up to 6000 feet high between the Muldrow and Straightaway glaciers, in the park's western reaches. The remainder are scattered over large areas. Cows seem to prefer mountainous areas near glaciers and snowfields because they're more protected from predators. Others, however, choose spruce forests. Caribou calves are especially vulnerable to predation their first two weeks of life, when they're unable to outrun wolves and bears.

By mid- to late June, bulls as well as cows and calves have moved high into the mountains to escape insects (though they remain in separate groups). Caribou, more than any other large Denali mammal, are plagued by mosquitoes and flies. Two species in particular, warble flies and nostril (or bot) flies, cause them great discomfort. As Murie noted, "On sunny days when the flies are very active, the movement of the herds is drastically influenced. The large herds may seek a high, breezy ridge, or a snowfield, to minimize the attack."

The insects begin to ease by mid- to late July and the caribou again disperse, only to re-form large groups in September for the start of the rut. After mating has ended, the caribou migrate to wintering ranges; many travel to the Outer Range's northern foothills, while others head for the lowlands west of Wonder Lake.

Wolf (*Canis lupus*)

To those who love wilderness, few experiences are as exciting as seeing or hearing wolves in the wild. And nowhere in Alaska do visitors have a better chance of encountering a wolf or hearing its howl than Denali National Park. Even here, the odds were extremely low until the 1990s, when (for reasons that are still uncertain) increased numbers of wolves began to frequent the park road corridor. Moving into the second decade of the twenty-first century, wolves still aren't seen as often as Denali's other large mammals; but some years between a quarter and half of all visitors who travel deep into the park (to the Toklat River or beyond) have spotted wolves (the average was 23 percent between 1999 and 2011). In 2010, park officials estimated that between 20,000 and 30,000 visitors were seeing wolves each summer. The odds may be even higher for backcountry trekkers, but probably not much. If nothing else, hikers and backpackers are more likely to find wolf sign: tracks, scat, or abandoned dens.

Given the wolf's present popularity with Denali visitors, it's hard to imagine that between 1929 and 1952 park rangers killed at least seventy wolves as part of a predator-control program intended to protect then-McKinley National Park's ungulates, particularly sheep. Even the renowned naturalist and conservationist Adolph Murie, champion of Denali's "wilderness spirit," participated in limited control programs to boost sheep populations. The year 1952 marked the end of Denali's wolf-control era, and wolves are now protected from any human harvest in the park's 2.1-million-acre wilderness core. However, a subsistence harvest occurs outside protected areas and a small percentage of Denali's wolves are annually killed by hunters and trappers, both in the preserve and on adjacent state lands (when wolves roam beyond the park's boundary).

Based on research and monitoring studies conducted since 1986, researchers tell us that Denali's wolf population is highly dynamic. The number of wolves estimated to inhabit the 6-million-acre park and preserve has ranged from a low of 46 to a high of 169 (wolf counts are normally lowest in early spring, because mortality is highest in winter, and they're largest in late summer/early fall, after pups are born). The number of packs monitored on the Alaska Range's north side since 1986 has ranged from four to twenty, with the number of identifiable packs since 1990 varying from nine to twenty.

More evidence of flux: twenty new packs were formed and sixteen died out during a twelve-year period between 1986 and 1997. Only two packs—the East Fork and McLeod Lake—maintained their continuity throughout that time, though even they experienced many changes. The East Fork, for example, had as few as six and as many as twenty-nine members during that time frame.

The best known of Denali's packs is the East Fork, first studied by Murie in 1940–41 and discussed, in great detail, in his landmark book *The Wolves of Mount McKinley* (published in 1944). As wolf researcher L. David Mech and his co-authors wrote in their own 1998 book *The Wolves of Denali*: "The East Fork Pack is of great interest to park staff and visitors, being the most readily observable pack in the park and carrying the legacy of Murie's study and writing.... The wolves regularly travel, make kills, and occupy rendezvous areas within sight of the park road." And most of their range is in wide-open country, which increases viewing opportunities. Since the early 2000s, a second family group, the Grant Creek Pack, has become even more visible than East Fork wolves, partly because its alpha pair has denned remarkably close to the park road for several summers. For the best chance of seeing a wolf, visitors should be especially alert anywhere from Teklanika to Eielson.

Denali's wolf packs, like those elsewhere, live their lives in territories that they mark and maintain in three main ways: scent marking, howling, and aggression. However, there is usually some overlap in the territories of neighboring packs. Wolves will readily kill interlopers that invade their territories. In fact, it appears that wolves killing other wolves is their main cause of death, usually occurring along pack boundaries. In the late 1980s, a pack of ten wolves completely wiped out a neighboring pack of eight. Known territories within the park (as measured by researchers) have varied from 190 to 1160 square miles (500 to 3000 square kilometers). The larger areas reflect packs that are heavily dependent on caribou and follow their annual movements.

Highly social predators, wolves depend on cooperation to survive. Led by the alpha, or dominant, male and female, Denali's wolves prey mostly on ungulates: sheep, moose, and caribou. Young, old, sick, and injured animals are most commonly taken, but when the circumstances are right—as in deep-snow winters—healthy adults are also sometimes killed. When enough food is available, a wolf can consume up to one-fifth its body weight in meat. Other species that fill out a wolf's diet include snowshoe hares, ground squirrels, voles, mice, lemmings, marmots, and porcupines.

A wolf pack's year is divided into two main seasons: summer and winter. Pregnant females seek out a den in May, which then serves as a base for the next two months. Normally only the alpha female becomes pregnant, but in some instances two or three females in the same pack will produce pups (usually in separate dens). The East Fork Pack had multiple pregnancies every year between 1988 and 1991. Born the second or third week in May, litters average four to five pups.

While the moms look after the newborns, other members of the pack disperse to hunt; sometimes they join in small groups or pairs, but most often go alone. By midsummer, the pups are moved to an aboveground rendezvous site, where they sleep, eat, play, and begin to explore their world. Wolves are known for their play behavior, and adults as well as pups engage in "play fights" and other forms of fraternizing.

By late September or early October, the pups are ready to travel and the pack becomes a nomadic group that moves about its territory in search of prey. Traveling at a steady pace of 5 miles per hour, wolves may cover up to 45 miles in a day. They tend to go in single file, the most efficient way of traveling through snow.

At birth, a wolf weighs less than 1 pound. By the time they reach adulthood, males will average 80 to 120 pounds, females about 10 percent less. Gray is their most common color, but their coats can also be white, coal black, brown, or some combination. Few Denali wolves live beyond age three, and the odds are about one in a thousand that any given wolf will live to nine or older. Most, as mentioned, are killed by other wolves; some die from starvation, avalanches, drowning, or human hunters and trappers.

Moose (*Alces alces*)

Visitors don't have to travel far into Denali National Park to see North America's largest member of the deer family. A study of shuttle- and tour-bus driver sightings between 1980 and 1990 showed that nearly half of all moose seen from the park road were spotted along the first 15 miles.

Moose may be seen almost anywhere in Denali's wooded entrance area: in the Riley Creek campground, near the visitor center and other facilities, even in the middle of the road. And what a sight they are: mature males stand up to 7 feet

A bull moose rests in the taiga forest after a September snowfall. This bull has been radio-collared to help biologists learn more about the species' habits.

high at the shoulders and weigh 1000 to 1500 pounds; in summer and fall, they'll also carry antlers that on the biggest bulls reach 60 to 70 inches across and weigh up to 70 pounds. Cows are only slightly smaller, weighing 700 to 1100 pounds. Besides being the largest of Denali's wildlife, moose also are among the strangest looking: their massive bodies are supported by tall, spindly legs, and their large heads sit on short necks and sport big ears and long, bulbous noses.

Though moose frequent the forested entrance area, seeing them is not a sure thing despite their great size. A park road study done between 1999 and 2011 found that only 40 percent of bus passengers saw moose during their Denali visit.

Visitors were more likely to see moose in the 1970s, says Vic Van Ballenberghe, who has studied Denali's moose for more than three decades. Back then, approximately 300 of the animals occupied Denali's wilderness core, east of the Teklanika River. By the mid-1990s, the number had plummeted to 125. The main reason: bear predation. Sometime in the mid-1970s, for reasons that remain unclear, Denali's grizzlies learned to be efficient killers of moose calves. And as the years went on, they took a great toll on the moose population. Some years, up to 90 percent of the moose born during the May–June calving period were killed by bears within weeks of their birth. By the 1990s, grizzlies accounted for more than half the calf mortalities, while wolves killed a small percentage and others died from accidents, malnutrition, congenital defects, or unknown factors.

Since the mid-1990s, the grizzly kill of newborn moose has declined substantially, perhaps because calves have become fewer in number and harder to find. By 2010, Van Ballenberghe notes, "we could find very few documented instances of grizzlies killing calves" in the entrance area. Consequently, the moose population in that area has stabilized at about 120 to 125 animals.

Those calves that survive the first few months of life grow quickly: 30 to 35 pounds and cinnamon colored at birth, they will weigh 300 to 400 pounds by fall and have darker brown coats like those of adults.

A note of caution: Cow moose are extremely protective of their young, one reason that park naturalists issue "moose warnings" to Denali visitors. Never should a moose family be closely approached; and if a moose charges—whether male or female—the best strategy is to run for cover. Once you've left a moose's "personal space," the animal will end its charge.

Unlike the entrance area, high grizzly predation didn't occur in Denali park's patchily forested northwestern corner, where moose numbers have largely remained stable. In all, the park's moose population north of the Alaska Range is estimated to be about 1300 animals; many others inhabit the wooded areas of South Denali, where they may be seen in Denali State Park or along the Parks Highway and Petersville Road corridors.

Though the areas most heavily populated by moose are far from the park road, the best bet for visitors remains the paved entrance-area roadway, which is bordered by high-quality moose habitat that includes a mix of taiga forest and thickets of willow, the primary food of moose. Special favorites include the diamond-leaf and felt-leaf varieties. Other plants eaten by Denali's moose include grass, alder, dwarf birch, and aspen. One other area with good moose-viewing potential is the Wonder Lake area, where they can sometimes be seen feeding in the lake or tundra ponds.

The best times to see Denali's moose are late May to early June, when they're on the move looking for new plant growth, and late August through September, during the rut. The rut is an especially fascinating time to observe moose. It begins, like clockwork, in late August, when bulls begin to lose the velvet from their antlers. This is also when they dig "rutting pits," shallow, elongated depressions into which they urinate. Both bulls and cows may wallow in such pits or splash the urine-mud mixture onto their antlers, head, neck, and shoulders.

Around September 1, dominant bulls stop feeding and begin their search for cows. At mid-month, bulls start to actively herd cows into breeding groups and they also become more vocal. Their grunts—described by biologists as "croaks"—are made while traveling alone, during courtship, or in response to rival bulls.

Breeding normally begins the last week of September and reaches a peak about October 1. The rut then gradually winds down and ends by October 10.

The breeding groups of cows are sometimes called harems, but they are more of a loose aggregation: "The bulls don't really have control over the cows," says Van Ballenberghe. "A cow can leave a bull if she's serious about it." The largest aggregation he has seen numbered thirty-four moose: twenty-two cows and twelve bulls. Besides the dominant bull, other males—called "satellite bulls"—hang out along the margins and sometimes breed with cows on the periphery.

It's nearly impossible for a bull to stay in charge of an aggregation throughout the rut. During the peak, the dominant bull may be challenged several times during the day—and the fighting eventually takes a toll. "It's sort of like being in a bar," Van Ballenberghe comments. "Sooner or later, somebody's going to come along who's tougher."

Confrontations normally begin with displays and threats and eventually escalate into sparring and, sometimes, fierce fights. Injuries are part of the ritual. About one-third of the dominant bulls are harmed, some fatally. Few bulls live beyond age ten or eleven, while the average life span of cows is fifteen to sixteen years and some live to be twenty or older.

When the rut has ended, the moose split up. Younger bulls remain with the cows, while the more dominant bulls go off by themselves in loose groups of up to ten animals.

Red Fox (*Vulpes vulpes*)

Widely distributed throughout the Denali region, red foxes are frequently seen by both backcountry trekkers and road-bound visitors. Despite their name, adult foxes come in silver, "cross," and red color phases. Kits, meanwhile, are charcoal gray when born, except for the white-tipped tail. The adult fox's large, white-tipped bushy tail (one-third to nearly one-half its total body length) is perhaps the most reliable way to distinguish it from Denali's wolves and occasional coyote.

Red foxes are commonly spotted along Denali Park Road, sometimes with a ground squirrel, or several, firmly gripped in their jaws. If seen in early to mid-summer, such a fox is likely to be a parent, hunting for its litter of kits.

Foxes may den in either forest or tundra, and they produce litters of four to ten kits in early May. Mom stays at home for the first few weeks but then helps with the hunting. The parents visit the den less and less often as summer passes, and eventually the kits begin exploring on their own.

Mice, lemmings, ground squirrels, snowshoe hares, and ptarmigan are all important to the red fox's diet. They also feed on blueberries and crowberries when available. Despite their comparatively small size—less than 4 feet long, and 6 to 15 pounds in weight—adult foxes do not appear particularly troubled by larger predators. As Adolph Murie notes in *Mammals of Denali*, "Foxes appear to be well able to take care of themselves. They can outrun the grizzly, wolf, and wolverine. When the golden eagle swoops at him he stands on watch with his bushy tail erect and straight as a ramrod. The eagle dares not strike."

Snowshoe Hare (*Lepus americanus*)

Named for their long back feet, snowshoe hares, like some other northern animals, are masters of disguise. In summer, their coats are predominantly brown. But as summer gives way to autumn and winter, they shift to an all-white wardrobe that provides ideal camouflage for Denali's snowy landscape. To escape detection by predators, hares sit perfectly still, depending on their ability to blend with the surroundings. They also have protruding eyes that give them nearly 360 degrees of vision and ears that move independently of each other.

They are preyed upon by several species—foxes, martens, hawks, owls, and occasionally wolves—but their primary foes are lynx, who over the millennia have developed a special taste for snowshoe hares. Another, less likely, mammal preys on newborn hares: red squirrels.

Snowshoe hares prefer brushy and forested habitat, and they may be seen along trails or the edge of the park road in Denali's wooded entrance area. Some years hares are highly visible, other years they're rarely seen. It depends on where the snowshoe hare population is in its decade-long boom-and-bust cycle.

Because females can produce up to three or four litters in a year, hares have the ability to quickly boost their population. When food is abundant (hares eat grasses, leaves, and plant buds in summer, aspen and willow bark in winter), production and survival rates increase and the number of hares grows. So do the number of predators. Eventually, the population becomes too large for the available habitat, and a combination of predation, starvation, and disease causes a population crash.

Lynx (*Lynx canadensis*)

One of Denali's more secretive creatures, the lynx is the only member of the cat family to inhabit the park. A resident of the taiga forest, the lynx's fate is closely tied to its primary prey, the snowshoe hare. As Adolph Murie expressed it, "Nature has bestowed on the lynx a snowshoe fixation so that he spends his nights and days thinking and dreaming of hare dinners. So dependent has he become on the hare for his main course that his numbers flourish and wane in the wake of hare statistics." Despite that dependence, lynx will also prey on ptarmigan, ground squirrels, and mice. On rare occasions, they've also been known to attack Dall sheep. During the winter of 1907–8, when the hare population had crashed, naturalist Charles Sheldon twice witnessed lynx hunting Dall sheep;

in one instance, a lynx killed a young Dall ram that outweighed it by nearly 100 pounds.

When first observed, the lynx may seem to be an oddly shaped creature: it has long thick legs, extra-large feet, and a comparatively small body. Though strange in appearance, that physique is ideal for travel in deep snow and hunting hares. With great stealth, the lynx quietly stalks its quarry; when it gets within striking distance, the cat uses its agility and long legs to pounce and grab its prey. While its brown and gray body may seem strangely shaped, the lynx is a graceful creature to watch. And its face is an attractive one, with large, yellow eyes, long, delicate whiskers, a shaggy, streaked throat "ruff," and black tufted ears.

Unfortunately for visitors, the lynx is rarely seen, even by those who spend lots of time in Denali's backcountry. In his book *Denali Journal*, wildlife photographer and author Tom Walker writes, "A great silver, ear-tufted lynx, padding silently over the snow, is my fantasy. I have seen very few free-roaming lynx in the wild.... Yet I can easily envision their yellow eyes burning in venatic zeal."

Wolverine (*Gulo gulo*)

Weighing only 15 to 40 pounds (adult males weigh considerably more than females), wolverines have earned a reputation for their great strength, endurance, and ferocity. In *Alaska's Mammals*, Dave Smith reports that Denali naturalists once watched a wolverine drag an adult Dall sheep down a mountain, then across a braided river, and up a steep bank: more than 2 miles in all. Chased by snowmobiles in other parts of Alaska, they have run more than 40 miles through deep snow without stopping. By some accounts, wolverines will even occasionally drive bears and wolves away from carcasses they've claimed, though the researchers who know wolverines best say that's unlikely; despite their fierce nature, wolverines will avoid confrontations with larger predators whenever possible.

The largest land-dwelling members of the weasel family, wolverines have stocky, heavily muscled builds, bushy tails, and wear coats of long, dark brown hair. Because of this, they bear a vague resemblance to grizzly cubs (except for the longer tails). They are also sometimes confused with marmots. Those who get a good look, however, will notice the broad, creamy to yellowish-tan stripe that runs along both sides of the wolverine's body; sometimes, a whitish collar can be seen across the throat.

Even where their populations are healthy, wolverine numbers are small. Mostly solitary animals, they need a lot of room to make a living. And not just any ground will do. Even more than grizzlies and wolves, wolverines need large expanses of wilderness to thrive. Males stake out territories of up to 240 square miles, females half that. They inhabit a variety of terrains, from lowland forests and river bottoms to alpine tundra and high mountain ridges. They may walk

30 to 40 miles in a day while looking for prey or carrion and are also said to be good tree climbers.

Their desire for vast wild spaces, solitary nature, and tendency to avoid humans have earned wolverines a reputation for being "elusive." They're rarely seen in the wild, even by researchers who study the animal.

Although they prey on small mammals and birds, wolverines are primarily scavengers that lead a feast-or-famine life and will consume as much food as possible when it's available. Even their scientific name, *Gulo gulo*, means "glutton," though their allegedly gluttonous nature, like their ferocity, has been exaggerated in what some call the "legend of wolverine," perpetuated over time by trappers, hunters, and other outdoorsmen. If there's more food than a wolverine can eat at one sitting, the animal will cache it for future meals. Powerful jaws and sharp teeth enable wolverines to consume even bones, hide, and hooves.

Wolverines mate in early to midsummer, with two to four young born between January and March. Most that survive to adulthood live five to seven years, though some survive to twelve or thirteen.

Though much has been learned about wolverines in recent decades, those who know the animal best say that much still remains to be learned about its life history.

Hoary Marmot (*Marmota caligata*)

A resident of Denali's alpine areas, the hoary marmot is best known for its high-pitched alarm call, which has been compared to a traffic cop's whistle. The approach of a fox, grizzly, wolf, golden eagle, or human into marmot country is almost certain to provoke a loud whistle from this woodchuck-like member of the rodent family. For that reason, the marmot is sometimes appropriately called "the whistler."

Weighing anywhere from 8 to 20 pounds, marmots have black feet (the *caligata* in its Latin name means "boots"), a bushy tail, large incisors, a black patch across the nose, and two-tone fur: they are gray over the shoulder region and chest and light brown on the back and hips. Like the grizzly bear, the marmot's fur has a grizzled appearance, as if frosted with gray. Marmot coats provide excellent camouflage for the bouldered talus slopes where they make their homes. Social animals, they live in colonies within the boulders. In summer, they can often be seen sunning themselves on a favorite rock and, more rarely, engaged in wrestling matches. Tom Walker describes one such bout in *Denali Journal*: "They tumbled to the ground, rolled madly about, then stood again, their mouths still clamped together. A forward thrust by the larger marmot and the two went over, the attacker thrown as if by judo. The smaller one was up in an instant and the chase resumed. This wrestling continued for the next half hour."

Alpine hikers have a good chance to see marmots, which are scattered through Denali's foothills. In places, they've become habituated to humans and will allow a close approach. Good places to see marmots include Savage River, Primrose Ridge, the East Fork of the Toklat River, the hillside near Eielson Visitor Center, and Polychrome Pass where marmots can often be seen near the park road.

Marmots eat grasses, flowers, and roots and in turn are preyed upon by wolverines, foxes, wolves, grizzlies, and golden eagles. Like ground squirrels and bears, they are hibernators that pass the winter in their underground dens.

Arctic Ground Squirrel (*Spermophilus parryi*)

The ubiquitous ground squirrel is one of Denali's crowd pleasers. Residents of tundra, mountains, and occasionally even forested areas, ground squirrels are

commonly seen along the park road as they stand erect on hind legs or lie on their bellies, and they are ever-present moochers at the Eielson Visitor Center, where humans are cautioned to resist their charming demands for food.

Underground dwellers that spend much of the year in hibernation, Denali's ground squirrels awaken to warming temperatures in April. Males are the first to arouse themselves, and they compete with each other for prime den sites that offer the best in food and good drainage. Mating occurs in late May, and anywhere from five to ten young are born in June. At birth they weigh one-quarter ounce; as adults, 1 to 2 pounds. The fur of ground squirrels is yellowish brown, often with flecks of gray that give their coats a grizzled appearance like those of marmots.

Among the most visible of Denali National Park's mammals, ground squirrels are a favorite food of many predators, including bears, wolves, foxes, and eagles.

Ground squirrels are important prey for a variety of Denali predators: golden eagles, hawks, weasels, foxes, lynx, wolverines, wolves, and grizzly bears. The latter sometimes spend hours digging in the tundra for squirrels, throwing dirt and rocks high in the air as they excavate squirrel dens.

Red Squirrel (*Tamiasciurus hudsonicus*)

Unlike ground squirrels, these woodland residents remain active year-round. For that reason, red squirrels spend much of their summer preparing for Denali's long, cold season. Commonly seen—and heard—in the entrance area's forests, red squirrels depend heavily on spruce cones to survive winter's scarcity.

Squirrels begin their harvest in the latter half of July. Climbing to the tops of trees, they cut cones from branches, then flip them with mouth or paws to the forest floor. For reasons of efficiency, they often harvest spruce twigs with ten or even twenty cones attached. Hundreds of cones soon begin to pile up on the forest floor; these are eventually stockpiled in a main cache or midden.

Located at the base of one or more spruce trees, middens usually are riddled with holes, where squirrels have tunneled into their food supplies. Some are impressively large, up to 12 feet long, a couple feet wide, and a foot deep. Besides cones, middens may also include plant buds, berries, and another red squirrel favorite: mushrooms.

Red squirrels are tree nesters, and they use a variety of materials to build their nests: grasses, shredded bark, bird feathers, and mammal hair. One squirrel in the entrance area went so far as to carry an almost-full roll of toilet paper into a tree.

When they're not working, sleeping, or eating, red squirrels are likely chattering or churring. Very talkative sorts, they're almost impossible to miss in the forested areas around Riley Creek Campground, Horseshoe Lake, and the entrance area's trail system. They are also abundant in the forested areas of South Denali, such as Byers Lake in Denali State Park.

Beaver (*Castor canadensis*)

The largest of Denali's—and North America's—rodents, adult beavers may weigh up to 60 pounds and measure 3 to 4 feet long, including the broad, flat tail. Besides using their tails when swimming, beavers slap them against the water when alarmed by potential dangers. Other aquatic adaptations include large, webbed hind feet, an ability to remain underwater for up to 15 minutes, eyes protected by transparent lids, ears and nose that can shut tightly underwater, and flaps of skin behind their buck teeth that keep water from going down their throats when chewing.

Residents of Horseshoe Lake, in Denali's entrance area, beavers also inhabit many of the tundra ponds in the park's western areas, and their lodges and dams are readily seen from the park road between Eielson and Wonder Lake.

In South Denali, beavers and their lodges can be seen along the shores of Denali State Park's Byers Lake. The beavers themselves are most visible in late summer and early fall, when they busily cut and cache willows, aspens, poplar, alder, and birch for the winter season. Though they're nocturnal animals (not an easy thing to be in midsummer, when the sky above Denali never completely darkens), beavers often emerge from their homes in late afternoon and remain active through the evening.

Some beavers excavate dens into the banks of rivers and lakes, but they're better known for their lodges, which may be up to 12 feet wide and several feet high. Thick walls of branches and mud protect beaver families from both predators and the weather. Perhaps more than anything else, though, beavers are known for their dam construction. The dam must make the beaver's pond deep enough that it doesn't freeze solid in winter. The dams, which may be hundreds of feet long and several feet high, also provide protection from predators, which include wolves, wolverines, lynx, and grizzlies.

While they are slow and generally clumsy on land, beavers will sometimes travel hundreds of yards to harvest wood for building or food. At Horseshoe Lake, they've been observed climbing a steep gravel bank, more than 100 feet high, to cut willows and other browse for winter storage.

BIRDS

Though Denali is much better known for its mammals than its birds, the park is home to a large, cosmopolitan avian community. Approximately 166 species have been identified in Denali National Park, though only about two dozen remain here year-round. The great majority spend their winters in warmer climes all around the world and then come to Alaska for the breeding season. Some birds, like the northern wheatear, migrate here from Asia. Another species, the long-tailed jaeger, comes from Hawaii on a 3000-mile open-ocean flight. Wandering tattlers spend their winters in Peru, Swainson's thrush in Mexico, and Wilson's warblers in Nicaragua. But the greatest long-distance traveler is the arctic tern, which annually flies about 24,000 miles in its round-trip travels between Alaska and Antarctica. What follows are descriptions of Denali's more common and highly visible birds. A complete list of species is given at the back of the book. Visitors may wish to consider two other helpful resources. One is *Birds of Denali: An Introduction to Selected Species*, by Carol McIntyre, Nan Eagleson, and Alan Seegert; this sixty-four-page book features forty-four species, from year-round residents that demonstrate a variety of adaptations to life in the subarctic, to others that draw birders to Denali because they're rarely seen elsewhere in North America. Another handy reference is the *Bird Checklist of Denali National Park and Preserve*, a pocket-sized pamphlet that includes all of the species identified in Denali.

Golden Eagle (*Aquila chrysaetos canadensis*)

With a wingspan of up to 7.5 feet, the golden eagle is the largest and highest-profile raptor to commonly be seen in Denali National Park. Unlike the fish-eating bald eagle, the golden is an inland bird that prefers mammals and ptarmigan. The Denali region north of the Alaska Range is prime golden eagle habitat, and researchers have identified well over 100 nesting territories. They generally nest on mountain cliff faces or atop high rock outcroppings, but occasionally they'll nest in trees; whatever the spot chosen, nests consist of branches piled up to several feet high and with grasses, lichens, and feathers interwoven with the sticks. Breeding pairs may have from one to more than a dozen nests within their territories.

The plumage of adult birds is entirely dark brown, except for the top of the head, which is golden (hence the name). Immature birds have a broad white band at the base of the tail, and white patches are visible on the undersides of their wings when fully spread.

From the park road, golden eagles are most likely to be spotted soaring high above the tundra, but visitors may also see the birds swooping low over alpine ridges as they hunt for food. Polychrome Pass and Eielson are two areas where soaring eagles are often observed. The eagles' favorite summer prey is ground squirrels, but they also regularly eat marmots, snowshoe hares, and ptarmigan; other prey includes porcupines, red foxes, other birds, and even an occasional Dall sheep lamb or caribou calf. Hares and ptarmigan are especially important prey in late winter and early spring, when golden eagles have begun to nest, and ground squirrels and marmots are still hibernating.

Golden eagles are migratory birds, and those that inhabit Denali in summer spend their winters from British Columbia to northern Mexico. Some have been tracked as far east as Kansas and South Dakota. They return to Denali each year between late February and April. Females lay one to three eggs the last week of April, and chicks hatch in late May or early June. The young fledge and take their first flights by August. Most of the eagles depart for wintering grounds in late September to early October, with fledglings heading south independent of their parents and siblings.

Bald Eagle (*Haliaeetus leucocephalus*)

Rarely seen north of the Alaska Range, the bald eagle is a fish-eating bird that prefers coastal areas. It's fairly common in the South Denali region, particularly in mid- to late summer, when salmon are moving up the Susitna River and its many tributaries. If you're lucky, you may see one flying overhead while driving the Parks Highway or while stopped at one of Denali State Park's campgrounds or Denali-view pullouts. Mature bald eagles are easy to identify, with their white heads and tail. Younger birds that haven't developed the distinctive markings of adults may be confused with golden eagles, in places where their ranges overlap.

Other Raptors

A variety of hawks, falcons, and owls inhabit the Denali region. The most common hawk is the northern harrier (*Circus cyaneus*), which has a wingspread of 3.5 to 4.5 feet and can most easily be identified by its white rump patch. Adult males are mostly gray, while females are brown on top and buff below. Immature birds have rusty brown undersides. The northern harrier nests in open country and can often be seen as it glides low over the tundra and alpine ridges in search of small prey, particularly mice and voles.

Among the falcons, both the American kestrel (*Falco falconidae*) and merlin (*Falco columbarius*) are considered "fairly common" residents of Denali. Both frequent forested areas and have foot-long bodies with wingspans of about 2 feet. The kestrel has a striking black-and-white face pattern, reddish-brown tail and back, and blue-gray wings; when hunting, it characteristically hovers above the ground, wings beating rapidly. The merlin, which feeds primarily on smaller birds, is described as blue-gray above, with tan-and-brown streaked underside. Some visitors may also see the peregrine falcon (*Falco peregrinus*), an "occasional" resident of Denali; like the golden eagle, it's a cliff nester and frequents open country. Known for snatching birds from midair, peregrines may fly low over the ground or perch on high cliffs when hunting. Both peregrines and golden eagles share airspace with the gyrfalcon (*Falco rusticolus*), the world's largest falcon; unlike the other two, they are year-round residents. And rather than making their own nests, gyrfalcons inhabit unused ones built in previous years by eagles.

Denali's most common owl, the short-eared (*Asio flammeus*), prefers open tundra. Sometimes confused with the northern harrier, the short-eared owl lacks the white rump patch and flies with deep, mothlike wing strokes. Unlike most owls, the short-eared often hunts in midday for rodents and small birds. In Denali's forested entrance area, visitors may see—or hear—the great horned owl (*Bubo virginianus*) and northern hawk owl (*Surnia ulula*).

Willow Ptarmigan (*Lagopus lagopus alascensis*)

The most abundant of the three ptarmigan species to inhabit Denali, the willow ptarmigan is, without doubt, the most highly visible of all Denali's bird species. Alaska's state bird is frequently seen along the park road as it moves in and out of willow thickets that border the gravel roadway. Like a few other species that inhabit Denali, the willow ptarmigan changes color with the seasons. In winter, both males and females have all-white plumage. By midsummer, females are mottled dark brown to black and golden brown; males are mostly reddish brown but retain white wings and belly. The willow ptarmigan is the only member of the grouse-ptarmigan family in which the male stays with his female partner as she incubates the eggs and rears the young. As Robert Armstrong

A willow ptarmigan skirts the brushy edge of the Denali Park Road.

says in *Alaska's Birds,* "He hides near the female and viciously defends her and her eggs from all intruders. While these attacks are usually aimed at gulls preying on the eggs and new-born chicks, willow ptarmigan have been known to attack humans and even grizzly bears.... If the female is killed, the male will continue caring for the chicks." As summer progresses, families band together; by fall they may form groups of 100 or more.

Willow ptarmigan, appropriately, inhabit willow thickets as well as tundra, where in summer they feed on willow leaves and catkins, flower heads, other shrubs, and berries. They are preyed on by a variety of species: gyrfalcons, peregrine falcons, golden eagles, snowy owls (occasionally found in Denali), and foxes.

Though not as abundant, rock ptarmigan (*Lagopus mutus*) and white-tailed ptarmigan (*Lagopus leucurus*) also inhabit Denali. They too shift colors with the seasons; in summer, rock ptarmigan are mottled brown, while white-tails are more gray than brown and have their distinctive white tails. Both of these species tend to inhabit higher elevations than the willow and are most commonly found in upland tundra and along high mountain ridges. All three species are known for their loud, distinctive clucking and cackling calls.

Mew Gull (*Larus canus*)

The most widely distributed gulls in Alaska, mew gulls are the most abundant seabird to seasonally inhabit the Denali region. A small gull, the mew has a white head and body, gray wings that are black-tipped, yellow bill, and greenish-yellow legs. It can be found in tundra lakes and ponds, along river bars, and almost anywhere that people gather. Teklanika rest stop, campgrounds, Eielson Visitor Center, and Wonder Lake are popular gathering spots. They feed on mice and voles, insects, eggs, and human foods (though people are not allowed to feed gulls or any other Denali wildlife). Besides the mew gull, Denali is summer home to several other members of the jaeger-gull-tern family, though only the long-tailed jaeger (*Stercorarius longicaudus*) is considered fairly common.

Predatory birds, jaegers feed on rodents and smaller birds, as well as their eggs. Adults have black-capped head, gray body and wings, white breast and the long, streaming tail feathers for which they are named. Ground nesters, they inhabit open tundra country.

Sandhill Crane (*Grus canadensis*)

These large, long-necked and long-legged wading birds don't spend much time in Denali. In fact, they merely pass through on their seasonal migrations. But in fall, they are among the region's most conspicuous wildlife. After spending their summers on the Yukon–Kuskokwim Delta, the cranes pass along the Alaska Range on their migrations south. They can be observed flying overhead in large flocks that form V-shaped to straight-line formations. Usually they're heard before seen. As naturalist Robert Armstrong describes it, they make "loud, trumpet-like calls that sound like a cross between a French horn and a squeaky barn door."

Sometimes flocks of cranes will intersect upwelling air masses and their V's will temporarily disintegrate as the birds circle upward hundreds or even thousands of feet, while carried by the rising air.

Up to 4 feet long, with 6-foot wingspans, adult sandhills have blue-gray plumage with a red face and forehead. In flight, their long necks are stretched out and their legs trail straight behind. At peak migration, hundreds or even thousands may pass through the skies above Denali.

Waterfowl

A wide variety of loons, ducks, geese, and swans inhabit the Denali region's tundra ponds and lakes, though most—including four species of loon and two species of swan—are uncommon to rare in the national park. Waterfowl are most easily observed in Wonder Lake and the ponds adjacent to the park road between Eielson Visitor Center and Wonder Lake. Among the more common species are the horned grebe and several ducks: green-winged teal, mallards, northern pintails, American widgeon, greater and lesser scaup, oldsquaw, Barrow's goldeneye, surf scoters, and white-winged scoters. Waterfowl may also be seen in Denali State Park; the most accessible site is Byers Lake, accessible from the Parks Highway. Here, several species nest each summer, including trumpeter swans, common loons, and common mergansers.

Shorebirds

More than two dozen shorebird species have been identified in the Denali region during the summer season, though only a half dozen are considered common. Among them are the lesser yellowlegs, common snipe, and red-necked phalarope, summer residents of tundra lakes and ponds. Like waterfowl they are most readily observed along the stretch of road between Eielson and Wonder Lake. Semipalmated plovers are more likely to be seen along the sand and gravel bars of Denali's large braided rivers, while two other common species, American golden-plovers and least sandpipers, are found in tundra surroundings of Denali state and national parks.

Songbirds

More than sixty species of songbirds inhabit Denali in summer. They include some of Alaska's best-known year-round residents—ravens, black-billed magpies, boreal and black-capped chickadees, and common redpolls—and others that travel thousands of miles in their annual migrations. As a group, they inhabit every imaginable niche, except the highest snow- and ice-covered reaches of the Alaska Range. Among the more common visitors are ruby-crowned kinglets, Swainson's and varied thrush, American robin, yellow-rumped and Wilson's warbler, American tree sparrow, white-crowned sparrow, and dark-eyed junco. Most of the migrants arrive in May to early June, to coincide with the explosion of insect life, and begin to leave in August.

PLANTS

Denali National Park's subarctic environment limits the number of species that can survive in this northern region. The park's 6 million acres are home to only about 650 species of flowering plants; the number of species jumps to more than 1500 if mosses, lichens, and liverworts are included. By contrast, a similar area in the tropical locale of Costa Rica supports more than 9000 plant species. Descriptions of the Denali region's more common visible forest and tundra plants are provided below, and a checklist of common plants is presented at the back of the book. Helpful references include Verna Pratt's *Wildflowers of Denali National Park*, Janice Schofield's *Alaska's Wild Plants*, and Les Viereck's *Alaska Trees and Shrubs*.

TREES

Denali's taiga forest includes only a handful of tree species, including two evergreens and a few common deciduous species. Though the variety of trees is small, forested lands comprise a substantial part of the Denali ecosystem.

Spruce

The most abundant trees, by far, are the white spruce (*Picea glauca*) and black spruce (*Picea mariana*), members of the pine family. Spruce trees are abundant in South Denali, the wooded entrance area, and along much of the park road to Igloo Creek (about mile 34). Both spruces are well adapted to harsh northern environments; among their adaptations is a shallow root system, which allows the trees to gain nutrients from thin layers of soil; this is especially important where permafrost comes close to the surface. White spruce prefers drier, well-drained, and less acidic soil free of permafrost, while black spruce grows well in boggy areas with acidic standing water and underlain by permafrost. Black spruce trees tend to be shorter (rarely more than 30 feet high) and have a narrow, spindly shape; one Denali naturalist has described them as "Dr. Seuss spruce; scraggly looking things." Their branches characteristically point toward the ground, and younger twigs are covered by a fuzz of dark brown hairs. Upper branches often—but not always—form "crow's nest" clusters. Black spruces have more rounded, egg-shaped cones and shorter, blunt, four-sided needles. White spruces may grow much taller than black spruce, up to 80 feet or higher in protected areas. They also are straighter and more conical in form, and their young twigs are smooth and shiny, not hairy. White spruce cones are more cylindrical than those of black, and their four-sided needles are longer and stiffer.

Paper Birch *(Betula papyrifera)*

Abundant in some parts of the entrance area and especially on Denali's south side, paper birches are easily distinguished by their white, peeling, paperlike bark. (The bark is sometimes yellowish to creamy brown.) Small to medium-sized deciduous trees that prefer well-drained soils, birches have green heart- to-diamond-shaped leaves with sharp points and toothed edges. In fall their leaves turn golden yellow.

Balsam Poplar *(Populus balsamifera)* and Black Cottonwood *(Populus trichocarpa)*

These closely related species are often found in river bottoms, but may also grow on hillsides, in mixed spruce-hardwood forests. Poplars are medium-sized trees that may grow to 50 feet, while cottonwoods may approach heights of 100 feet in the South Denali area. Mature trees of both species have gray bark that is rough, thick, and deeply furrowed. The larger trees often have no branches for up to half the tree's height. In midsummer, they produce large cottony seed pods (poplar pods have two parts, cottonwoods have three). Poplars and cottonwoods have large, green, shiny, arrowhead-shaped leaves; in fall, they turn bright yellow. The leaves of cottonwoods are the largest in the Denali region and may reach 2 to 3 inches long.

Quaking Aspen *(Populus tremuloides)*

Small to medium deciduous trees up to 30 to 40 feet high, aspens have chalky, whitish-green, smooth bark and oval, waxy green, finely toothed leaves that flutter or "quake" in the slightest breeze. In autumn, aspen leaves may turn brilliant yellow to orange. Aspens grow in moist-to-dry, well-drained soils and are often found on south-facing hillsides and along creek bottoms. Aspens may reproduce without seeds; parent trees send out underground shoots and "suckers" grow from these into new, genetically identical trees. A stand that has grown from a single parent is called a clone.

SHRUBS

Willows, alder, and dwarf birch are the most common shrubby plants that visitors will encounter north of the Alaska Range and are especially abundant—and thick—in the park's transitional ecotone, while the prickly devil's club has a substantial presence in South Denali.

Willow

At least two dozen species of willow have been identified in the Denali region. Some, like the arctic willow (*Salix arctica*), hug the ground; others, for instance the diamond-leaf willow (*Salix planifolia*) may form tall bushes and a few, like the felt-leaf willow (*Salix alaxenis*), reach tree size in favorable conditions. Willows grow in dense thickets along streams, trails, and the park road and also grow thickly in the transitional zone between forest and tundra, as well as in moist tundra. Willows that grow in dry alpine tundra are usually low to the ground and more widely scattered. (In general, the higher and drier the

One of many willow species to inhabit the Denali region, this ground-hugging tundra shrub creates a cottony mass as it goes to seed in late summer.

locale, the smaller the willow.) Whatever their size, willows produce soft catkins, which are actually columns of densely packed flowers without petals. Their leaves, which come in various shades of green, are smooth-edged, unlike those of alder. Willows are an important food for several wildlife species, particularly moose and ptarmigan. Because the species tend to hybridize, identification of willow species can often be a challenging task. In fall their leaves turn yellow.

Alder (Alnus crispa)
Another shrub that grows in dense thickets and on occasion reaches tree size, alders can be recognized by their smooth gray bark, marked by thin white horizontal lines (called lenticels); their green, tooth-edged leaves; and clusters of small, hard cone-like fruits, which are bright green when formed and dark brown to black when dead. The alder is an important colonizing plant, because it's a nitrogen fixer; that is, it absorbs nitrogen from the air and transfers it to the soil.

Dwarf Birch (Betula nana)
A low, spreading shrub that may grow up to 2 or 3 feet high, the dwarf birch is found on moist soils of both rocky alpine slopes and wet tundra. In summer its leaves are rounded, hairless, and green, with wavy toothed edges. In fall they turn copper red.

Devil's Club (Echinopanax horridum)
A resident of the wetter South Denali region, devil's club is a prickly forest shrub that grows 4 to 8 feet tall and often forms dense thickets. Hikers should beware of this plant: its large, platter-sized and maple-shaped leaves have spines on their stems and veins, and its pale brown "trunk" is covered with needles. In late summer, bright red berries grow in a bunch at the devil club's top; favored by black bears, they're bitter to humans.

BERRIES
Found in both forest and tundra, berries are an important food source for a variety of wildlife, from black bears and grizzlies to songbirds. Some are important subsistence foods, too, especially blueberries and cranberries.

Bog Blueberry (Vaccinium uliginosum)
Especially popular with grizzlies and humans, blueberries occur in wooded areas; moist, boggy tundra; and dry, alpine meadows. Depending on the terrain, Denali's bog blueberry may be a ground-hugging mat or a bush that grows up to 1.5 to 2 feet high. Pink, bell-shaped flowers bloom in late May to mid-June, and

dark blue, slightly tart berries up to a half inch in diameter (though usually smaller) begin to ripen in July.

Soapberry (*Shepherdia canadensis*)

Another grizzly favorite, this berry is one that most people avoid: to us it has a bitter, soapy taste. Like blueberries, soapberries grow in a variety of habitats: open woods, gravelly river bottoms, and mountain slopes. Up to 3 feet high, the soapberry bush has rusty scales on new growth and the bottoms of its oval, dark green leaves. The plant's tiny yellow flowers bloom in late May to mid-June, and bright, translucent, fire-engine-red berries ripen in late July to August.

Lowbush Cranberry (*Vaccinium vitis-idaea*)

Also known as the mountain cranberry, this plant is widely distributed in Denali's open woodlands, moist tundra, and alpine meadows. A ground-hugging plant that may be 1 to 6 inches high, the lowbush cranberry has small, shiny, oval evergreen leaves. Pink or white bell-shaped flowers form in June, and round, maroon berries ripen in August to September.

A ripe blueberry, ready for eating. Blueberries are a favorite food of both grizzlies and humans; in Denali National Park they begin ripening in July.

Pumpkin Berry (*Geocaulon lividum*)

A woodland plant that's also known as timberberry or northern comandra, the pumpkin berry can be found along trails in Denali's entrance area. Leaves grow on stems up to 6 inches high; small green flowers are produced in May to early June, and orange berries that resemble miniature pumpkins ripen in July. Crunchy to eat, pumpkin berries have a pea-like taste. Some Denali residents like to use them in salads.

WILDFLOWERS

More than 150 species of wildflowers have been identified within the Denali region. Only twenty or so species, arranged by color, are identified here, but they are among the most common and/or striking of the park's flowers. A more complete listing is provided at the back of the book. Verna Pratt gives a much more detailed treatment in *Wildflowers of Denali National Park*.

BLUE TO VIOLET

Forget-Me-Nots

Three different species are found within the park. The alpine forget-me-not (*Myosotis alpestris*) blooms in alpine meadows from late June to late July. Flowers grow at the end of stems up to a foot high; there they form clusters of tiny, sky-blue flowers with a white inner ring and yellow center. The mountain forget-me-not (*Eritrichium aretioides*) is a high alpine plant with rounded, rosette-like leaves, found in loose, moist scree and tundra. This forget-me-not blooms from mid-June to early July; growing in mound-like mats, it produces bright blue, five-petaled flowers with dark yellow "eyes." Finally, the splendid forget-me-not (*Eritrichium splendens*) grows in sandy areas near tree line. It too forms mounds, with narrow, hairy leaves. Its five-petaled bright blue flowers (also with a yellow eye) grow on stems up to 3 inches long.

Bluebells (*Mertensia paniculata*)

Also known as chiming bells, this flower blooms in open woods and moist meadows from mid-June to early August. Bluebells grow up to 2 feet high and have long, hairy, dark green leaves. The flowers are bell-shaped and hang downward from the stem; they are pink when the flower first buds, later turning blue.

Monkshood (*Aconitum delphinifolium*)

Another plant that grows both in moist meadows and open woods, the monkshood grows 10 to 30 inches high, with deeply "toothed" leaves and bluish-purple flowers that are hood- or helmet-shaped and scattered up the stem. It usually blooms from late June into August. A subspecies called the dwarf monkshood grows on rocky alpine slopes and may only be an inch or two high; usually it bears a single flower. This plant, it should be noted, is highly poisonous if eaten.

Larkspur (*Delphinium glaucum*)

The larkspur is among Denali's taller wildflowers: it grows 2 to 5 feet high in either moist woods or moist alpine meadows. Like the monkshood it has deeply divided leaves and blooms from late June into August. The larkspur grows dark bluish-purple flowers along its upper stem, with their petals joined to form a spur. Also like the monkshood, it is poisonous.

Arctic Lupine (*Lupinus arcticus*)

A widely distributed plant, the arctic lupine grows in meadows from mid-June until late July. Up to 8 inches high, the lupine has leaves that grow like the spokes of an umbrella. Its flowers are light to dark blue or purple with a white patch at the base of the petals; they grow on a long, thick, spiky stem. The lupine's hairy seed pod is probably poisonous if eaten.

PINK TO MAGENTA

Prickly Rose (*Rosa acicularis*)

A prickly shrub that may grow up to 4 feet high, this wildflower grows in open woodlands between mid-June and early July. Its flowers are 2 to 3 inches across with five pink, rounded petals. It also bears a dark-red, edible fruit, called a rose hip, which is high in vitamin C.

Frigid Shooting Star (*Dodecatheon frigidum*)

Shooting stars are found in wet tundra and alpine meadows from early June through mid-July. The flowers do indeed have a "shooting star" shape; they are mostly pink to magenta, with white to yellow rings next to the black stamens, and they grow at the end of leafless stems up to 10 inches high. Large bladelike leaves grow at the flower's base.

Fireweed

Two forms of fireweed grow in Denali. Tall fireweed (*Epilobium angustifolium*) is broadly scattered in meadows, open forests, and along roadsides. It can therefore be easily spotted along the park road. Up to 5 feet high, it has bladelike leaves that grow alternately on the plant's stem. Bright pink to magenta flowers have four rounded petals and four long, pointed purple sepals. The flowers bloom up the stem as summer progresses, and tall fireweed is said to be an indicator of winter's approach as the uppermost flowers blossom. The dwarf fireweed or river beauty (*Epilobium latifolium*) prefers gravelly areas along rivers and alpine meadows. This variety is shorter and often has a bushy appearance. Its flowers are similar in appearance to those of tall fireweed, though sometimes larger. Both species bloom from mid-June through mid- to late August.

Woolly Lousewort (*Pedicularis kanei*)

A short woolly plant that grows up to 10 inches high (but is usually shorter), this wildflower blooms from late May to late June in dry, gravelly, or rocky tundra.

Tundra rose blossoms brighten an alpine meadow in the northern foothills of the Alaska Range.

When young, it is covered by woolly white hairs that help to keep the plant warm. Featherlike leaves grow around the stem, from which numerous dark pink flowers grow.

Moss Campion (*Silene acaulis*)

The moss campion is most commonly found on dry, gravelly alpine slopes where it forms ground-hugging cushions. Narrow, bright green leaves grow in dense mats and small, pink, five-petaled flowers bloom from early June through mid-July.

YELLOW

Tundra Rose (*Potentilla fruiticosa*)

Also known as shrubby cinquefoil, this wildflower grows in bogs, in alpine meadows, and on scree slopes. It forms many branched shrubs 1 to 3 feet high, with narrow blue-green leaves and reddish, peeling bark. The five-petaled flowers are bright yellow, and they bloom from mid-June into August.

Arctic Poppy (*Papaver lapponicum*)

The cup-shaped flower of the arctic poppy is lemon yellow in color and grows at the end of a hairy, leafless stem 6 to 10 inches high. The leaves at the flower's base are hairy and lobed. The poppy's flower, which blooms from mid-June to late July, follows the sun as it moves across the sky, and its cuplike shape acts as a parabolic reflector that focuses the sun's rays to the center of the flower and helps to warm it.

WHITE AND CREAM COLORED

Mountain Avens (*Dryas octopetala*)

A widespread alpine flower, mountain avens prefer rocky, well-drained mountain slopes. They often grow in dense mats whose small, narrow leaves are dark green and have wavy edges. The white flowers normally have eight petals; they bloom from mid-June to mid-July on 2- to 4-inch stems. Like poppies, they track the sun as it moves across the sky.

Canadian Dogwood (*Cornus canadensis*)

Primarily a woodland plant, the dogwood grows close to the ground (up to a few inches high) and blooms from mid-June to late July. Four to five large green leaves form a whorl near its top, while tiny flowers form a cluster in the middle of four white bracts (leaves).

Narcissus-Flowered Anemone (*Anemone narcissiflora*)

A resident of tundra meadows, the narcissus-flowered anemone blooms from early June to late July. The plant's stems grow in clumps, each up to a foot high, with hairy, divided leaves near the base. White flowers up to 1.5 inches wide grow at the ends of the stems.

Richardson's Saxifrage (*Boykinia richardsonii*)

This plant is also called bear flower, for obvious reasons: grizzlies like to eat it, especially when the plant is still young and tender. The bear flower grows near streams in alpine meadows and blooms in July and August. Up to 2.5 feet high, it has large, toothed oval leaves at the base of the stem; white flowers with maroon sepals grow along the plant's spiky stem.

A backpacker follows the gravelly margins of a large, braided stream, while crossing open ground in Denali National Park's vast wilderness.

PART II   EXPLORING

DENALI

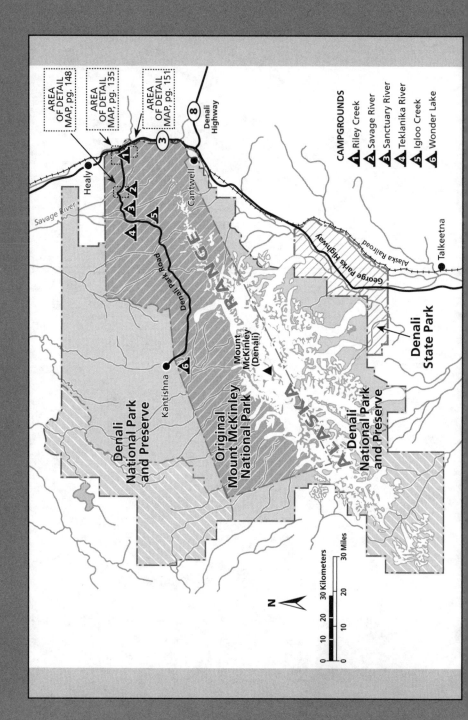

CAMPGROUNDS
1 Riley Creek
2 Savage River
3 Sanctuary River
4 Teklanika River
5 Igloo Creek
6 Wonder Lake

AREA OF DETAIL MAP, pg. 148
AREA OF DETAIL MAP, pg. 135
AREA OF DETAIL MAP, pg. 151

Denali Highway

Healy

Cantwell

Savage River

Alaska Railroad

George Parks Highway

Talkeetna

Denali Park Road

Denali State Park

Kantishna

Denali National Park and Preserve

Original Mount McKinley National Park

Mount McKinley (Denali)

ALASKA RANGE

Denali National Park and Preserve

N

30 Kilometers
30 Miles
0 10 20 30

Chapter 4

EXPLORING THE NATIONAL PARK ENTRANCE

The small sliver of Denali National Park and Preserve along the first 15 miles of the Denali Park Road from the Parks Highway to Savage River is the transition between a world where the customary conveniences of civilization—paved roads, telephones, restaurants, hotels, electricity, Internet connections—can be found, and a uniquely preserved world where the landscape is dominated by wildlife and wilderness.

Visitors seeking a wilderness experience may be tempted to dismiss the entrance area as a necessary transit stop while waiting for a bus trip into the "real Denali." But although it has more amenities than the rest of the park, the entrance area provides a tantalizing taste of all the park has to offer. Here it is possible to explore nearly all of Denali's major terrain types (except glaciers and the park's highest and most forbidding peaks)—from glacial river to taiga forest, from wet and dry tundra to high alpine ridges. Visitors can walk forest trails, traipse across tundra, struggle up rugged mountainsides, or take a plunge down a whitewater river. All of the park's large mammals may be encountered here: grizzlies, caribou, Dall sheep, wolves, and especially moose. The park's long history is preserved in historic buildings, ranger programs, and sled dog demonstrations. And when the sky is clear, Denali viewers can glimpse The High One's uppermost slopes from the park road. In short, Denali's entrance area offers a microcosm of the entire park experience.

The entrance may satisfy those visitors who travel to the park with little time. Others will find it a welcoming introduction to the magical landscape that awaits them past the Savage River and the edges of the park road.

PARK ENTRANCE RESOURCES AND INFORMATION
Visitor Services

Below is a summary of non-park facilities and amenities a visitor can find in and around Denali National Park's entrance area. See "Visiting Denali," in the book's introductory section, for park contact information.

Food and Lodging

Numerous hotels, restaurants, and other stores are located outside Denali National Park, along the Parks Highway between Cantwell and Healy. For more details, contact the Greater Healy/Denali Chamber of Commerce (907-683-4636; www.denalichamber.com). Another option is to consult the *Denali Summer Times*, a visitor-oriented newspaper that's published annually and provides information on a wide array of visitor services (800-478-8300; ncountry@gci.net; www.denali101.com).

Communication

Cell phone and Internet/wireless connections are possible throughout most of the entrance area and along the Parks Highway corridor, though there may be some "blackout" areas where those technologies don't function.

Post Office

A post office is located inside the entrance area, near Riley Creek Campground.

Riley Creek Mercantile

Located next to the Riley Creek Campground (about a quarter-mile from the Parks Highway entrance), the mercantile includes a general store along with laundry facilities and showers. There are also recycling bins (for aluminum, plastic, and batteries) and a sewage dump station. Campground reservations may be made here.

Park Entrance Fees

The general entrance fee to visit Denali National Park is $10 per person (youths fifteen and younger get in free), good for a seven-day stay. The fee is collected at the Wilderness Access Center when visitors purchase bus tickets or make campground reservations; those neither traveling into the park on buses nor staying in campgrounds pay their entrance fee at the Denali Visitor Center. Visitors can also buy a $40 Denali Annual Park Entrance Pass, good for an entire year from the date of purchase; another option is the "America the Beautiful Annual Pass," which costs $80 and is accepted at all national park units or other

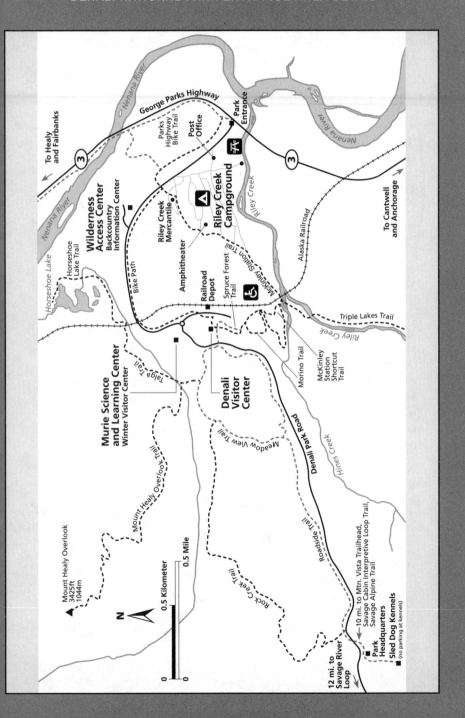

federal recreational sites. U.S. citizens and permanent residents with disabilities can obtain a free lifetime access pass. And those who are sixty-two or older can purchase a senior pass for $10, good for the remainder of that person's lifetime.

Getting Around the Entrance Area

Visitors are allowed to drive their vehicles throughout the Denali entrance area (to the Savage River turnaround at mile 15), but there are other options as well:

By Foot

The entrance area's trail system connects the visitor center to several other facilities, including the Riley Creek Campground, the railroad depot, the Wilderness Access Center, Murie Science and Learning Center, park headquarters, and the sled dog kennels.

By Bus

Three free shuttle buses provide entrance-area transportation. The Riley Creek Loop Shuttle links all major visitor facilities, approximately every 30 minutes; stops include the Denali Visitor Center bus stop, Wilderness Access Center, Murie Science and Learning Center, Riley Creek Campground, Riley Creek Mercantile, and Horseshoe Lake/Taiga/Mount Healy Overlook Trailhead. The Sled Dog Demonstration Shuttle provides transportation to the sled dog kennels and leaves from the visitor center bus stop 40 minutes before each show. Several times a day the Savage River Shuttle leaves from both the visitor center bus stop and the Wilderness Access Center and takes passengers to the Mountain Vista Trailhead (mile 13) and the Savage River turnaround/recreation area (mile 15).

Denali *Alpenglow*

The *Alpenglow* is a newspaper-like visitor guide that's valuable both while visiting Denali and when planning trips to the park. Produced by Denali National Park staff and published by Alaska Geographic, the *Alpenglow* provides information on Denali's campgrounds, bus system, hiking trails, and other visitor facilities, as well as backcountry permits, bear "awareness," and more. Besides being available at the national park and Alaska Public Lands Information Centers in Anchorage, Fairbanks, and Tok, the *Alpenglow* can be downloaded from the Denali National Park website (www.nps.gov/dena/parknews/newspaper.htm).

LEARNING ABOUT THE PARK
Denali Visitor Center

The Denali Visitor Center and its surrounding "campus" is an essential first stop for travelers who are arranging their own visits. Open from mid-May through mid-September (8 AM to 6 PM daily), the visitor center (mile 1.5 of the park road) is the park's main "welcome and information" hub.

Completed in 2005, the heart of Denali's entrance area facilities includes both the main building and a nearby restaurant, bookstore/gift shop, bus stop, railroad depot, and large parking area. Most of the entrance area's forest trails can be easily reached from the center, and many of the ranger programs also occur here (or use the center as a starting point).

Not only does the center prepare visitors for their trips into Denali, it offers inspiration and interpretation through a variety of programs and displays. Inside the main building, visitors can speak with park rangers and view *Heartbeats of Denali*, a 20-minute film shown repeatedly throughout the day that explores the park's seasons, landscapes, and wildlife. The visitor center also includes a huge exhibit area, with natural history and cultural displays that introduce visitors to (among other things) the legacy of Charles Sheldon, Adolph Murie, and other Denali legends; the park's role as a "living laboratory" to study wolves, eagles, glaciers, plant communities, and much more; Dall sheep as a symbol of Denali's wildlife riches; and the connections that different groups of "Denali's people" have to the landscape and its natural riches, from Athabascan Indians to Euro-American explorers, miners, mountaineers, scientists, and park visitors.

Among the most impressive exhibits are the large dioramas displaying Denali's forest and tundra ecosystems and the plants and animals that inhabit them, from charismatic grizzlies, caribou, and golden eagles to the tiny creatures that are often overlooked, like ruby-crowned kinglets, voles, collared pikas, and wood frogs; even certain insects are featured, from mosquitoes to warble flies (while the former pester humans and other animals, the latter especially torment caribou). Also on display are the rocks and fossils that underlie the park's "living" landscape.

Other features: a large relief map of Denali and surrounding areas, displayed on a large circular table, with natural history information, additional maps, and artwork displayed along its edges; a timeline of the park's human history; a kids' corner that features a junior ranger program; and information on the park's ranger programs (see sidebar "Ranger Interpretive Programs" for more details).

The Park Service notes that the Denali Visitor Center (like some other park buildings constructed in 2005 and beyond) boasts a number of sustainable features and demonstrates the agency's commitment to environmental sustainability. These include photovoltaic solar panels on the center's south-facing side, and the use of renewable or recycled materials for building components.

Murie Science and Learning Center

Located a short walk from the Denali Visitor Center, the Murie Science and Learning Center (MSLC, mile 1.4) is part of a national effort to enhance the use of science in national parks and to share ongoing research more effectively with the public. Though located in Denali, the Murie Center coordinates with eight other national parks in arctic and subarctic Alaska.

The MSLC is the only one of Denali's visitor facilities that is open to the public year-round; it therefore also serves as a visitor-contact and information center during the park's winter season (from late September through mid-May it's open from 9 AM to 4 PM daily, except for major holidays). The peak season/ summer hours are 9:30 AM to 5 PM daily. The center features an exhibit area that highlights current scientific research in Denali (for instance, there's a substantial wolves-and-humans display), a classroom, and office space for visiting scientists. There are also several computer stations where visitors can watch digital slide shows on a variety of topics, from wolves to wildland fires.

A "team" of non-governmental partners helps support the center's research and educational activities. Summertime interactive courses include teacher training, field seminars, and youth camps. An "Experience Denali" program introduces participants to Denali while encouraging them to see the park through

Located less than a mile from the Parks Highway, Denali's Wilderness Access Center is the starting point for shuttle bus trips into the park.

a scientist's eyes and explaining current research efforts. Field seminars are led by a wide variety of Denali experts, from researchers to naturalists and authors.

Wilderness Access Center

The Wilderness Access Center (WAC) serves the needs of visitors who wish to arrange bus trips into the Denali wilderness, reserve spots at campgrounds located along the park road, or plan overnight treks into the park's vast backcountry wilderness. Located at mile 0.75 of the park road, the WAC is open from mid-May through mid-September (5 AM to 7 PM daily for bus departures and 7 AM to 7 PM for ticket purchases). This is also the starting point for shuttle bus trips into the park. (The shuttle bus system is described in more detail in Chapter 5's section, "Getting Around by Bus.") And it's where backpackers obtain the backcountry permits required for overnight trips into the wilderness. (Permits are available in the Backcountry Information Center, adjacent to the WAC; more details on backcountry permits are provided in Chapter 6, "Hiking the Backcountry.") Besides its other functions, the access center has a gift shop, coffee stand, and general information desk.

ENTRANCE AREA CAMPGROUNDS

Two of Denali National Park's campgrounds are located within the entrance area, including one that has facilities for group camping. The Riley Creek and Savage River campgrounds are accessible by private vehicle, and sites are by reservation only. (Campgrounds deeper in the park are described in Chapter 5, "Traveling the Park Road.")

Ranger Interpretive Programs

During their stay in Denali, visitors are invited and encouraged to join rangers for a wide variety of interpretive programs, ranging from the wildly popular sled dog demonstrations to informal campground talks (on topics ranging from glaciers to grizzlies and tundra plant communities), visitor center slide shows, guided trail walks, and Discovery Hikes that take participants away from roads and trails, into the heart of Denali's wilderness core. All but the "disco hikes" are free and do not require pre-registration. Schedules posted at the visitor center show when and where such activities occur and give brief descriptions of their content. These programs help visitors more fully understand and appreciate the park's wildlife, plant communities, wilderness setting, landforms, and human history.

Sites at Riley Creek and Savage River may be reserved in advance beginning December 1, either by going online at www.reservedenali.com or by calling the concessionaire, 800-622-7275 within the United States and Canada, or 907-272-7275 from international locales or while in the Anchorage area. Requests can also be made by fax (907-264-4684; fax forms can be downloaded at www.nps.gov/dena) or by mail, to Doyon/Aaramark Joint Venture, 2445 West Dunlap Avenue, Phoenix, AZ 85021; mailed requests must be received at least 30 days before the reservation dates.

Prepaid reserved tickets can be picked up at the Wilderness Access Center (WAC, mile 0.75). Those who arrive at Denali without campground reservations must go to the WAC to reserve sites.

RILEY CREEK CAMPGROUND

Location:	0.25 mile west of the Parks Highway
Number of sites:	146; accommodates both RVs and tents
Season:	Year-round; limited facilities September–May
Water:	Yes (but not in winter)
Facilities:	Flush and vault toilets, plus a sewage dump station adjacent to Riley Creek Mercantile
Fee:	$14 per night for tent sites, $22 for RVs up to 30 feet long, $28 for RVs 30 to 40 feet long
Emergency:	Contact camp host or park staff
Reservations:	All sites are assigned; reserve in advance online or by phone, fax, or mail, or after arriving at the park, at the WAC or Riley Creek Mercantile (located next to the campground, the mercantile has a store as well as laundry and shower facilities)

SAVAGE RIVER CAMPGROUND

Location:	Mile 13
Number of sites:	33; RVs and tents
Season:	May through September, weather dependent
Water:	Yes
Facilities:	Flush and vault toilets
Fee:	$22 per night or $28 for RV "pull-through" sites
Emergency:	Contact camp host or park staff
Reservations:	All sites are assigned; reserve in advance online or by phone, fax, or mail, or after arriving at the park, at the WAC

SAVAGE RIVER GROUP CAMPGROUND

Location:	Mile 13
Number of sites:	3 group sites, 9–20 people; tents only
Season:	May through September, weather dependent
Water:	Yes
Facilities:	Vault toilets
Fee:	$40 per night
Emergency:	Contact camp host or park staff
Reservations:	Must be reserved in advance, by phone or online only

Campground Regulations

Fires are allowed only in established grates. Firewood may be purchased at Riley Creek Mercantile. Cutting live vegetation or standing deadwood is prohibited, as is the use of power saws.

Pets must be leashed at all times and are not allowed on trails, river bars, the backcountry, or buses. Dispose of feces in garbage cans. Secure pet food inside vehicle or food locker.

Quiet hours are between 10 PM and 6 AM. Generators may be operated only between 8 AM and 10 AM and 4 PM and 8 PM. Keep in mind that even with long days, people still need their sleep.

Check-in time is after 11 AM and checkout time is 11 AM.

Food Storage and Wildlife

Improper food storage and sloppy camping can lead to unnecessary and potentially harmful conflicts with Denali's wildlife, particularly bears. For the safety of visitors and animals alike, observe the following principles:

- Keep a clean camp. Wash dishes immediately. Discuss the matter of dishwater disposal with a ranger or your campground host.
- Do not cook directly on fire grates; use foil and dispose of it (and other trash) properly in the bear-resistant garbage containers provided at each campground.
- Store and cook food away from sleeping areas.
- All food, cooking utensils, and ice chests, as well as scented toiletries and cosmetics, must be stored in hard-sided vehicles or in the food lockers provided.
- Do not feed any animal, birds included. Not only will they become a nuisance, they will grow dependent on an unnatural food supply.

Visitors are reflected in Horseshoe Lake, located in Denali National Park's entrance area and easily accessible from a forest trail.

ENTRANCE AREA HIKING TRAILS

Several developed trails, ranging from easy to strenuous, are located in Denali's entrance area (degree of difficulty is based on Park Service ratings). The trailheads of most are within easy walking distance of the visitor center at mile 1.5, while three others are in the Savage River area, between miles 13 and 15. Hikers are reminded that they may encounter bears or moose even along the road corridor; more than once, bears have killed moose in the entrance area woods. It's therefore wise to remain alert and make noise (see "Visiting Denali" for a more detailed discussion of hiking in bear country). Hikers should also be prepared for rapid weather changes. Recommended items include day pack, water, snacks, sunglasses, sunscreen, warm hat, sturdy boots, thick socks, layered clothing, raingear, field guides, trail guide or map, insect repellent, binoculars, and camera.

Denali Walks, an award-winning book written by Alaskan author Kris Capps (Alaska Geographic, 2007), provides comprehensive descriptions of Denali National Park's established trails, along with information on weather, safety, wildlife viewing, detailed maps, and tips on how visitors can help Denali remain wonderfully wild.

EASY

BIKE (AND WALKING) PATH

Route: Connects the Denali Visitor Center and Wilderness Access Center to the park entrance and the Parks Highway Bike Trail; also forms a 3-mile (4.8-kilometer) loop with the McKinley Station Trail. Gravel path, 10 feet wide; wheelchair accessible.

Length: 1.7 miles one way (2.7 kilometers)

Elevation change: 150 feet

Time: 45 minutes one way

Highlights: Skirting the forest edge, this path is primarily used by walkers and bikers moving from one facility to another, but it does provide opportunities to view entrance-area plant communities and occasionally, wildlife. (See map, page 135.)

PARKS HIGHWAY BIKE (AND WALKING) TRAIL

Route: Begins at park entrance and goes to Nenana River Bridge and tourist-oriented "business district" centered along the Parks Highway 1–1.5 miles from the entrance, with lodging and visitor services. Paved path, 10 feet wide; wheelchair accessible.

Length: 1.6 miles one way (2.6 kilometers)

Elevation change: 100 feet

Time: 45 minutes one way

Highlights: The bike trail provides some excellent views of Nenana River and, now and then, river-runners along its route between the park and nearby business district. (See map, page 135.)

SPRUCE FOREST TRAIL

Route: Begins at Denali Visitor Center trailhead, connects with McKinley Station and Taiga trails. Gravel path, 6 feet wide; wheelchair accessible.

Length: 0.27 mile round-trip (0.4 kilometer)

Elevation change: None

Time: 15 minutes round-trip

Highlights: This very short connector trail passes through spruce forest, with wildflowers and berries in season. (See map, page 135.)

Park rangers have been giving sled dog demonstrations for decades. Here, tourists visit the sled dog kennels in June 1939.

MOUNTAIN VISTA TRAIL

Route: Begins at mile 13 of the park road, just before the Savage River Campground. Trailhead area includes a large parking lot, restrooms, natural history displays, wooden benches, and picnic tables (including some that are sheltered). Gravel path, 4 feet wide; wheelchair accessible.

Length: 0.6 mile round-trip (1.0 kilometer)

Elevation change: Negligible

Time: 30–45 minutes round-trip

Highlights: Among the park's newer trails, this one passes from taiga forest into lowland tundra and the banks of the Savage River, offering a variety of habitats, while linking into a historic road and airstrip used by some of the park's earliest tourists. Once out of the forest, the trail provides sweeping 360-degree views of the surrounding landscape, from the Outer Range to the foothills of the Alaska Range; on a clear day, visitors can see 20,320-foot Denali gleaming brightly in the distance. Wildlife viewing opportunities include moose in the forest, grizzlies wandering the edges of the forest-tundra ecotone, and Dall sheep on distant alpine hillsides. Smaller critters include snowshoe hares, red and ground squirrels, ptarmigan, northern harriers hunting small rodents, and a host of songbirds. Wildflowers are seasonally abundant, from lupine and monkshood to river beauty (dwarf fireweed) and wild pea. Traveling out the trail, visitors can move from road-accessible amenities to the edge of an expansive wilderness; some may even choose to leave the trail and walk along the Savage River's stream bed, in the tracks of hare and moose and grizzly. (See map, page 148.)

SAVAGE CABIN INTERPRETIVE LOOP TRAIL

Route: Begins near mile 13, across from Savage River Campground. Gravel path, 6 feet wide; wheelchair accessible.

Length: 0.25 mile

Elevation change: Negligible

Time: 30 minutes or less

Highlights: Several displays have been placed along this quarter-mile path, focused on such varied topics as the park road and bus system; the "wilderness guardians" sled-dog patrols and cabin system; Denali's designated wilderness; and the importance of spruce trees to park rangers on patrol (as shelter and fuel for stoves). As the name suggests, the trail also provides access to the historic Savage River cabin (described in detail elsewhere in this chapter). (See map, page 148)

Ranger John Rumohr stands beside the Savage River Patrol Cabin in this undated photo. Cabins were built in the 1920s and 1930s for winter sled dog patrols.

EASY TO MODERATE

TAIGA TRAIL

Route: Begins at the Denali Visitor Center, connects to Rock Creek, Horseshoe Lake, and Mount Healy Overlook trails. Gravel path, 2 feet wide.

Length: 0.9 mile one way (1.5 kilometers)

Elevation change: 75 feet

Time: 30–45 minutes one way

Highlights: This trail passes through spruce-aspen forest, with wildflowers in spring and summer, berries in late summer and fall; it also provides access to three other trails across Denali Park Road from visitor center complex and presents opportunities to see taiga wildlife. (See map, page 135.)

MCKINLEY STATION TRAIL

Route: Begins at either the Denali Visitor Center or Riley Creek Campground; connects with Bike Path to form a 3-mile (4.8-kilometer) loop. Gravel path, 4 feet wide; wheelchair accessible.

Length: 1.6 miles one way (2.6 kilometers)

Elevation change: 100 feet

Time: 1 hour one way

Highlights: Takes visitors through taiga forest, with opportunities to see wildflowers and wildlife, and also passes near historic building remains, Riley Creek, and the railroad trestle over Riley Creek. (See map, page 135.)

MEADOW VIEW TRAIL (PART OF A LARGER LOOP)

Route: Connects with Rock Creek and Roadside trails to form a 1.6-mile loop with the Denali Visitor Center. Gravel path, 2.5 feet wide.

Length: 0.3 mile one way (0.5 kilometer)

Elevation change: None

Time: 1 hour round-trip (entire loop)

Highlights: This short connector path provides views of meadows and mountains and presents opportunities to see wildflowers and, occasionally, wildlife. (See map, page 135.)

A large bull moose moves through the taiga forest in Denali's entrance area, one of the best places to spot the park's moose.

SAVAGE RIVER LOOP

Route:	Begins at mile 15 of the Denali Park Road. Footpath with roots and rocks, 2 feet wide; first 0.5 mile is gravel path; wheelchair accessible.
Length:	2 miles round-trip (3.2 kilometers)
Elevation change:	Negligible
Time:	1.5 hours round-trip
Highlights:	Unlike other entrance-area trails, this one passes entirely through tundra, with expansive views of the surrounding hills. It also provides opportunities to see or hear tundra wildlife; possibilities include Dall sheep, grizzlies, caribou, howling wolves, whistling marmots, and soaring golden eagles. Here too is an opportunity to observe tundra plant communities, including wildflowers. Trail follows Savage River downstream, then crosses bridge and returns to park road.

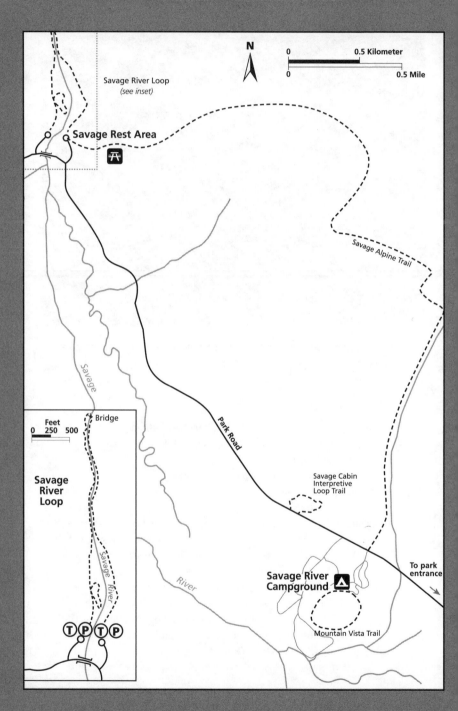

MODERATE

HORSESHOE LAKE TRAIL

Route: Begins at mile 0.9 of the park road, near the railroad track crossing; can be reached from either Taiga Trail or Bike Path. Footpath with roots and rocks, 5 feet wide.

Length: 1.5 miles round-trip (2.4 kilometers)

Elevation change: 250 feet

Time: 1–1.5 hours round-trip

Highlights: With distant views of the Nenana River and close-up looks at an oxbow lake, beaver dam and lodge, this trail also presents good opportunities for wildlife viewing, from forest birds and beavers to squirrels and moose. See the sidebar "A Guided Walk to Horseshoe Lake" in this section for a more detailed description of what can be found and experienced here. (See map, page 135.)

ROCK CREEK TRAIL

Route: Combined with Taiga Trail, connects the Denali Visitor Center to park headquarters and the sled dog kennels. Gravel path, 2.5 feet wide.

Length: 2.4 miles one way (3.8 kilometers)

Elevation change: 400 feet

Time: 2 hours one way (uphill)

Highlights: Hikers following this trail move through mixed taiga forest, with stands of spruce and birch trees. Here there are wildflowers and berries in season, plus views of Horseshoe Creek and Healy Ridge. Visitors will find increased quiet and solitude away from the park road (when compared to Roadside Trail). (See map, page 135.)

ROADSIDE TRAIL

Route: Combined with Taiga Trail, connects the Denali Visitor Center to park headquarters and the sled dog kennels. Gravel, 3 feet wide.

Length: 1.8 miles one way (2.9 kilometers)

Elevation change: 350 feet

Time: 1 hour one way

Highlights: Mixed taiga forest, with stands of aspen, paper birch, and spruce. Less elevation gain than Rock Creek Trail when walking uphill to headquarters area. (See map, page 135.)

MODERATELY STRENUOUS

TRIPLE LAKES TRAIL

Route: One trailhead is located near mile 232 of the Parks Highway; the other begins near the Hines Creek Bridge, at its intersection with McKinley Station Trail. Footpath with rocks and roots, 2 feet wide; the first 0.75 mile from Hines Creek is gravel, wheelchair accessible.

Length: 8.6 miles one way (13.8 kilometers)

Elevation change: About 1000 feet

Time: 5 hours one way

Highlights: The longest of the entrance-area trails, Triple Lakes provides panoramic views of Riley Creek, the Nenana River, Alaska Range foothills, the railroad, and highway corridor. Hikers will find spruce and birch forests and a series of three tranquil forest lakes, with opportunities to see wildflowers and wildlife (especially waterfowl, beavers, squirrels, moose, and spruce grouse), pick berries, and experience solitude miles from roads and entrance area facilities. (See map, page 151.)

SAVAGE ALPINE TRAIL

Route: This trail connects the Mountain Vista Trailhead area (mile 13) with the Savage River turnaround/parking area (mile 15). Hikers are encouraged to use the free Savage River Shuttle bus, which stops at both ends of the trail. Footpath with rocks; 2 feet wide.

Length: 4.1 miles one way (6.6 kilometers)

Elevation change: 1550 feet

Time: 3–4 hours one way

Highlights: The trail gives hikers an opportunity to walk through high alpine tundra and look for tundra wildlife, including sheep, hoary marmots, ground squirrels, collared pikas, northern harriers, and golden eagles. In spring and summer hikers can also discover a wealth of wildflowers, while in late summer and fall, berries may abound. At higher elevations there are sweeping views of both Outer and Alaska ranges' peaks, and on a clear day, 20,320-foot Denali can be seen rising high above its mountain neighbors, some 70 miles to the southwest. (See map, page148)

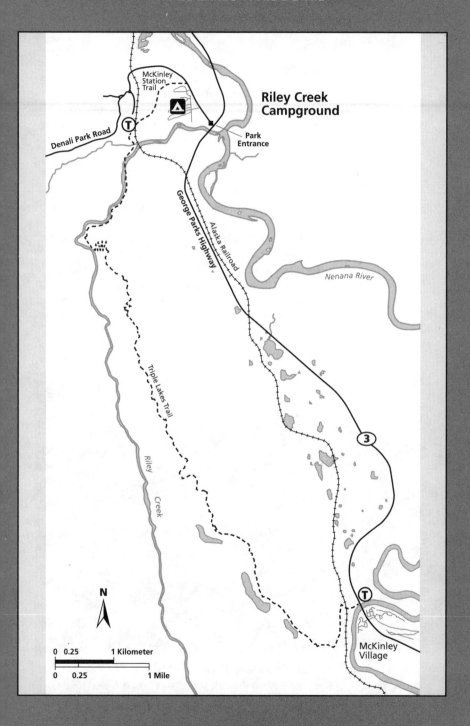

McKinley
Station
Trail

Riley Creek
Campground

Denali Park Road

Park
Entrance

George Parks Highway

Alaska Railroad

Nenana River

Triple Lakes Trail

Riley Creek

3

McKinley
Village

N

| 0 | 0.25 | 1 Kilometer |
| 0 | 0.25 | 1 Mile |

STRENUOUS

MOUNT HEALY OVERLOOK TRAIL

Route: Connects with Taiga Trail on the north side of the park road and leads through the forest uphill into subalpine and alpine zones, finally reaching the overlook at 3425 feet. Footpath with rocks and roots; 2 feet wide.

Length: 4.5 miles round-trip (7.3 kilometers)

Elevation change: 1700 feet

Time: 3–4 hours round-trip

Highlights: Hikers willing to get an uphill workout will be rewarded with spectacular views of the Denali National Park entrance area, the Nenana River Valley, Healy Ridge, and other alpine ridges. Denali can be seen in the distance on clear-sky days. Once in the high alpine, ambitious hikers have the opportunity to do some ridge walking and tundra exploring beyond the end of the developed trail; good opportunities to see tundra wildlife. (See map, page 135.)

Born on the southern side of the Alaska Range, the Nenana River is popular with river-runners as it flows north along the eastern edge of Denali National Park.

GUIDED RIVER RAFTING ON THE NENANA RIVER

A half dozen companies guide raft trips down the Nenana River from June through mid-September. Most are based within a mile of Denali National Park's entrance area. A list of guide outfits is included in the *Denali Summer Times*. Several are also listed in *The Milepost*. (You'll find contact information for both publications earlier in "Visiting Denali.")

For those who would prefer to do the Nenana River on their own, Andy Embick's *Fast & Cold: A Guide to Alaska Whitewater* includes detailed information on raft and kayak put-ins and take-outs. Another good source of information is Karen Jettmar's *The Alaska River Guide*. Both books (see "Recommended Reading") include descriptions of the Nenana River and information on such things as difficulty, access, trip lengths, and necessary maps.

According to Embick, Nenana River put-ins near Denali National Park's entrance area include Slime Creek (mile 220), Carlo Creek (mile 223.9), McKinley Village (mile 231.1), and the Jonestown Bridge near Riley Creek (mile 238). Take-outs are possible along the next 3 miles; once entering the Nenana Gorge at about mile 243, no take-outs are possible until reaching the community of Healy, another 6 to 7 miles north.

Down the Nenana River

The eastern boundary of Denali National Park is defined by the swift, cold, and silty Nenana River. The Nenana is an unusual river, as it arises from a southward-flowing glacier on the south side of the Alaska Range, flows west along the base of the mountains, and then cuts north through the range to the Tanana River instead of joining the Susitna like other major south-side glacial rivers. The canyon carved by the Nenana provides one of the few relatively easy passages through the Alaska Range.

Many broad, calm rivers in Interior Alaska were used historically, and are still used today, for regular transport by explorers, miners, fishermen, traders, and Native Alaskans. The upper Nenana is a different kind of river. Passing through the Alaska Range, the combination of the narrow canyon and the debris deposited by rock slides and side streams creates a fast-flowing river with many rapids, waves, and rocks. Much of the water comes from melting of Nenana Glacier ice; only a few degrees above freezing, it carries a heavy load of gray silt ground out of the mountains by the glacier. Travel through the Nenana Canyon by water is downstream only, and only by those who are prepared for a whitewater adventure. Although the river lies outside of the National Park Service's jurisdiction, a float down the Nenana provides an excellent and somewhat unusual way to experience

(continued)

Down the Nenana River (continued)

the park's mountain scenery, and to catch sight of the occasional moose, caribou, or other wildlife. The trip will also instill a greater understanding of the dynamics (and temperature!) of the park's glacial rivers.

Several rafting companies based along the Parks Highway near the park entrance guide trips down the river. There are generally two options: a quiet, scenic wilderness float on relatively mild waters, or the wet-and-wild Canyon Run through Nenana Gorge, which has ten major whitewater rapids along one 11-mile stretch. Each raft trip lasts about 2 hours; they can also be combined into a 4-hour river journey.

Though the gorge is considered thrilling and splashy, it has few tricky hazards; plus there's room to maneuver through obstacles and time for boaters to recover between its biggest rapids. To experienced river runners, that makes it relatively safe. The greatest challenges are the 10- to 12-foot-high (and sometimes taller) waves, and large holes—troughs where water recirculates, threatening to hold or flip rafts. Never should the river be taken lightly: rafters and kayakers occasionally end up in the icy water, which can be a bone-chilling and life-threatening experience. Some river-runners have died here.

The canyon trip starts in a broad, glacially carved, U-shaped valley north and east of the park entrance. But once in the gorge, the Nenana is squeezed between near-vertical rock walls. River runners have bestowed names on the Nenana Gorge's most notorious rapids. Some—like Twin Rock, Train Wreck, and Splatter Rock—describe human or natural landmarks along the route. Others—like Ice Worm, Roostertail, and Coffee Grinder—are more descriptive of the rapids themselves. Entering the rapids, the raft slams into tall gravy-colored waves. People go up and down and get bounced around, and everyone gets splashed, but those up front get especially drenched as they take direct hits to the head and upper body. Such moments of high energy are spaced among longer intervals of relative calm.

This stretch of the Nenana is never far from either the highway or railroad. But deep within the gorge, surrounded by canyon walls, the only sound—besides occasional shrieking humans—is river music. In calmer stretches, the water makes a gentle lapping, gurgling song. Among the rapids it becomes a roaring, booming cacophony of crashing waves. The river at once puts the traveler in intimate touch with the tranquility, the challenge, and the powerful natural forces that created and continue to mold Denali.

EXPLORING THE TAIGA (MILE 1 TO MILE 7)

The entrance to Denali is nestled in a forest of primarily evergreen trees that spread out across the valley floors and sweep partway up the surrounding mountain slopes. This is the taiga or boreal forest, which covers an enormous swath of the northern hemisphere from Alaska to northern Canada, Europe, and Siberia. The dominant evergreen trees are white and black spruce, which are difficult to distinguish with a casual glance except by habitat: white spruce grow on well-drained soils, while black spruce compete better in boggier locations. In some places the spruce share space with deciduous aspen and birch trees and—by lakes or streams—with cottonwoods.

The beauty of the taiga is not only in its vastness, but in the details that are often hidden from all but careful observers. Small pearls of color may be the bloom of a pasque flower in early spring, a dwarf dogwood or prickly rose during the height of summer, or a blueberry in the fall. The chattering of red squirrels and songs of thrushes fill the air. More quietly, the large mammals of the forest move beneath the trees. Moose browse on willow leaves, red foxes and coyotes hunt small mammals, black bears and grizzlies pass among the trees like shadows while seeking out an omnivore's variety of foods, and beavers cut trees for food and the construction of dams and lodges. More challenging to spot is one of the forest's most stealthy predators, the lynx, as it searches for snowshoe hares. Signs of the park's long inhabitation by humans are evident too, in log cabins, railroad trestles, and other living relics from the park's pioneer days.

Denali National Park is distinguished as a mostly trail-less wilderness, but the entrance area has several short hiking trails for explorers of all ages and abilities. These trails (described above) allow visitors to immerse themselves in this pocket of the vast northern forest. The taiga offers a wealth of sights, sounds, smells, and startling discoveries; described below are some of the more evident ones. Those who prefer to travel with a guide should check at the Denali Visitor Center for listings of ranger-led walks.

Trees and Forest Succession

Despite the seemingly timeless expanse of spruce trees dominating the taiga, the composition of the forest does change regularly, albeit over a long period of time. Fire is the principal agent of change on a large scale, although smaller disturbances take place any time a tree dies and falls over. When a fire burns the existing forest cover, as happened in the Denali entrance area in 1924, it opens clearings in the spruce forest that are quickly occupied by fast-growing shrubs such as willow and alder. Aspen and paper birch trees also get an early start, growing well ahead of the spruce. A stand of aspen is therefore a relatively young forest. Small spruce trees eventually sprout beneath the forest canopy and grow taller than the aspen, shading out the leafy trees and ultimately replacing them entirely after eighty years or more. Try to identify disturbed areas in the taiga, and the reason for the disturbance.

The smooth, green-barked aspen are especially beautiful to see in the fall, when their leaves turn a brilliant yellow. Those who observe the trees throughout the growing season may notice that an entire clump of aspen will turn colors at precisely the same time. This is because the apparently separate trees are actually more like stalks of the same plant. Most aspen reproduce without seeds: a parent tree will send out underground shoots, which sprout into genetically identical plants.

The bark of the paper birch is always peeling in beautiful, thin strips. Native Alaskans traditionally used the bark of the birch to make baskets and other useful items. However, the bark is very much the birch's skin, and unnecessary peeling may damage the tree.

See the Forest Succession

Each of the trails listed below pass through successional forest areas; all are easy to moderate and distances given are one way. For more details, see "Entrance Area Hiking Trails" earlier in this chapter.

- Taiga Trail, 0.9 mile
- Meadow View Trail, 0.3 mile
- Rock Creek Trail, 2.4 miles
- Roadside Trail, 1.8 miles

Taiga Understory

The forest's understory presents wonderful opportunities for a treasure hunt. From the time the snow first melts from south-facing slopes in the spring, the taiga's gems begin to bloom. Common, long-flowering plants such as fireweed and bluebells are easy to find, but the taiga harbors dozens of harder-to-locate flowers such as shy maiden, twinflower, or rarely seen calypso orchids. In the fall, the flowers fade and are replaced by edible treasures: blueberries, lingonberries, crowberries. Suddenly it becomes evident that much of the forest floor is covered in berry bushes, although not all produce fruit each year.

Some parts of the taiga forest floor are covered in deep moss, or with the delicate brushes of horsetail, a primitive plant also called "scouring rush," because the silica content of its fronds make it excellent for scrubbing. Mushrooms may be very abundant for a few weeks in one season, virtually absent the next. Contrary to visual evidence, mushrooms do not grow in tree branches, though they do appear there frequently during years of abundance because red squirrels carry them into the trees to be dried for winter consumption.

See the Understory

While hikers can see examples of understory on nearly all the entrance area trails, here are a few (ranging from easy to moderately strenuous) that showcase it best. For more details, see "Entrance Area Hiking Trails" earlier in this chapter.

- Taiga Trail, 0.9 mile
- Horseshoe Lake Trail, 1.5 miles round-trip
- Rock Creek Trail, 2.4 miles
- Triple Lakes Trail, 8.6 miles

Animal Signs

Some of Denali's most charismatic animals roam the taiga, such as moose, bear, beaver, and lynx. However, they are difficult to see here because the dense forest means that sight-distances are very short, unlike in the parts of the park that are above tree line. Even if Denali's large mammals remain hidden behind the foliage of the forest, their signs are everywhere. Most trails boast the sawdust-filled nuggets of moose scat, resulting from a winter diet of willow twigs and aspen bark. Nearby are aspen trees missing strips of bark, or willows that have torn twigs where the moose dined. If a willow branch is more cleanly snipped, it is probably the work of a snowshoe hare. Don't wonder about waist-high snowshoe hares if a neatly cut branch seems too far above the ground; just imagine the hare standing on a 30-inch snowpack.

At lakes such as Horseshoe Lake and the Triple Lakes, there are many signs of one of nature's most remarkable engineers, the beaver. Approaching the lakes, it is possible to see the stumps of trees that have clearly been gnawed upon. In the lakes themselves are beaver lodges, mounds of logs and twigs where a beaver family lives year-round, and at Horseshoe Lake a series of beaver-created dams. All the lakes along Denali's entrance area trails are geologically formed; the Triple Lakes through glacial action, and Horseshoe Lake by the shifting Nenana River, which stranded a former channel as an oxbow lake. However, the beaver dams at Horseshoe Lake deepen the lake so that it does not freeze solid in winter, and the beaver family is able to swim from the lodge to its cache of food stored on the lake bottom, beneath the ice.

Note that most of the tree bark nibbled by animals is the bark of deciduous, leafy trees and shrubs, not the more common spruce. Spruce trees secrete a resin that makes their bark unpalatable to hares, moose, and beaver. Only the porcupine favors the spruce, eating the bark of young trees or climbing to upper branches where the resin is not so strong. If the bark of a spruce is stripped, it is

Beavers have left many signs of their presence in Denali's entrance area, especially along the margins of Horseshoe Lake and the Triple Lakes.

certainly the work of porcupines, which sometimes girdle trees, incidentally cutting off the flow of nutrients to the energy-producing branches and causing the tree to die. Other parts of the spruce are staples for different creatures. The spruce grouse lives almost exclusively on spruce needles during the winter. Red squirrels feast on the seeds of spruce cones, dropping the cone scales on the ground where they can accumulate into sizable middens, which are found near many trails. The territorial squirrels can frequently be heard voicing loud chattering or buzzing noises, trying to warn away human explorers who come too close.

See the Animals

Opportunities to see wildlife—or at least their "signs"—can be found along any entrance area trail, but the four below—ranging from easy to moderately strenuous—are among the best possibilities. As elsewhere, distances given are one way unless otherwise noted. For more details, see "Entrance Area Hiking Trails" earlier in this chapter.

- Taiga Trail, 0.9 mile
- Rock Creek Trail, 2.4 miles
- Horseshoe Lake Trail, 1.5 miles round-trip
- Triple Lakes Trail, 8.6 miles

See McKinley Park Station (Mile 1.5)

The site of the first park headquarters, this settlement at times hosted a railroad construction camp, a fox farm, road construction support facilities, and trappers' small cabins. The roadhouse of Maurice Morino was a fixture for many years, located on a homestead where Morino Campground is now. All of the early structures have vanished, leaving only a few old foundations, bits of chicken wire, and other remnants that can be detected by sharp-eyed observers. Even the original park headquarters has been entirely dismantled and removed. Only the railroad depot remains, although it has changed considerably since the station first opened in a converted railroad car in 1922.

Across the park road from the depot was the Denali Park Hotel. As far back as the 1920s, park planners and tourism promoters realized the need for an entrance area hotel if Mount McKinley National Park were to become a major visitor destination. Finished in 1939, the 200-room McKinley Park Hotel was built a short walk from the train station, then the entry point for nearly all park visitors (the George Parks Highway wouldn't be completed until 1972). The original hotel building burned in 1972 and was replaced by a modular structure more functional than luxurious. Renamed the Denali Park Hotel in 1980, it was closed after the summer of 2001, since modern hotels along the highway have eliminated the need for one inside the park.

PARK HEADQUARTERS HISTORIC DISTRICT (MILE 3.4)

When the first superintendent of Mount McKinley National Park arrived in 1921, there was already a small community clustered around the railroad tracks in the vicinity of the train depot. Known as McKinley Park Station, this tiny settlement (now abandoned but worth a visit) was the site of the first park headquarters at the base of the Riley Creek railroad trestle.

Harry Karstens's initial choice of Riley Creek as a site for a park headquarters proved less than ideal. Frigid air sinking into the creek bottoms makes them 10 to 15 degrees colder than nearby bench lands. In extreme subzero cold, the difference can be profound and potentially deadly. So in 1924, Karstens lobbied his superiors to move headquarters to "a beautiful spot, with ample room for expansion, one and two-thirds miles from the railroad" and along the new road being built into the park. Given the go-ahead, he and his staff built three log cabins, a barn, and utility shelters on a forested bench above Hines Creek—the site of the present-day headquarters. At an elevation of 2000 feet (610 meters), it benefits from the warm-air temperature inversions that commonly occur here in

Denali National Park's headquarters area, circa 1940. Located at mile 3.4 of the park road, most of the buildings were built from the 1920s through the 1940s.

winter. It also affords excellent views down Hines Creek and across the Nenana River to mountains that border the Yanert Valley, east of the park.

Over time, this upland headquarters site has proved an ideal spot for both administrative and residential needs. Today it remains part of a cluster of log and frame buildings tucked into the taiga forest. Among the existing structures are fourteen built between 1926 and 1941, leading to the area's designation as a National Historic District. Located at mile 3.4, the park's headquarters and historic district can be reached by personal vehicle, the Savage River Shuttle, the sled dog demonstration bus, or by foot along the Rock Creek or Roadside trails.

Many of the structures here were built from the mid-1920s through the 1940s as ranger cabins, workshops, barns, and sled dog kennels. Now they are used as employee housing, research offices, storage sheds, and the park's administrative headquarters. The oldest existing structure is the original superintendent's office, built in 1926; later moved and converted into a museum, it has served as park-staff housing since the 1960s. Two other log structures built during McKinley Park's "pioneer years" are today employee homes (close to twenty families live inside the park year-round). Other buildings are still in use for park business. They show the transition in construction methods from log to log veneer and board-and-batten, and reflect some of the changes that have taken place in Denali over the years.

Whimsically named by park staff, "The Overthere" is an example of early log construction. It served as a warehouse for more than five decades. Completed in 1928, the original building included a wide, double-bay sliding door that opened onto a log-loading platform. Its interior was remodeled in 1982 and now provides office and work space for interpretive rangers. Another example of log construction is "The Barn." Built in 1929, it was used as a shelter for horses and storage space for pack supplies until the park phased out the use of horses in the 1940s. It has since been used as a carpentry shop, sign shop, and storage space. Recently restored, it too now serves as office space for park staff.

Between 1929 and the early 1930s, the park made the transition from constructing buildings entirely of logs to using a combination of exteriors built with logs and interiors finished with board-and-batten sheeting. A building now used by Denali's commercial services staff is one example; originally a garage completed in 1931, this building's vehicle stalls were converted to offices in 1978.

Constructed in 1935, the park's current headquarters building shows mixed log and log-veneer construction. This eight-room building was originally built as a two-story ranger dormitory that its residents called the "Ranger Club." Today it holds the offices of the park superintendent and other top Denali administrators.

Although these buildings are not used for their original purposes, they stand as a record of the park's history. The one building still used for its original purpose is the sled dog kennels building, built in 1930.

NOTE: Buses make several round trips from the Denali Visitor Center bus depot to the sled dog kennels at park headquarters each day, making it possible to walk either the Rock Creek or Roadside Trail one way and ride back. The walk is mostly uphill from the visitor center to park headquarters, so make plans according to your desire for exercise!

The Sled Dog Kennels

Sled dogs have been an integral part of the Denali experience since the early 1920s, when Superintendent Harry Karstens and his rangers first mushed into the 1.4-million-acre wilderness on poaching patrols. Without their dog teams, Karstens and his rangers would have had no way to reach the park's most remote areas. From late fall through early spring, the dogs helped protect Denali's wildlife from illegal hunting.

Nowadays, poaching isn't the problem it once was. And throughout much of the north, snowmobiles have replaced dogs as the primary means of winter travel. But sled dogs, not machines, continue to be used on winter patrols into the heart of Denali's wilderness, where mechanized vehicles are not allowed. On modern patrols, rangers maintain and stock Denali's network of historic cabins, assist wildlife researchers, keep a winter route open from headquarters to Wonder Lake, and stay in touch with visitors and park neighbors.

Visitors can see Denali's sled dogs in action throughout the summer. Demonstrations are given from late May through the end of August at the park's kennels.

See the Sled Dogs

Visitors can see Denali's sled dog teams in action throughout the summer at the kennels, located behind park headquarters (mile 3.4). Short (30-minute) demonstrations are given three times daily during the peak visitor season (June 1 through the Labor Day holiday) with more limited offerings in the "shoulder" seasons of late May and the first half of September. There's little parking room in the headquarters area, but free shuttle buses transport visitors from the visitor center 40 minutes before each show. And of course you can walk the entrance-area trails to get there.

Approximately thirty dogs are housed at the kennels year-round. They are Alaskan huskies, wonderfully adapted to the severe conditions of northern winters, in which temperatures may plummet to –50°F (–45°C). Intelligent and athletic, these are working dogs that weigh 50 to 80 pounds and have dense winter coats, tough feet, wolfish faces, and bushy tails. And what they love to do most is run and pull. Overheating prevents them from doing much exercise in summer, but they're regularly taken on walks by park staff.

Sled dog demonstrations begin with a short talk that includes the historic importance of sled dog teams at Denali. Then, as the kennel of dogs erupts in a cacophony of yips, yelps, barks, shrieks, and howls, a handful of huskies are harnessed to a wooden sled that is outfitted with wheels for easier travel over bare dirt and gravel. (A single team on winter trips may use seven, eight, or even more dogs.) As on winter patrol, a ranger takes a spot on the sled's back runners and hangs on tightly as the excited dogs race around a short track built specifically for these demonstrations. The dry-land run lasts only 30 seconds or so, but it's a half minute of pure ecstasy for dogs that live to run.

EXPLORING THE TUNDRA (MILE 7 TO MILE 15)
Denali National Park is known for its wide, open vistas found above tree line, which allow for superb viewing of the Alaska Range and ease of seeing wildlife. These vistas cannot be found in the taiga forest except through occasional openings in the trees. However, the park road provides access to some excellent opportunities in the entrance area for exploring the land above the trees.

Along its first 7 miles, the park road is bordered by taiga, while passing through the forested Riley and Hines creek valleys. Ascending out of Hines Creek, the road enters the broader, higher Savage River basin as it approaches Denali's second major plant community, the treeless habitat known as tundra. Appearing uniform from a distance, tundra is a complex network of wildflowers, grasses, tussock-forming sedges, woody plants, mosses, and lichens.

Denali's tundra can be either wet or dry. Most in the entrance area is the wet variety, consisting of moisture-loving plants like willow and alder thickets, lush berry patches, or hummocky mounds of sedges and grasses, but dry tundra occupies higher alpine terrain.

It soon becomes clear that the tree line in this subarctic region is a variable, ill-defined thing. Within Denali National Park tree line ranges from 2700 feet (850 meters) on cooler, exposed, north-facing terrain, up to 3800 feet (1160 meters) on warmer, south-facing slopes. The vague zone between taiga and tundra is a transitional plant community in which stunted spruce trees are interspersed with dense willow thickets, berry bushes, and plants more closely associated with wet tundra.

The taiga–tundra transitional zone that surrounds much of the park road between miles 7 and 15 is prime moose habitat, providing both food and cover for the deer family's largest member. Moose especially favor the leaves of willow, which grow abundantly here. Moose are most often seen in spring and early summer, when they're looking for new plant growth, and in September, during the mating season, or rut. Using their massive antlers, rutting bulls battle each other for dominance—sometimes within sight of the road—as they herd cows into breeding groups. Confrontations begin with antler displays and escalate into sparring and, in some instances, fierce fights. As many as twenty to thirty moose, both males and females, may congregate during the rut.

Caribou occasionally pass through the entrance area's wet tundra and transitional zone during their seasonal migrations. They, in turn, may be stalked by wolves. Grizzlies appear in early summer to feed on fresh greens and stalk moose calves and in late summer to gorge on berries. The chances of seeing these animals are less here than deeper in the park, partly because of the thick brush.

More readily visible are smaller animals that frequent the shoulders of the road. Large numbers of sparrows, warblers, and other songbirds flit among the roadside bushes, while willow ptarmigan scurry in and out of the thickets for which they're named, feeding on willow leaves and catkins, berries, flowers, and other shrubs. White in winter, female willow ptarmigan become mottled brown in summer; males go from winter white to mostly reddish brown but keep their white wings and belly. Both ptarmigan and ground squirrels are favorite foods of red foxes, which sometimes walk the edges of the road, mouth filled with prey they're bringing home to their families.

Beyond mile 7 there are sweeping views of tundra, taiga, rocky foothills, and the Savage River as it pours out of mountains to the south. Dall sheep commonly graze tundra-covered foothills north of the road, appearing as tiny white pinpoints on distant slopes. Between miles 9.6 and 10.6 are the first roadside views of snow- and ice-capped Denali—weather permitting—as its pearly uppermost slopes rise above the darker foothills.

Savage River Patrol Cabin

At mile 13, just past Savage Campground, is another piece of Denali's cultural history: the Savage River cabin, one of fifteen historic patrol cabins within the park. Most were built between 1924 and 1935, some for road construction crews, others to provide shelter for rangers during winter mushing patrols. After the road's completion in 1938, all were used for patrols. Spaced 10 to 15 miles apart and located along Denali Park Road and the park's wilderness boundary, the cabins were intended to be within a day's journey of each other, even in marginal weather. A November 1927 patrol report by chief ranger Fritz Nyberg showed the clear need for such a cabin network:

> *The new cabin at Toklat and the dog-houses made this stretch of freighting much less disagreeable than heretofore. If there were several more of these cabins along the trails and along the boundary, patrol work could be carried out much more effectively. It is not fair to the rangers to ask them to patrol in the cold weather and get wet in the overflows and then have to spend the night out in the open under a spruce tree. Especially as they travel alone it is too dangerous to ask any man to do. This month Ranger [Grant] Pearson was caught in a blizzard in the Copper Mountain Basin with the nearest cabin or shelter of any kind 17 miles away. There was no timber in the basin for wood to make a fire and he had to double back 17 miles to the Toklat cabin, arriving late at night.*

Many of the historic cabins are still used by park rangers in winter while on sled dog patrol. In summer, only the one at Toklat (near mile 53 of the park road) is occupied full-time by rangers, though others at Igloo Creek and the Sanctuary River are intermittently used by both rangers and resource staff. Another, the East Fork cabin, is summer home to individuals participating in Denali's Artist-in-Residence program. And one—the Savage River cabin—is used in a "living history" program. At times when bus tours pass through, actors welcome visitors to the cabin and tell stories while playing the roles of legendary Denali personalities, like the park's founding father, Charles Sheldon, or Kantishna gold miner Fannie Quigley.

The Savage River cabin is furnished simply, in the way of most patrol cabins. There's little besides a table, chair, bed, wood-burning stove, shelves that hold various items (such as fur mittens and containers for tobacco and Epsom salts), several tools, and a pile of wood. Outside are snowshoes and skis, a sled, dog collars, and a wood-chopping station. When not being used, the cabin's windows are boarded over, with nails pointing outward to keep bears away. Near the cabin are the remains of doghouses once used on sled patrols.

Savage River's historic significance doesn't end with its patrol cabin. Horse packer and guide Dan Kennedy established the park's first visitor tent camp here in 1923, between the stream and the new park road. Kennedy sold his operation to the Mt. McKinley Tourist and Transportation Company in 1925, when park visitation jumped from 62 people to 206. According to historian William Brown:

> *The camp itself became a "tent house colony" during the summer. Dining hall, social hall, and tent houses took care of some 60 people at a time. Barns, a corral, and utility buildings completed the camp, which was served by running water.*
>
> *From this base, visitors could proceed on horseback, and later by Concord stages, on various loop trails into the Savage and Sanctuary rivers country. Spike camps allowed overnight wilderness experiences. More adventurous visitors could take guided pack-train trips into the park's farther hinterlands.*
>
> *...By 1929, the company's 22 buses, 9 touring cars, 4 stages, 2 trucks, and a trailer were pressed to the limit to handle visitors and logistics. At that, with only 150 to 200 visitors in the park at a given time, this was the golden age of park touring.*

Use of Savage Camp ceased after the park hotel was constructed in 1939, and all of the structures have been removed, leaving only roads and clearings south of Savage River Campground to remind visitors of the way people once visited the park.

See the Savage River Area

Four trails in the Savage River area provide excellent opportunities to learn more about its natural and cultural history. The trails listed below range from easy to moderately strenuous; more details can be found in the "Entrance Area Hiking Trails" section of this chapter. Distances are one way except where otherwise noted.

- Savage Cabin Interpretive Loop Trail, 0.25 mile
- Mountain Vista Trail, 0.6 mile round-trip
- Savage River Loop, 2 miles round-trip
- Savage Alpine Trail, 4.1 miles

Off-Trail Hikes

While the entrance area's developed trails provide easy access into the taiga forest—and, in the Savage River area, to the tundra—hikers can choose their own routes into the wildlands that border the park road beyond park headquarters. Although navigating in the taiga can be difficult, much of the hiking from mile 7 out to the Savage River is near or above tree line. The easiest way to explore these mixed forest–tundra flatlands—and reach the foothills beyond—is to follow one of the half dozen creeks that drain the Outer Range north of the road.

More than 50 feet wide in places, the creek beds are a mix of boulders, gravel, and sands. For most of the summer they are dry or have only a small flow of water. Walking the creeks is easier than navigating the often-dense thickets of waist-high birches and willows. Wildlife also frequently use these creek beds as travel corridors, so hikers have the opportunity to observe moose, grizzlies, caribou, wolves, foxes, and other animals.

Here as elsewhere in grizzly country, hikers should take precautions to avoid close encounters with bears. In 2012 a backpacker who ventured too close to a grizzly while photographing the bear was killed.

Throughout most of the entrance area, hikers must walk 3 to 5 miles to reach alpine tundra. But near the Savage River turnaround and parking lot at mile 15, it's a short—though strenuous—hike to alpine meadows and rocky ridges. The easiest option here is to take the Savage Alpine Trail and then either remain on that maintained path or head off-trail for more distant upland alpine bowls, ridgelines, and hilltops. Ambitious hikers can also head for high ground from the Savage River Loop (which itself passes through tundra while following the stream) or even the park road.

Visitors can also get a good taste of lowland tundra in the Savage area, by following the Mountain Vista Trail to a braided section of the Savage River that has large sand and gravel bars. This is easy walking, with expansive views of the surrounding hills (and, as noted in the trail description, the possibility of seeing Denali when the weather is right). Move just a few feet beyond the end of the developed path to get a taste of vast, untrailed wilderness.

Besides the popular Savage River area, it's also possible to climb to alpine tundra from the vicinity of the Denali Visitor Center. The Mount Healy Overlook Trail splits off the Taiga Trail not far from the Murie Science and Learning Center and winds through 1.5 miles of forest, then rises sharply through the taiga–tundra transition to tundra meadows and bare rock. Both steep and relatively long, the Mount Healy Overlook Trail is the best way to experience on foot the entire range of Denali habitats, finishing on a clear day with expansive views of both the Outer and Alaska Ranges, including The Mountain, shimmering brightly in the distance. Once in the alpine at Mount Healy (as at the Savage River), ambitious hikers can choose to go on their own off-trail explorations.

A Guided Walk to Horseshoe Lake

"Holy cow!" says naturalist Carrie Cahill as she greets the visitors who've gathered for a walk along the Horseshoe Lake Trail. "This is a really big group today." Forty-one of us, including a half dozen kids, stand at the trailhead on a calm, warm, dry, and surprisingly bug-free morning in late July—ideal conditions for a forest walk. Several people are in short-sleeved shirts; a few even wear short pants. Some carry packs, walking sticks, or binoculars, but no specialized gear is needed for this hike.

Before we move down the trail, Cahill has a few things to say.

"How many of you arrived today?" she asks. Several hands go up.

"How many are staying more than a day?" Most people raise their hands. "How many are staying at least two days?" About half the group. "A week?" Only two of us still have our hands raised.

"I'm happy most of you are staying at least a couple days," says Cahill, a spirited ranger with long brown hair, sparkling eyes, and an abundance of enthusiasm. "Did you know that the average stay at Denali is only one day? As you probably know, this is a really big park. I'm surprised people think they can see it in a day or two."

Next, a short quiz. "With this many people we're not likely to see wildlife. But if you were hiking this trail alone, you might meet a moose. Does everyone know what you'd do?"

"Run," someone shouts.

"Right," Cahill replies. "If you encounter a moose, get out of its way as quickly as possible. If you hang around, you could get run over. Now, what if you meet a bear?"

"Stand still," says a youngster.

"Very good," Cahill tells him. "Stand your ground and talk to the bear. And wave your arms slowly above your head. Let it know you're human. Never run from a bear; that's the worst thing you can do, because it could trigger the bear's predatory instincts. And remember this: you're more likely to get struck by lightning than touched by a bear."

Denali rangers repeat this message—run from moose, don't run from bears—before every naturalist program. Of all the park's critters, moose and bears are the two most likely to charge and injure a human if encountered at close range. The hazards of surprising a grizzly are well documented, but moose can be nearly as dangerous. This is especially true of cows with calves, and bulls during the autumn rut. Even with moose and bears, the odds of getting attacked are low, but it's always best to be cautious, to play it safe.

Next, Cahill tells us that we'll be seeing several varieties of edible berries and plants along the trail. Picking an occasional berry is fine, she says. "The only rule is that you have to eat everything you pick." One final piece of advice: "Be here, in Denali. If you find yourself thinking about other things, like your job or where you're going next, bring your attention back here. Notice what's going on around you."

I like that message: Be present. Pay attention.

The trail takes us into a forest of spruce, aspen, birch, and poplar trees. As we hike, our group stretches nearly the length of a football field, so Cahill stops frequently and has people gather around whenever she finds something of interest. Our first stop is among tall fireweed. A common plant with a tall stalk, long, willow-like leaves, and fuchsia-colored flowers, the fireweed blooms from bottom to top. As Cahill explains, it's one of Alaska's end-of-summer indicators. When the uppermost flowers have bloomed and gone to seed, "it's only six weeks 'til the first snowfall." Or so the story goes. Using fireweed to predict the weather, like anything else, can be tricky business. Still, it's a little unsettling that in late July the fireweed's flowers are already nearing the top.

Stopping at some aspen, Cahill suggests we touch the trees' bark. It feels velvety. Unlike most other trees, the aspen has chlorophyll in its olive-green trunk. In winter, when other food sources are rare, moose will eat the bark to gain necessary nutrients. Looking around, we see that many of this forest's aspens have had sections of their bark stripped away.

Later, Cahill introduces us to several types of berries: blueberries, crowberries, cranberries, pumpkin berries. The first three are among Alaska's most common berries, but pumpkin berries are new to me. Orange and creased, they do resemble miniature pumpkins. Cahill says they taste like green peas; she likes to put them in salads. I try one. Sure enough, it's crunchy and tastes like a pea.

Soapberries too are edible. In fact, these shiny red berries are a grizzly favorite. One researcher who analyzed bear scats estimated that grizzlies eat as many as 200,000 soapberries in a day, during their annual pre-denning feeding frenzy known as hyperphagia. Soapberries aren't as palatable to humans, though. As their name suggests, they taste something like soap.

Cahill's approach—go slowly, look around, pay attention—is effective. In a park known for its high peaks, expansive scenery, and big mammals, she has us looking closely at plants along the forest floor. We're starting to notice some of the Denali ecosystem's smaller—but critically important—

(continued)

A Guided Walk to Horseshoe Lake (continued)

components. We're opening our senses, learning natural history, making connections. Take willow, for example. Here's a plant, says Cahill, that's "an incredible thing for your outdoor pharmacy." Willows contain salicin, a natural aspirin substitute. Chewing their leaves can relieve headaches or muscle aches. A good thing to know when backpacking.

Besides producing natural painkillers, willows are the No. 1 food source for Denali's moose—and they benefit from being eaten. "To have a moose bite you is a good thing, if you're a willow," Cahill explains. "When the tops of their stems are bitten, willows compensate by growing two or three new shoots. What this does, in effect, is make the willow lower to the ground, but also denser and bushier. This is a good thing in a subarctic environment."

The trail eventually brings us to Horseshoe Lake. Thousands of years ago, this oxbow lake was part of the nearby Nenana River. But as the river carved a new course, this meandering section was cut off. Bordered by spruce, birch, and cottonwood forest, the lake and its environs provide shelter and food for many animals: beaver, muskrats, fish, ducks, squirrels, kingfishers, songbirds, grouse, moose, even a great-horned owl.

From a trail overlook we get a good view of the small U-shaped lake. Eventually, it will fill with sediments and become a meadow within the forest. And when enough time passes, the meadow will then fill with trees. Beyond the lake are the Nenana's roaring, gray, glacially fed waters; and beyond the river is a heavily commercialized stretch of Parks Highway, with hotels, restaurants, and other tourism businesses. Here, the line between wildness and development is sharply drawn, and Cahill uses this opportunity to briefly discuss Denali's growing pains. "There's been an explosion of tourism growth here," she says, "and that presents an interesting dilemma. How do we put on the brakes? How or when do we say 'enough is enough'? I don't have the answers. I don't know that anyone does. But I think it's important that we begin asking the questions."

HEALY AND THE STAMPEDE TRAIL

The nearest community to Denali National Park to offer year-round visitor services, Healy was settled in the early 1900s by prospectors, trappers, and commercial hunters. Among Healy's earliest buildings were a roadhouse, store, moonshiner's still, and café. The local population was boosted considerably when railroad workers built a construction camp nearby in 1920, and the young settlement was soon transformed into a full-fledged railroad town, complete with dormitory, mess hall, hospital, store, and blacksmith shop.

The railroad's looming presence also sparked development of several nearby coal mines. In 1922, workers completed a 4-mile spur that connected the railroad's main line with the Suntrana Mine, owned by the Healy River Coal Company. The spur allowed the company to expand its mining operations, begun in 1917, and to ship large quantities of coal north to Fairbanks. The mine also supplied local users, including those at Mount McKinley National Park.

The mine changed hands in 1943, when it was purchased by Emil Usibelli. Today, using state-of-the-art equipment and techniques, the Usibelli Coal Company extracts 1.5 million tons per year of coal from Alaska's only commercial coal mine. Some of it is used to fuel six Interior Alaska power plants; the remainder is sent by rail to Seward, then shipped to Chile, South Korea, and other Pacific Rim destinations.

Though it remains mostly a company town best known for its coal mine, Healy has many businesses that serve highway travelers and park visitors: gas stations, hotels, bed-and-breakfasts, restaurants, gift shops, auto repair shop, grocery store, RV parks. Many are open year-round.

A few miles north of Healy, on the highway's western side, is the historic Stampede Trail, which many years ago led to the Stampede Mine, once Alaska's prime producer of antimony. The mine ceased operations in 1970, and since 1980 its abandoned mill and other buildings have been located within Denali National Park's expanded borders. Much of the trail, too, is now within Denali, though its first 25 to 30 miles are outside the park.

Blazed in the 1930s by miner Earl Pilgrim, the Stampede Trail was upgraded to a road during the early 1960s in the hope that trucks could haul antimony ore from the mine year-round. Impassable bogs, melting permafrost, and flooding rivers ultimately stopped the road project, but not before 50 miles had been built. Since then, most of the route has largely disappeared, wiped out by brush, river washouts, and the boggy nature of the land. Only the first few miles of road/trail remain well graded; beyond that, the Stampede is largely overgrown and challenging to follow. Its primary users are hunters in fall, and snowmobilers, mushers, and skiers in late winter, when travel is easier. In recent years, a substantial number of explorers (many of them young and inexperienced in backcountry travel) have hiked out the Stampede Trail to visit "Bus 142," made famous by Jon Krakauer's best-selling book *Into the Wild* (later adapted into a popular film), about the life, journeys, and death of Chris McCandless, who as a young man ventured into Denali's wilderness and died there.

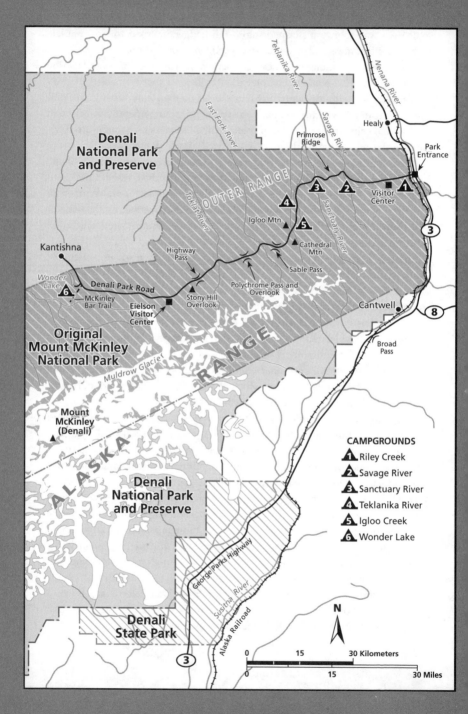

Chapter 5

TRAVELING
THE PARK ROAD

The Denali Park Road is a magical pathway that transports national park visitors from their familiar, civilized world into a timeless Alaska landscape. A trip down the park road offers a unique opportunity to view wildlife such as grizzlies, moose, caribou, Dall sheep, and wolves in their natural environment, with a backdrop of stupendous mountain scenery. Stretching more than 90 miles from the George Parks Highway to the former gold camp of Kantishna, the park road is the only developed route into the heart of Denali, but it is merely a narrow gravel thread in the midst of countless acres of wild land. Passing through all of Denali's major ecosystems—taiga forest, wet tundra, alpine tundra—it crosses large, braided rivers that pour out of the Alaska Range; it skirts the edges of brightly colored volcanic cliffs and is dwarfed by the surrounding landscape as it follows stream valleys into huge glacier-carved basins.

Only the first 15 miles of the road are paved. For the most part, the road intentionally remains a narrow and primitive—but safe—gravel pathway into the wilds, whose route largely follows the contours of the land. Naturalist and conservationist Adolph Murie, who worked to keep the road undeveloped in the 1960s, spoke of "the blessing of a road with a tempo in harmony with the enjoyment of flowers, lichens, wandering tattlers, and grizzlies." The Denali Park Road still largely retains such a harmony with its surroundings.

Nearly every road traveler sees at least some of Denali's large mammals as well as golden eagles, hawks, magpies, gulls, songbirds, marmots, ground squirrels, red foxes, beavers, and Alaska's state bird, willow ptarmigan. The farther one goes on the road, the less human traffic one encounters and the more wildlife one is likely to see. Besides the increased odds of seeing wildlife, the farther one goes, the closer the views (if the weather is right) of the great mountain, Denali.

A grizzly mom and her two cubs graze on plants near Sable Pass, an area where bus riders have a good chance of spotting families of bears.

PARK ROAD AREA RESOURCES AND INFORMATION

Visitors who wish to explore the Denali Park Road have their choice of either shuttle or tour buses. Visitors should note that pets are not allowed on buses, while bikes are permitted on shuttles and camper buses, but not tour buses.

Camper buses, intended for backpackers and campers, are described in Chapter 6, "Hiking the Backcountry." These are likely to be phased out as part of Denali National Park's new Vehicle Management Plan, scheduled to go fully into effect in 2015. If and when the park no longer employs camper buses, backpackers and campers will likely be directed to use Denali's shuttle buses.

Bus Tours

Three types of tours are offered. For all of them, drivers are expected to be interpretive guides. Passengers must stay on the bus except at designated rest areas, but buses stop for better viewing when wildlife is sighted. Snacks or box lunches are provided, and some tour buses are wheelchair accessible.

- **Tundra WildernessTours** emphasize wildlife viewing, along with descriptions of the park's landscape and its natural and cultural history. Trips normally go as far as the Toklat River (mile 53) and last 7–8 hours round-trip, but drivers will continue to the Stony Hill Overlook when The Mountain is visible.

- **The Denali Natural History Tour**, an abbreviated alternative (4–5 hours), goes only 17 miles from the park entrance to Primrose Ridge and presents an overview of the park's natural and human history. Big mammals are occasionally seen on this shorter tour, but the odds of finding wildlife are much smaller, and the views of Denali are not nearly as revealing as those farther west.
- **The Kantishna Experience Tour** takes visitors to that former gold-boom community at mile 92 on an 11–12-hour ride that offers a mix of wildlife and Denali viewing (when The Mountain is visible) along with the opportunity to learn more about Kantishna's history.

Round-Trip Costs

Adult fares are $113.25 for the Tundra Wilderness Tour; $66.50 for the Denali Natural History Tour; and $159 for the Kantishna Experience Tour; prices for those fourteen and younger are half the adult fare. The fare includes the park entrance fee and lunch. Buses depart throughout the day.

NOTE: Prices naturally vary from year to year, and it's common for fares to increase slightly from one year to the next. Those listed here were accurate at press time.

Dates of Operation

The Natural History Tour normally begins in late May, with the longer tours starting in early June; all three run through early to mid-September, weather permitting. A shortened version of the Tundra Wilderness Tour, the Teklanika Tundra Wilderness Tour (to mile 30) operates in the spring and fall shoulder seasons.

Reservations

A portion of tour-bus tickets are available for advance purchase, as early as December 1; the remainder are kept for purchase within two days of a scheduled trip. Tour bus tickets may be reserved in advance online (www.reservedenali .com); by phone (800-622-7275 within the U.S. and Canada, 907-272-7275 from international locales or while in the Anchorage area); by fax (907-264-4684; fax forms can be downloaded at www.nps.gov/dena); or by mail (Doyon/Aramark Joint Venture, 2445 West Dunlap Avenue, Phoenix, AZ 85021; mail requests must be received at least thirty days before the travel date). When at the park, tour bus tickets can be purchased at the Wilderness Access Center (WAC, mile 0.75, in the entrance area). Prepaid reserved tickets can also be picked up at the WAC.

Shuttles

A less-expensive alternative to the tours is the shuttle bus system. Primary turn-around points are:

Igloo Creek Campground, pictured here, is one of three campgrounds along the Denali Park Road designated for tent campers only; the others are Sanctuary and Wonder Lake.

- Toklat (mile 53, 6.5 hours round-trip)
- Eielson Visitor Center (mile 66, 8 hours round-trip)
- Wonder Lake Campground (mile 85, 11 hours round-trip)
- Kantishna (mile 92, 13 hours round-trip)

As with tours, wildlife viewing is emphasized, and buses stop when animals are sighted. Shuttle bus drivers are not required to be interpretive guides, but many actively look for wildlife and offer knowledgeable insights. A notable shuttle bus advantage: flexibility. Passengers can get off wherever they choose (except when large animals are nearby) to explore the park on their own and then catch another shuttle—space permitting. Waits for later shuttles may last an hour or more. Most shuttle passengers make Eielson their endpoint, particularly when the weather is wet and overcast. The 38-mile round-trip ride between Eielson and Wonder Lake adds 3 hours of travel. The extra time is worth it, especially when Denali is visible, or in late August and early September, when the tundra burns with autumn's colors and caribou bulls, velvet hanging from bloodied antlers, frequent this section of road. Throughout the summer, the Eielson–Wonder Lake drive presents a look at beaver ponds and associated wildlife not seen along other stretches of road. The Kantishna shuttle provides at look at this historic gold-boom area and adds a couple more hours of travel.

Round-Trip Costs
Adult-fare prices are $24.50 to Toklat, $31.50 to Eielson, $43.25 to Wonder Lake, and $47.25 to Kantishna. Prices for young adults (fifteen to seventeen) are half that, and those fourteen or younger travel for free. Prices include reservation fee but not park entrance fee. Buses depart throughout the day.

NOTE: Prices naturally vary from year to year, and it's common for fares to increase slightly from one year to the next. Those listed here were accurate at press time.

Dates of Operation
Beginning and ending dates depend on the destination (because the park road may not be open to the farthest destinations until slightly later in the season). As a general rule, shuttle buses run to Toklat from late May through mid-September, while the Eielson shuttle normally begins operation around June 1, and the Wonder Lake–Kantishna shuttles start about a week after that.

Reservations
Advance reservations are recommended. The methods and contact information are the same as for tour buses (see above).

What to Bring on Bus Trips
The following items will make your bus trips more pleasurable. Remember that lunch is provided on tour buses, but that no food or beverage is available on shuttles.
- Warm clothing
- Rain jacket and pants
- Sturdy walking shoes
- Insect repellent and/or head net
- Binoculars and/or camera gear
- Water or other nonalcoholic beverages
- Snack foods and/or lunch

PARK ROAD AREA CAMPGROUNDS
Four of Denali National Park's campgrounds are located beyond Savage River. Sanctuary River (mile 23) and Teklanika River (mile 29) campgrounds are in open forest, near tree line, and close to glacially fed streams. Igloo Creek Campground (mile 34) is in denser spruce forest beside a clearwater creek. Wonder Lake

Campground (mile 85) is on a tundra-covered ridge; one side overlooks Wonder Lake, and the other looks out on the McKinley River and Denali. Individual sites are hidden from the road, though within a short walk. Only Teklanika Campground is accessible by private vehicle, with a required three-day minimum stay for those who drive themselves here (shorter stays are possible for campers who take the bus to Teklanika). Other campgrounds must be reached by camper bus.

Reservations

Campsites may be reserved in advance beginning December 1, either by going online (www.reservedenali.com) or by calling the concessionaire (800-622-7275 within the United States or Canada, and 907-272-7275 from international locales or while in the Anchorage area). Requests can also be made by fax (907-264-4684; fax forms can be download at www.nps.gov/dena) or by mail (Doyon/Aaramark Joint Venture, 2445 West Dunlap Avenue, Phoenix, AZ 85021; mailed requests must be received at least thirty days before the reservation dates).

Prepaid reserved tickets can be picked up at the Wilderness Access Center (WAC, mile 0.75 in the entrance area). Those who arrive at Denali without campground reservations must go to the WAC to reserve sites.

SANCTUARY RIVER CAMPGROUND

Location:	Mile 23
Number of sites:	7; tents only
Season:	May through September, weather dependent
Water:	Creek water, must be treated
Facilities:	Vault toilets
Fee:	$9 per night
Emergency:	Contact park staff or bus driver
Reservations:	Reserve sites in person at the WAC or Riley Creek Mercantile

TEKLANIKA RIVER CAMPGROUND

Location:	Mile 29
Number of sites:	53; RVs and tents
Season:	May through September, weather dependent
Water:	Yes
Facilities:	Vault toilets
Fee:	$16 per night; minimum 3-night stay for vehicle campers
Emergency:	Contact campground host, park staff, or bus driver
Reservations:	All sites assigned; reserve in advance online or by phone, fax, or mail, or in person at the WAC or Riley Creek Mercantile

IGLOO CREEK CAMPGROUND

Location:	Mile 34
Number of sites:	7; tents only
Season:	May through September, weather dependent
Water:	Creek water, must be treated
Facilities:	Vault toilets
Fee:	$9 per night
Emergency:	Contact park staff or bus driver
Reservations:	Reserve sites in person at the WAC or Riley Creek Mercantile

WONDER LAKE CAMPGROUND

Location:	Mile 85
Number of sites:	28; tents only
Season:	June through September, weather dependent
Water:	Yes
Facilities:	Flush toilets
Fee:	$16 per night
Emergency:	Contact campground host, Wonder Lake Ranger Station (2 miles west), or bus driver
Reservations:	All sites assigned; reserve in advance online or by phone, fax, or mail, or in person at the WAC or Riley Creek Mercantile

Campground Regulations

Beyond Savage River, fires are allowed only at Teklanika Campground, in established grates. Firewood may be purchased at a store near the entrance area. Cutting live vegetation or standing deadwood is prohibited, as is the use of power saws. All other campgrounds allow stoves only; no open fires.

Pets are not allowed on trails or buses, so beyond Savage River they can be brought only to the Teklanika Campground (by those who drive their own vehicles). There, they must be leashed at all times. Please dispose of feces in garbage cans. Secure pet food inside of vehicle or in food locker.

Quiet hours are between 10 PM and 6 AM. Generators may be used at Teklanika only from 8 AM to 10 AM and 4 PM to 8 PM. Checkout time is 11 AM.

Day hikers stand in an alpine meadow, among early blooming June wildflowers, as they explore Denali National Park's tundra near the Eielson Visitor Center.

Food Storage and Wildlife

Improper food storage and sloppy camping can lead to unnecessary and potentially harmful conflicts with Denali's wildlife, particularly bears. For the safety of visitors and animals alike, observe the following principles:

- Keep a clean camp. Wash dishes immediately. Discuss gray water disposal with a ranger or campground host.
- Store and cook food away from sleeping areas.
- All food, cooking utensils, and ice chests, as well as scented toiletries and cosmetics, must be stored in the food lockers provided or, at Teklanika, in hard-sided vehicles.
- Do not feed any animal or bird. Not only will they become a nuisance, they will grow dependent on an unnatural food supply.

Drinking Water and Giardia

Transmitted through the feces of many mammals, the intestinal parasite *Giardia lamblia* occurs in waters throughout the Denali region and may result in nausea, diarrhea, and intense cramping if it enters the body. Where potable water is unavailable, the best precaution is to boil all stream or lake water for at least 1 minute, use a filter specifically designed to remove such microorganisms, or add iodine tablets to the water. If using a filter, avoid glacial water whenever possible, because the fine sediments in the water may clog your filter.

PARK ROAD AREA HIKING TRAILS

While most of Denali beyond the entrance area lacks defined and maintained trails, a couple of hiking trails can be found at the Eielson Visitor Center, and another near Wonder Lake.

EASY

TUNDRA LOOP TRAIL

Route: Begins at the Eielson Visitor Center and loops through the nearby tundra. Graveled footpath, 3 feet wide.

Length: 0.5 mile (0.8 kilometer)

Elevation change: Negligible

Time: 30 minutes

Highlights: The setting of dry alpine tundra displays a mosaic of plants, including beautiful wildflowers; animals that may be seen here range from ground squirrels and foxes to golden eagles, caribou, Dall sheep, grizzlies, and wolves. Spectacular views of Denali (when the weather cooperates) and other Alaska Range foothills and mountains.

EASY TO MODERATE

MCKINLEY BAR TRAIL

Route: Begins at road about 0.25 mile from Wonder Lake Campground. The trail leads through spruce forest and passes several ponds en route to the banks of the McKinley River. Graveled footpath, 3 feet wide.

Length: 2.5 miles one way (4 kilometers)

Elevation change: Negligible

Time: 1–1.5 hours one way

Highlights: From the river, on a clear day, hikers have sweeping views of 20,320-foot Denali and other Alaska Range peaks. Whatever the weather, hikers may see wildflowers and wildlife (including black bears, which are sometimes encountered along the trail) and, in late summer, pick blueberries, which are abundant here. Mosquitoes too are abundant for much of the summer, so hikers are advised to bring plenty of bug repellent and/or head nets. (See map, page 172.)

STRENUOUS

THOROFARE RIDGE TRAIL

Route: Begins at the Eielson Visitor Center and climbs, in zigzag fashion, up nearby Thorofare Ridge. Footpath, 2 feet wide.

Length: 1 mile one way (1.6 kilometers)

Elevation change: 1000 feet

Time: 30 minutes to 1 hour one way

Highlights: The ridge trail provides an opportunity for more ambitious hikers to go higher into the alpine and, for some, to go off-trail to even greater heights; like the Tundra Loop Trail, this also presents spectacular views of Denali (when the weather cooperates) and other Alaska Range foothills and mountains. Animals that may be seen here range from ground squirrels and foxes to golden eagles, caribou, Dall sheep, grizzlies, and wolves.

BIKING THE PARK ROAD

In recent years, an increasing number of people have explored Denali National Park by bicycling all or part of the park road. To enhance cyclists' "Denali experience," park staff offer these guidelines and tips:

- Cyclists may ride on park roads and the designated Bike Path between the Nenana River (in the Parks Highway corridor) and the Denali Visitor Center, as well as in parking areas and campground loops. Bicycles are prohibited on all other trails.
- Cyclists should stay attuned to the road surface, traffic, and changeable weather conditions while cycling. They should also travel single file, keep to the right, and obey traffic regulations.
- Cyclists are asked to move to the right and slow down or stop when encountering motor vehicles on the road.
- Bikes can be transported on the free Savage River Shuttle, on camper buses, and on shuttle buses that travel to the Eielson Visitor Center at certain hours in the morning. Space is limited, however, and cyclists should check availability at the Wilderness Access Center.
- Bike racks are provided at campgrounds, rest areas, and visitor centers. Cyclists who wish to go day-hiking in the backcountry should carry their bikes at least 25 yards from the road and hide them from view. If leaving a bike overnight, tag it with contact information.
- Bikers who wish to camp outside an established campground must obtain a backcountry permit at the Backcountry Information Center.
- Wild animals are curious and opportunistic. Cyclists should not leave

food or other scented items at their bikes unattended. Use storage lockers provided at campgrounds and other locations or use a bear-resistant food container, provided free with a backcountry camping permit.

- Be familiar with wildlife distance regulations; if an animal changes its behavior in your presence, you're too close.
- If a bear appears near you or your planned route, do not try to outride it. Stop and dismount. Keep all your gear with you and back away slowly. Wait for the bear to move away. If there is a motor vehicle nearby, use it as a barrier between you and the bear.

EXPERIENCING DENALI'S PARK ROAD

Denali National Park is unusual among national parks in that travel along the park road is generally restricted to buses, in order to preserve wildlife-viewing opportunities. Personal vehicles are generally permitted on the road's 15-mile paved section only. With few exceptions, visitors must take either a shuttle or a tour bus when traveling beyond Savage River. Depending on their choice of bus, passengers can ride as few as 17 or as many as 92 miles into the park, on journeys that range from 4 to 13 hours round-trip. (Destinations, costs, and reservations for both tours and shuttles are detailed under "Park Road Area Resources and Information" at the beginning of this chapter.)

When choosing destinations, visitors may wish to consider that the landscape opens up, with expansive tundra vistas, beyond Sable Pass (mile 39.1), and that the best park-road views of Denali—The Mountain—are between Stony Hill (mile 62) and Wonder Lake (mile 85). Wildlife watching too is generally better deep in the park.

Although the park bus system doesn't have the flexibility and comfort of touring by personal vehicle, it offers certain advantages, especially for wildlife viewing. Buses put passengers much higher, making it easier to see beyond brush-lined stretches of road, and increase the odds of wildlife sightings because of the many sets of eyes looking for animals. A study to determine frequency of wildlife sightings from shuttle buses—which take visitors to mile 53 and beyond—found that between 1999 and 2011, 84 percent of passengers saw grizzly bears (the odds being especially high on trips to Eielson, mile 66, and beyond); 91 percent saw caribou, 82 percent Dall sheep, 40 percent moose, and 23 percent wolves (the odds of seeing wolves, like bears, greatly increases for those going deeper into the park). By cutting down on traffic, the bus system also lessens the likelihood that animals will be chased from the road corridor.

Whether by shuttle or tour bus, trips along the park road give visitors the opportunity to observe Denali's diverse wildlife in their natural surroundings while traveling deep into a wilderness that has changed little since the first pioneering expeditions passed through the region in the early 1900s. This section offers a park-road perspective of Denali's landscape and wildlife between Savage River (mile 15) and Kantishna (mile 92). The 77 miles of road beyond Savage River are divided into the following eight sections based on landscape features, plant communities, wildlife assemblages, cultural history, and road characteristics. (The park road's first 15 miles are described in Chapter 4, "Exploring the National Park Entrance.")

While the park road generally trends east–west as it moves deeper into the park, it has many twists and turns, and along some stretches runs north–south. The Alaska Range roughly parallels the road to the south, and Denali stands to the southwest. Because visitors will have changing perspectives as they use this guide both on their outbound trip and on their return, directions to landforms and other points of interest are given as compass bearings rather than left or right of the road.

Primrose Ridge: Savage River to Sanctuary River (Mile 15 to Mile 23)

Pavement gives way to gravel at Savage River, though the park road retains its two-lane width. Through long curving stretches of flat terrain and gently sloping grades, the road hugs the base of Primrose Ridge, a foothill of the Outer Range to the north. It climbs gradually from 2500 feet at the Savage River, up and across a 3000-foot bench covered in dense willow thickets and scattered spruce, overlooking a vast valley that stretches to the base of the Alaska Range foothills. The road then winds down the other side of the ridge to 2600 feet at the Sanctuary River. Small groups of caribou pass through the Savage and Sanctuary river valleys on seasonal migrations, while tundra-dwelling creatures such as marmots and Dall sheep feast on alpine vegetation high on Primrose.

The Savage River bridge (mile 15) is an excellent site at which to observe the difference between landscape sculpted by water and that shaped by glaciers. South of the bridge, the river winds through a broad, U-shaped valley that was scooped out by ice some 70,000 years ago, as an immense glacier flowed out of the Alaska Range to nearly where the road is now. Just north of the bridge, the Savage River squeezes into a narrow channel and cuts through a steep-sided, V-shaped canyon typical of stream erosion—evidence that the glacier didn't extend this far.

Just west of Savage River and north of the road is Primrose Ridge. Nearly 6 miles long and barely more than 5000 feet (1525 meters) at its highest point, Primrose is part of the nonglaciated Outer Range, a group of hills uplifted 5 to 6 million years ago and separated from the Alaska Range by lowlands south of the road. Though geologists consider the Outer Range to be a young landform, many of its gray to pale green rocks—visible along parts of Primrose—are

The Savage River and bridge, seen from an alpine lookout. Visitors may drive their own vehicles as far as the Savage River, 15 road miles into Denali.

among the Denali region's oldest. First deposited more than 500 million years ago, they've been deformed and reshaped numerous times since then.

Hoary marmots—large, grizzled, gray-and-brown rodents closely related to woodchucks—are abundant on Primrose's flanks. Social animals, hoary marmots live in colonies along the ridge's rocky ribs and give a high-pitched, piercing whistle when alarmed. They're hunted by a variety of predators—wolves, grizzlies, foxes, wolverines, and golden eagles—and so never stray far from their subterranean homes.

Caribou sometimes cross the lowlands south of Primrose Ridge and the road. If it's early summer, they are likely to be bulls, distinguished by their towering racks of antlers, up to 5.5 feet high and 3 feet wide. Caribou cows (also antlered, but with small spikes 12 to 18 inches long) and their young appear near the park road later in the summer, after spending the early months of the calves' lives in the high foothills of the Alaska Range.

As the park road climbs out of the Savage River valley, it crosses a bench that looks out upon a sweeping panorama to the south. Stretching southwest to northeast as far as the eye can see is the northern edge of the Alaska Range, the great mountain chain that culminates in Denali. Arcing 600 miles across the state, the range is a mix of sedimentary, volcanic, and granitic rocks that have been uplifted by the violent collision of Earth's crustal plates for the past 60 million years.

On its descent to the Sanctuary River, the road comes to Sanctuary River Campground (mile 23). Located beside the turbid and fast-flowing glacial stream, this campground is one of the park's smallest—and most primitive, without potable water or electricity. Sanctuary's seven sites are reserved for tent campers, who get here by camper bus, a type of shuttle designed to transport backpackers and campers. (If camper buses are phased out by 2015, campers will be directed to use Denali's shuttle bus system, described earlier in this chapter.) There's also a small log cabin here; visible from the road, it was built in the 1920s as a road-construction cookhouse and storage cache and now serves as a ranger station and patrol cabin. (See Chapter 4 for more on the park's historic cabins.)

Teklanika: Sanctuary River to Teklanika River (Mile 23 to Mile 31)
The park road passes through, or just slightly above, valley bottoms along this 8-mile stretch, at elevations below 3000 feet. Flat to gently sloping, the road is bordered by taiga forest and a transitional habitat of mixed spruce and wet tundra. Moose and black bears inhabit the spruce forest, and wolves and caribou pass through these wooded valleys on their seasonal travels. But here, as in much of Denali, the most abundant and highly visible resident is the arctic ground squirrel.

Similar in appearance to prairie dogs, these yellowish-brown squirrels frequent the shoulders of the road, scouring the ground for seeds, roots, plant stems, insects, and other food items to scavenge. When they're not eating, arctic ground squirrels often stand at attention, chattering loudly. They have good reason to be attentive; near the bottom of Denali's food chain, they're a favorite food of many meat eaters: foxes, wolves, grizzlies, wolverines, lynx, gyrfalcons, and golden eagles.

The moose within these forested valleys most often remain hidden among the spruce. Cows especially are cautious in summer, after giving birth to one or two calves in late May or early June. During their first few weeks of life, the calves are especially vulnerable to wolves and grizzlies.

Singly or in packs, wolves move like shadows through the forest as they stalk moose, hunt squirrels, or trail the caribou that migrate through these valleys.

Among the more curious landscape features along this stretch of road is a wooded area south of the road at mile 23.7, just past the Sanctuary River bridge, where black spruce trees tilt haphazardly in all directions to create a "drunken forest." Such tilting is due to the permafrost beneath the forest floor. In summer, the upper layer of permafrost melts, freeing the soil from its frozen matrix. Sometimes the soil sinks into spaces left by the melting ice, forming depressions. A tree standing next to such a depression will lose some of its support, causing it to lean.

The Teklanika Campground is on the road's north side at mile 29. The second largest of the park's campgrounds, this is the only one open to both tent and RV camping beyond the entrance area (see "Park Road Area Campgrounds" for more details); sometimes shuttle buses will stop here (as at other campgrounds) to pick up passengers. One mile later, bus riders get their first break at the Teklanika rest stop, 30.2 road miles into the park. Caribou, grizzlies, or even wolves sometimes use the riverbed below as a travel corridor, and mew gulls almost always hang around the parking area, seeking handouts. (Feeding gulls or any other animals is prohibited in the park; see the wildlife viewing guidelines at the end of the Introduction.)

A mile beyond the rest stop is the bridge across the Teklanika River, one of the park's large braided streams. Flowing north out of the Alaska Range and fed by glacial runoff, these streams carry immense quantities of silt, sand, and larger rock fragments in their opaque, brown-to-gray waters, and carve sinuous patterns as they rush through broad valleys a mile or more wide. Over time, these sediment-rich rivers have built enormously wide streambeds over which the streams migrate back and forth, constantly shifting shape with the seasons.

South of the bridge, the Teklanika drainage is closed to visitor entry. Scattered along the road, such closures are intended to protect the park's wildlife from human intrusion. In some places, such as here, closed areas protect denning mammals or nesting birds; other closures are intended to keep people away from grizzly or wolf kills and food caches or rutting moose. Depending on the circumstances, closures may last a few days or the entire summer. Teklanika's closure is normally summer-long.

Igloo Forest and Canyon: Teklanika River to Sable Pass Closure Sign (Mile 31 to Mile 38)

Beyond the Teklanika River crossing, the road narrows from two to one-and-a-half lanes and rises, first gently and then steeply, as it follows Igloo Creek to the Sable Pass closure. As it ascends, this north–south section of road enters a canyon between two prominent Outer Range peaks, Igloo and Cathedral, and the surrounding plant communities change, first from lowland taiga forest into transitional ecotone and then into tundra. The forest is home to a variety of woodland animals, including moose, porcupines, red squirrels, snowshoe hares, songbirds, and owls, and the Outer Range peaks beyond are heavily populated with bands of Dall sheep.

Igloo Forest is the name given to the lowland taiga west of the Teklanika River. Moose feed on patches of willow, porcupines waddle slowly along the forest floor or climb trees while foraging for plants, and great horned owls nest in spruce cavities and perch on branches as they hunt hares, voles and other rodents, songbirds, and even smaller owls.

At mile 34.1, still in lowland spruce forest, the road passes Igloo Campground, another small backpackers' haven. Next it enters Igloo Canyon, a rocky ravine that slices through the Outer Range. Four miles long and only a few hundred yards wide in most places, the canyon is a major wildlife "highway" used by grizzlies, wolves, and caribou as well as the abundant sheep.

For much of its way through Igloo Canyon, the park road is bordered by the steep slopes of Igloo and Cathedral mountains (located west and east of

Don't Miss the Dall Sheep

Congregating in bands of up to fifty or sixty animals, the sheep prefer to feed in high alpine meadows bordered by rugged rock faces and cliffs. If threatened by predators, they use their superior mountain-climbing skills to escape among the protective rocks. Ewes give birth in late May, and the newborn lambs are especially vulnerable to predators. Mature rams, as well as ewes, lambs, and younger rams, use the ridge, but they stay in their own "bachelor groups" until the early winter rut. Though usually far above the road, the sheep occasionally graze nearby it, making the playful antics of lambs or the large curling horns of mature rams easy to observe.

A hiker holds onto his hat while being battered by high winds as he ascends a rocky ridge on Sable Mountain, in Denali National Park's Outer Range.

the road, respectively). Just under 5000 feet (1525 meters) in elevation, the peaks are painted red, orange, yellow, and brown by iron-stained volcanic rocks. Both mountains provide excellent habitat for Dall sheep; Cathedral Mountain is where naturalist Charles Sheldon shot and collected his ram "specimens" in 1906.

Climbing out of Igloo Canyon, the road passes Tattler Creek (mile 37.5), a small tributary stream named after the wandering tattler, a mostly gray migratory shorebird that prefers to breed far inland, along rocky creek beds in alpine and subalpine habitat. The first wandering tattler nest ever found by scientists was discovered along Denali Park's Savage River in 1923. Beyond Tattler Creek, the road approaches the wide tundra expanses of Sable Pass, the gateway to grizzly country.

Sable Pass: Closure to East Fork River (Mile 38 to Mile 43.5)

The park road bends back to the west as it leaves the Outer Range and ascends to 3900-foot Sable Pass, one of Denali's prime grizzly bear habitats. Bordered by tundra meadows and alpine swales with dense willow thickets, the road then gently descends along straightaways and broad curves as it follows a tributary creek to the glacially fed East Fork River, elevation 3200 feet (980 meters). North of Sable Pass and looming over this section of road is the Outer Range's 6000-foot (1830-meter) Sable Mountain, a massive, dark, domelike peak. Broad tundra benches to the south rise gradually to meet jagged foothills of the Alaska Range. And far in the distance, visible from the pass (mile 39.1), Denali's shimmering summit rises into the subarctic sky. Grizzly bears frequent the Sable Pass area throughout summer, grazing on tundra plants and hunting ground squirrels.

Historically heavily used by grizzlies, especially females with cubs, Sable Pass is where many park visitors see their first bear. Because the area has been known as a grizzly feeding ground—and a place where bus passengers may see bears at close range—a critical habitat wildlife closure has been established here, prohibiting anyone from leaving the road from about mileposts 38 to 43.

Leaving Sable Pass and dropping down into the drainage of the East Fork River, the road at mile 43 passes two log cabins, including one used in the late 1930s and early 1940s by biologist Adolph Murie while he studied Denali's East Fork wolf pack. Over the years, the East Fork pack has ranged in size from only a few wolves to a remarkable twenty-nine (one of the largest family groups ever recorded in North America), while roaming over an area as large as 800 square miles (2000 square kilometers). That so few wolves need such a large territory shows how sparse prey is in the Denali region. The park's sheep, caribou, and moose are highly visible not because of their vast numbers, but because of their size, the abundance of undisturbed habitat, and the fact that much of the terrain is above tree line.

Don't Miss the Grizzlies

Though they'll eat other mammals when the opportunity presents itself, Denali's grizzlies have a plant-rich diet. In spring and early summer, they depend heavily on the roots of certain tundra plants; a wildflower called the Eskimo potato is one favorite. Using their long claws and powerful neck and back muscles, the bears pull back mounds of earth, then delicately expose the roots.

While root-pulling is a rather ho-hum routine task, grizzlies dig furiously when chasing squirrels in their dens, tossing large clumps of soil and even boulder-sized rocks into the air as they excavate holes several feet wide. As often as not, the squirrels escape. Later in summer, grizzlies consume enormous quantities of blueberries and soapberries.

Sow grizzlies with cubs are frequently seen near the road. Numbering from one to four (most commonly two), the cubs may be blond to dark chocolate brown in color. They'll remain with their mother for two-and-a-half to three-and-a-half years; when weaned, they'll lead a mostly solitary life, except for mating or, if females, having cubs of their own.

A thick layer of low-lying clouds shroud the northern foothills of the Alaska Range, seen here from the Polychrome Pass area.

Smaller in number than their prey and well camouflaged, Denali's wolves blend easily into the landscape; but since the 1990s, packs denning near the road have provided some excellent viewing opportunities, especially from the East Fork River to the Eielson area. For many years members of the East Fork pack were the most frequently seen of Denali's wolves, but beginning in the early 2000s, the Grant Creek wolves have also spent much of their summers in the park road corridor, thrilling visitors as they chase prey, play among themselves, and take care of their young.

Polychrome Pass: East Fork River to Toklat River (Mile 43.5 to Mile 53)

After crossing the East Fork—another of Denali's large braided rivers—the road becomes a narrow, curving track that rises from 3200 to 3600 feet (980 to 1100 meters). As it ascends to Polychrome Pass, the road cuts into the southeastern flanks of Polychrome Mountain and runs along the edge of precipitous cliffs that plunge hundreds of feet to the East Fork valley below. Beyond Polychrome Pass, the road gradually drops to the braided Toklat River (elevation 3100 feet). Golden eagles build nests on Polychrome's cliff faces and feed on marmots that den among the boulders and in rock slides. Wolves, caribou, and grizzlies cross both the East Fork and Toklat valleys on their seasonal passages.

Polychrome Mountain, as the name suggests, presents a multicolored landscape. Here, as at Cathedral Mountain, volcanic eruptions 60 to 70 million years ago formed an array of rocks known to geologists as basalts, andesites, and rhyolites. Though they've been warped, tilted, and uplifted by tectonic forces, these Outer Range rocks remain interlayered in brilliant bands of yellow, orange, black, brown, white, and even purple or lavender. Many are brilliantly exposed in road cuts.

On their ascent to Polychrome Pass, bus passengers are presented one of Denali's most spectacular vistas. Upon reaching a designated overlook site, they're allowed to briefly exit the bus and breathe in the sweeping panorama, take photographs, and/or explore a small trail, uphill of the road, that loops among tundra wildflowers and presents additional views of more distant Outer Range mountains. Far below the road, and to the south, broad lowlands once covered by glaciers and now dissected by stream channels flow from the Alaska Range foothills toward Polychrome Mountain. Six branches of the East Fork River flow across these alluvial plains, which range up to 5 miles wide.

Huge boulders—some of them larger than a house—are scattered across the plains. Dropped by retreating glaciers about 10,000 years ago, they are fittingly called "erratics." Geologists can match these boulders with their "parent rocks" in the Alaska Range, making it possible to trace the glaciers' paths. Sometimes the shrinking glaciers also left large blocks of ice behind; as the ice melted, it formed depressions in the ground, and these pockets eventually filled to form the kettle ponds that speckle the lowlands below Polychrome Pass. Unnamed remnants of the glaciers that once flowed across the valley bottom appear in the distant foothills as pale blue fingers or banded black-and-white tongues dirtied by rock debris.

Don't Miss the Golden Eagles

Golden eagles build tall stick nests on the faces of cliffs and soar on hot-air updrafts, known as thermals, that lift off Polychrome Mountain. Dark brown in color except for golden plumage on the backs of their necks, adult golden eagles have wingspans of up to 7.5 feet. Ground squirrels, snowshoe hares, and ptarmigan are their most common prey, but golden eagles will also sometimes dive-bomb Polychrome's plump, grizzled marmots.

Seen from the park road near the Eielson Visitor Center, massive Denali rises above the McKinley River and foothills newly dusted by a September snowfall.

Early morning sunlight illuminates the autumn. The fall color change may begin in early August and usually peaks in early September.

Backcountry skiers roped together cross the Alaska Range's Ruth Glacier while exploring the Don Sheldon Amphitheater, a huge glacial bowl surrounded by soaring granitic spires, towers, and massive rock faces.

As they prepare for winter's hibernation, Denali National Park's grizzly bears may consume hundreds of thousands of berries in a day.

Found along the shores of Denali State Park's Byers Lake, this pile of scat is rich in blueberries and high-bush cranberries.

Lichens brighten a boulder on Denali National Park's tundra.

The author looks north toward Denali from the Peters Hills, Denali State Park.

This view looking west from Denali State Park's Kesugi Ridge shows Byers Lake surrounded by forested lowlands; in the distance are the Chulitna River and foothills of the Alaska Range.

A willow ptarmigan sits on a willow branch along Denali Park Road. Alaska's state bird gets its name from its close association with willow thickets.

Left: A bull moose and two cows keep company in a grassy meadow below the northern foothills of the Alaska Range during the annual fall rut.

Following several days of downpours, sunlight breaks through thick clouds and a rainbow arcs across an alpine basin in the Alaska Range's northern foothills.

Top: Seen from Polychrome Pass, a September storm drops snow on Alaska Range foothills, heralding winter's approach.

Right: A September snowfall drapes foothills of the Alaska Range, along Denali Park Road. Snow may fall even in summer, particularly at higher elevations.

Climbers follow the West Buttress on their way to high camp, located at 17,200 feet along the most popular route to the summit of North America's highest peak.

Dall sheep rams stand atop outcrops of rock in Denali National Park's Outer Range. The wild white sheep may be seen in the foothills along the park road.

A signpost, rock cairn, and backpacker register mark Tarn Point, along Denali State Park's Kesugi Ridge Trail.

A backpacker carrying a heavy load travels across tundra in early summer, while exploring Denali National Park's Outer Range.

A hiker stands atop Sable Mountain in Denali National Park's Outer Range, with the East Fork of the Toklat River and Alaska Range foothills in the background.

The hoary marmot is sometimes known as "the whistler," because of its characteristic high-pitched alarm call.

Despite their delicate beauty, alpine wildflowers must be hardy to survive in high mountain meadows.

Top: A nearly full moon hangs over Divide Mountain. Located near mile 52 of the park road, Divide Mountain separates branches of the Toklat River.

Left: Rising from the forest floor near Troublesome Creek in Denali State Park, these ferns are gradually unfurling, fed by increased hours of daylight.

Denali is partially hidden by clouds in this evening view from Reflection Pond, near Wonder Lake.

A monkshood blooms in an alpine meadow. Found in both moist woods and meadows, monkshood flowers from late June into August.

As the bus descends from Polychrome Pass to the Toklat River, it passes the "Porcupine Forest" at mile 51.8. During an especially severe winter in the 1950s, a large number of porcupines became trapped in this small forested area. To survive, they ate tree bark—and consumed so much that most of the spruce trees here eventually died. Now only their gray skeletons remain.

Down in the flats, the road parallels one of the Toklat River's braided channels, filled with fast-moving, sediment-rich waters. The Toklat drainage is a major animal highway used by grizzlies, caribou, wolves, and smaller mammals. Gravel bars along the road attract grizzlies in late summer because they have an abundance of soapberries; bitter to humans, these oval red berries are a favorite grizzly food. Earlier in the summer bears are more likely to be in the nearby tundra, digging for roots or ground squirrels.

Across the Toklat River bridge is the Toklat rest area. This is the usual turnaround point for Tundra Wilderness Tour passengers (the tour continues on to Stony Hill when The Mountain is visible) and also a stop for shuttle buses, with toilets, interpretive displays, and a large wall tent with books and other Denali-related items for purchase. Downstream and out of view is the site of a cabin (now crumbled and decaying) built in 1907 by the "father" of Denali National Park, hunter-naturalist-conservationist Charles Sheldon. The buildings barely visible in the trees on the west side of the Toklat are housing for National Park Service employees who work at the west end of the park road.

Highway Pass and Stony Hill: Toklat River to Eielson Visitor Center (Mile 53 to Mile 66)

From the Toklat River, the park road ascends to Highway Pass (mile 58.3), at 3980 feet (1210 meters) the highest point along the road. This is wonderfully open country, where grizzlies and caribou graze on tundra-covered slopes and wolves roam the hills. Beyond Highway Pass is 3900-foot (1190-meter) Stony Hill Overlook; 62 miles into the park, it's a superb place to gaze upon The Mountain. To go farther, visitors must take a shuttle bus, the Kantishna Experience Tour, or make travel arrangements with one of Kantishna's backcountry lodges. From Stony Hill, the road crosses 3950-foot Thorofare Pass (mile 64.5) and then drops slightly on the final approach to the Eielson Visitor Center, elevation 3733 feet (1140 meters). When skies are clear, Denali is a massive, overpowering presence throughout this four-mile stretch of road.

Only 37 miles southwest of Stony Hill Overlook, Denali rises bright and gleaming above the tundra and Alaska Range foothills that front it. In afternoon light, the mountain shines with a pearly luminescence that gives it an ethereal quality and increases its contrast with the surrounding landscape and azure sky. It's easy to understand why early pioneers called Denali the "great ice mountain." In late evening or early morning, Denali glows rather than shimmers, in

A gray and roiling branch of the braided Toklat River carries huge amounts of glacier silt from the Alaska Range's northern foothills.

colors that shift between gold, rose, and purple.

From Stony Hill, the park road can be traced as a thin brown line that skirts the southern flanks of 5629-foot (1720-meter) Thorofare Mountain as it crosses broad, tundra-covered Thorofare Pass on its way to the Eielson Visitor Center. Caribou gather near the pass to graze on grasses, sedges, and willow leaves. In July the area draws post-calving groups of cows, adolescents, and reddish-brown calves, born in early to mid-May. Post-calving groups usually number a few dozen caribou or less but occasionally exceed 100 animals.

Shuttle buses reach Eielson Visitor Center after 4 hours of travel. Many turn around here; others, after a 30-minute stopover, continue to Wonder Lake, 19 miles and 60 minutes away. Passengers ticketed for Wonder Lake who don't want to finish the trip can seek a seat on another return shuttle here.

Eielson sits on a knoll that overlooks the Thorofare and McKinley river valleys, whose glacial streams flow west from the darkened foothills of the Alaska Range. The view includes several high, snow-capped mountains—Wedge Peak (10,240 feet), Mount Brooks (11,940 feet), and Mount Silverthrone (13,220 feet)—and the Denali massif itself, only 33 miles distant. From here a vertical rise of nearly 18,000 feet is exposed, from the 2500-foot bottom of the braided McKinley River to the 20,320-foot top of the continent.

Named in honor of pioneer bush pilot Carl Ben Eielson, the center is the only visitor facility, besides campgrounds and rest areas, between park headquarters and Kantishna at the end of the park road. The site was initially occupied by a tent camp, which operated from 1934 to 1948. Ten years later, work began on the visitor center, which opened to the public in 1960. The original center was demolished in 2005 and a modern building with a smaller imprint was completed in 2008. Though nearly twice the size of the former building in square footage, the new visitor center is built into the hillside so that it blends into the landscape, while providing unobstructed views of the tundra and surrounding mountains. The ground surrounding the center acts as a blanket, reducing the building's heating and cooling needs. Other energy-saving/sustainable features include renewable or recycled materials; rooftop photovoltaic solar panels; large south-facing windows that capture the sun's heat and provide "passive" solar heating; and a system that emphasizes renewable energy and water conservation.

As before, Eielson's primary role is as an interpretive center: a place where visitors can gain new perspectives or see up-close what they have watched out the bus window. The facility includes several natural and cultural history exhibits, including a 12-foot-diameter interactive model of "The High One." Other features include an art exhibit, dining area, seating for interpretive programs, plus two nearby trails; one is an easy half-mile loop, the other climbs a thousand feet up Thorofare Ridge (see "Park Road Area Hiking Trails" earlier in this chapter).

Park rangers answer questions, give mini-talks, lead daily tundra walks, and keep an eye on visitor–wildlife interactions. Eielson's concentration of people can have unexpected repercussions on the local ecosystem. Ground squirrels fatten on the leftovers of human picnics and in turn lure in predators like foxes, which lose their normal shyness of people. Even worse, bears sometimes come to Eielson seeking people-fed ground squirrels, posing a danger both to people and, ultimately, to the bears themselves. Visitors are therefore urged to be very careful and not leave any food where animals can get to it.

Muldrow Glacier: Eielson Visitor Center to Wonder Lake (Mile 66 to Mile 85)

West of Eielson Visitor Center the park road becomes a narrower and bumpier route with several sharp curves. It parallels the braided McKinley River while gradually dropping toward Wonder Lake (elevation 1985 feet) and Wonder Lake Campground (mile 85, elevation 2090 feet). As it descends, the road passes from alpine tundra into boggy lowland tundra and the transitional ecotone of willow-alder thickets and open forest. Beavers dam streams, migratory waterfowl nest and breed in tundra ponds, and moose feed on pond plants and willow leaves. Visible to the south along this entire stretch of road are Denali's North Peak and 14,000-foot-high (4270-meter) Wickersham Wall, one of the world's largest rock faces. Flowing off Denali's northeastern flanks is the Muldrow Glacier, ascended by the first mountaineers to reach the mountain's summit.

A view from Denali Park Road in early autumn, looking east up the Thorofare River Valley, toward the foothills and snowcapped mountains of the Alaska Range.

Don't Miss the Beavers

Some ponds are the work of beavers, whose dams and lodges are common along this stretch of the road. Slow and clumsy on land, beavers are excellent swimmers who can remain underwater for up to 15 minutes at a time—long enough to swim a half mile or more. The ponds created by their dam-building efforts provide refuge from a spectrum of predators: wolves, wolverines, lynx, and bears. From late summer into fall the beavers busily gnaw down willows, cottonwoods, and other woody plants and transfer their cuttings to food caches for the long winter ahead. When ponds freeze over, the beavers remain comfortable in their lodges, whose thick walls combine branches with mud and rocks.

Beavers often share their tundra ponds with another skilled mammalian swimmer: muskrats build burrows along the shore and sometimes move, uninvited, into beaver lodges. Moose wade knee-deep or even belly-deep into beaver ponds and dunk their heads to feed on aquatic plants, while several varieties of ducks build nests and rear their young along the water's edge. Hiding in the grassy fringes of many ponds are wood frogs, the only amphibians to inhabit Alaska's Interior.

The largest glacier on the Alaska Range's north side, the Muldrow begins as a bluish-white field of ice high on Denali's northeastern flank and ends as a dark jumbled mass 32 miles later on the tundra plain, less than a mile from the road. The glacier's upper reaches can't be seen from the road, and its lower portions are not easily distinguished from surrounding tundra. The glacier's hummocky lower section is heavily covered with morainal debris it has carried out of the mountains. And much of that rock and dirt is now covered with alder, willow, soapberry, and other tundra plants.

Twice during the 1900s, and most recently in 1956–57, the Muldrow surged forward at tremendous speeds—at least by glacial standards. Scientists measured movements of up to 1100 feet per day as middle sections of the glacier dropped 180 feet and then flowed over lower, more stagnant sections. In all, the Muldrow advanced 5 miles before resettling into a more quiescent state.

As it continues west of the Muldrow's snout, the park road enters flatter country. Foothills of the Outer and Alaska ranges recede, giving way to rolling tundra and forested lowlands dotted with lakes and ponds, many of the kettle variety seen near Polychrome Pass.

Wonder Lake comes into view at mile 83.6. A huge kettle pond, it nestles, dark and narrow, among low rolling hills. During the Pleistocene Ice Age, glaciers extended far beyond the present terminus of the Muldrow Glacier into the Kantishna Hills. The advancing ice flowed over a resistant ridge of rock at the southern end of what is now Wonder Lake, then gouged the weaker rock beyond it. When the climate warmed and the glacier retreated, a massive chunk of ice got left behind. As the ice melted, the hollow it left filled with water to produce Wonder Lake.

Lake trout, burbot, and freshwater sculpin inhabit Wonder Lake's waters year-round, while diving birds like loons, grebes, and mergansers feed on the fish and other aquatic creatures when they arrive in summer to nest and breed. Beavers build lodges, moose feed on aquatic plants, caribou graze on the surrounding tundra, and songbirds feast on the area's abundant insect life.

Because the terrain is low and wet, Wonder Lake's environs are ideally suited to mosquitoes; campers need a lot of insect repellent, head nets, and bug jackets, especially during the June–July mosquito peak. By late August most mosquitoes have died, though warm afternoons may produce swarms of biting flies.

Those who camp at Wonder Lake or who want to explore this area by foot can take the 2.5-mile McKinley Bar Trail, which begins about 0.25 mile from the campground and leads to the McKinley River (see "Park Road Area Hiking Trails" earlier in this chapter).

For most visitors who've ventured this deep into Denali's wilderness, the drive ends near Wonder Lake Campground, the last of Denali's roadside

Two big-antlered bull caribou feed side by side on tundra plants in early fall, not far from Wonder Lake near the end of the Denali Park Road.

campgrounds. However, some shuttle buses and also the Kantishna Experience Tour buses do follow the park road to Kantishna.

Mining Ruins and Wilderness Lodges: Wonder Lake to Kantishna (Mile 85 to Mile 92)

From the Wonder Lake turnaround, the park road winds several more miles past a ranger station and Wonder Lake's outlet—another excellent place to spot water birds, moose, and aquatic mammals—to the former gold-boom town of Kantishna.

Now surrounded by parkland, this early 1900s mining district is the site of another sort of boom: ecotourism. A handful of wilderness lodges operate on private inholdings in or near Kantishna; there are no public facilities besides an airstrip. Those who travel this far will get the chance to visit the restored house that Fannie and Joe Quigley occupied during Kantishna's gold-boom days.

After a 30-minute rest stop, visitors begin the long drive back to Denali's entrance (5 hours from Wonder Lake, 6–6.5 from Kantishna). Now headed west–east, the return trip presents new perspectives on the landscape, new opportunities to observe the park's wildlife as they go about their lives in a still-pristine wilderness of tundra, forests, river valleys, glaciers, and ice-capped mountains. The possibilities for discovery are endless, no matter the season, weather, time of day, or place along the road.

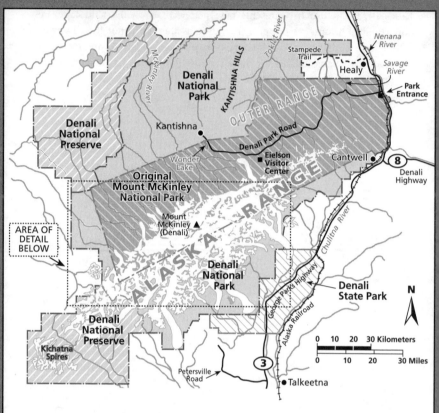

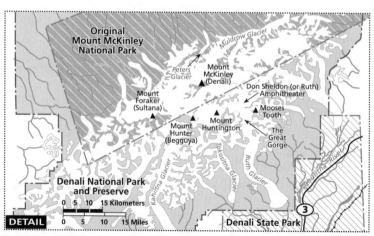

Chapter 6

HIKING THE BACKCOUNTRY

A river rushes out of the mountains in braided channels that meander across a mile-wide valley. Upriver a few miles is the pale blue remnant of glacial ice that feeds the murky stream. Silver strands of waterfalls drop from dark, jagged hills that enclose the basin, rising several thousand feet above the valley bottom. Lifted by warm currents of summer air, a golden eagle spirals overhead, searching the landscape below for prey. Breezes swirl along the hilltops, where natural gardens of blue, yellow, and purple wildflowers form bright patches on mostly bare rocks.

Dall sheep rams with massive, curling horns graze in verdant alpine meadows. Far below the sheep, a blond grizzly nonchalantly digs roots from lowland tundra as nearby ground squirrels stand erect, communicating in alarmed voices. There are no sounds here except the rush of water and wind, the chatter of squirrels, the chirps of songbirds. And there is no evidence of human presence: no signs, buildings, trails, or—for most visitors to Denali's backcountry—other people. Hikers who venture only a mile from the park road can quickly find themselves immersed in wild solitude.

Hiking in the backcountry of Denali National Park and Preserve is very different from hiking in most of the United States. Most of the park's easily accessible wildlands are within a legally designated wilderness area, where human disturbance is intended to be very limited. At Denali, this legislative mandate is taken seriously, even to the point that the National Park Service has generally chosen not to build or maintain trails in the wilderness. That means cross-country travel is required for backcountry adventures. Added to the usual Alaska challenges of avoiding encounters with bears, climbing steep slopes, and surviving inclement weather are the challenges of route-finding without guidance from trail markers; fording rivers; and finding secure footing on a variety of ground cover, from gravel bars to tussocks to alpine tundra.

Hiking cross-country provides a true challenge of wilderness exploration—and great solitude since there are no trails to concentrate travelers.

Most hikes in Denali National Park begin from the park road, although innovative hikers can find other points to enter the park. Hiking from the park road has the distinct advantage of using the shuttle bus system for transport. Because the buses drop off and pick up anywhere along the road, hikers do not have to worry about vehicle shuttles, planning circular routes, or retracing steps—a unique and positive feature of hiking in Denali!

BACKCOUNTRY RESOURCES AND INFORMATION

Before visiting Denali, backpackers may wish to research the wide range of backcountry possibilities; information is available at the park's online "Backcountry Camping and Hiking Guide" (www.nps.gov/planyourvisit/map.htm). The guide shows a map of Denali's backcountry units and provides a unit-by-unit description, with information on backpacker quota (if relevant), appropriate topographic maps, tips and special features, access, and routes/hiking corridors for each unit. Because popular areas may be filled when they reach the park, backpackers should give themselves several destination options.

Permits

To obtain a backcountry permit at the Backcountry Information Center (BIC):

- **Check the quota board to determine which units have openings.** Denali's backcountry is divided into eighty-seven units; in forty-one of those, only a limited number of backpackers are allowed each night. During peak season, many units may be full for several days, and others may be closed because of wildlife activity. Large hiking groups must be prepared to split up.

- **Read the backcountry description guides** for help in choosing a unit and consult a topographic map while planning your route. Keep in mind the lack of developed trails in this immense country, where even a 5-mile hike can mean an exhausting day. Map-reading skills are invaluable.

- **Consult with a ranger**, but staff will provide only general advice; in the end, the choice of a destination and the success of your trip rests with you.

- **Watch the park's 30-minute backcountry safety video,** which also discusses such topics as camp selection, proper behavior in bear country, minimum-impact camping, river-crossing techniques, and wildlife ethics.

- **Attend a safety talk,** given by a backcountry ranger. All members of a party must both watch the safety video and attend the safety talk. Only then will they receive their free backcountry permit and bear-resistant food container (BRFC). Made of hard, durable plastic, these black cylindrical canisters are designed to keep Denali's grizzlies from getting

A backcountry explorer peers through binoculars while scanning Denali's land-scape. Hikers should be prepared for cold, wet weather even in summer.

into campers' food and garbage. Containers should be returned promptly at the end of a trip.

Once a unit has been chosen and approved, backpackers are advised to purchase the appropriate 15-minute USGS **topographic maps** (at 1:62,500 scale, 1 inch = 1 mile) and mark unit boundaries and any relevant wildlife closures on their maps. Such maps can be purchased at either the BIC or the Alaska Geographic store (though topos can also be ordered online at http://store.usgs.gov, Denali explorers won't know which quads to obtain until they've chosen a backcountry unit at the park).

The final step is to **purchase a camper bus ticket** at the Wilderness Access Center adjacent to the BIC. Camper buses transport campers and their gear into the park and will drop backpackers at their chosen starting points. Reboarding is on a space-available basis on any shuttle bus; backpackers should be prepared to wait up to an hour and sometimes more.

NOTE: Camper buses are likely to be phased out as part of Denali National Park's new Vehicle Management Plan, which is scheduled to go fully into effect in 2015. If and when the park no longer employs camper buses, backpackers and campers will likely be directed to use Denali's shuttle buses.

Backpacking Gear Essentials

For overnight trips into Denali's wilderness, the following items should be carried in addition to the day-hiking essentials. See "Visiting Denali" in the Introduction for a full list of the ten essentials.

- **Bear-resistant food container.** This is provided with backpacking permits.
- **Food.** Large daily portions plus several days of extra emergency rations are recommended. Double layers of plastic bags reduce food and garbage odors that attract bears. Avoid scented, spiced, or smoked foods, such as bacon or fish.
- **Stove, fuel, cooking gear.** Campfires are not permitted in the Denali wilderness, and all cooking must be done on stoves. White gas is available at the Riley Creek Mercantile, near the park entrance.
- **Water filtration system.** Pack either a filtration system, SteriPen, or iodine tablets.
- **Footwear.** Take extra socks. Other extras include neoprene socks and gaiters to keep feet dry and a pair of comfortable soft-soled shoes to minimize impact at campsites.
- **Sleeping bag and pad.** For any overnight summer trip, a bag rated to 20°F (–7°C) is suggested.
- **Tent.** Your shelter should have a waterproof floor, rain fly, and protection from biting insects.
- **Other items.** Sunglasses, water bottle, flashlight, drinking cup, litter bag, windbreaker, groundcloth, cooking pot, pot gripper, eating utensils, personal toilet items, rain cover for pack, hiking shorts, trekking pole(s), watch, towel, binoculars, camera with extra memory cards and batteries, notebook and pencil.
- **Plastic bags.** Pack clothes, sleeping bag, and emergency gear in plastic bags to protect them during rainstorms and river crossings.

Some backcountry travelers also prefer to bring GPS (global positioning system) units to help track their location and/or satellite phones for emergencies. Cell phones generally won't work in Denali's wilderness.

In Case of an Emergency

The degree of self-reliance of backcountry travelers largely determines whether their trips will be a dream or nightmare. Through careful pre-trip planning and safety-conscious decisions in the field, backpackers and hikers can minimize unexpected crises. When the unexpected does happen, a person or group's backcountry savvy and resourcefulness—what Alaskans call "skookum"—will determine the outcome. If hikers or backpackers fail to check in from a backcountry trip, rangers will NOT initiate a search until a specific request is made; those who've brought a satellite phone into the backcountry should only call for help when they can't resolve an emergency or other problem on their own. In case of emergency, or while waiting for help, visitors can:

- Provide first aid.
- Conserve energy and body heat.
- Stay near a water supply.
- Signal or mark location.
- Use bright clothing, a tent fly, or a smudge fire for smoke to get rescuers' attention.
- Make the location visible.
- Send or go for help.
- Remain calm. Think, plan, and organize.

Suggestions in this guide assume backpacking visitors to Denali's backcountry are capable and experienced. A good pocket reference for wilderness users is Adventure Medical Kits' *Wilderness & Travel Medicine: A Comprehensive Guide*, Fourth Edition, by Eric A. Weiss, MD.

EXPLORING THE BACKCOUNTRY

This chapter provides guidance for those who intend to explore Denali National Park by foot and off trail, whether on a day hike, guided hike, or overnight backpack (see also the "Hiking Basics" section in the Introduction). The guidance may be less than expected since it consists primarily of general geographic descriptions, advice on cross-country travel, and safety and minimum-impact information. Unlike most hiking guides, there are no specific routes or destinations given here, but that is for the best.

In Denali, letting someone else make your travel plan when exploring off trail and beyond the road corridor would compromise your experience. Much of the Denali backcountry is scenically spectacular, and many areas present opportunities to climb hills or mountain peaks, traipse up river valleys, and encounter wildlife. What the Denali backcountry offers visitors is the opportunity to truly explore, instead of simply following a path, trail, or route that thousands of other people have traveled before. You don't have to spend a lot of time trying to figure out the "perfect" destination in Denali's backcountry. Once you've stepped off the edge of the road, you have likely already found it (though it is certainly true that some of the park's areas present easier hiking and backpacking than others).

Visitors can face the challenges and reap the rewards of backcountry travel whether they walk 1 mile or 100 miles into Denali's wilderness. Those who have little backcountry experience, or wish to learn more about this wild northern ecosystem, can join ranger-guided Discovery Hikes. Others will choose to independently explore the backcountry, from day hikes that may last a few hours to weeks-long backpacking expeditions.

Day Hiking

Even a mile (or less) from the park road, hikers can find places free of human traffic and noise, places of solitude and pristine landscapes. It may be a quiet tundra meadow, a rocky creek bottom, or a narrow alpine ridge with views of glacial valleys and distant snowcapped mountains. Within an hour's walk from the road, hikers are more likely to share the landscape with wild animals than with other people. A selection of park road–accessible trails is offered in Chapter 5. Hiking off-trail, the possibilities are infinite: follow moose, grizzly, or wolf tracks along sandy stream bottoms (and sometimes see the animals themselves!), climb high above tree line, nap among delicate mats of wildflowers, walk ridgelines that go for miles and miles, or study the bleached antlers of a caribou.

Day hikers do not need backcountry permits and are not constrained by the unit system described for backpackers below. They simply obtain a shuttle bus ticket in advance and ask the driver to drop them off at their place of choice (although they must stay out of designated wildlife closures). Hikers then can choose their own routes and length of journey, and return to the road for pickup. (See "Choosing a Backcountry Destination" later in this chapter to learn more about the possible areas to explore.)

NOTE: Even on the shortest of day hikes, visitors must remember that Denali's weather can change rapidly—and dramatically—from bright, warming sunshine to chilling downpours or even snowfall.

Discovery Hikes

Even day hikers must be prepared to deal with untrailed backcountry, stream crossings, grizzlies, and sudden mountain storms. While contributing to Denali's appeal, such challenges may present an intimidating obstacle to visitors who lack the expertise or confidence to step beyond the park road on their own.

There is an alternative for inexperienced backcountry travelers and others who would like to learn more about the park's natural history while exploring its wilderness in the company of a knowledgeable guide: Discovery Hikes. Limited to a maximum of eleven people (to minimize impacts on the wild but often fragile landscape), these ranger-led hikes take park visitors into the unknown and help them learn the nature of Denali's animals, plants, and geology. At the same time, rangers teach the basics of safe backcountry travel.

From 3 to 5 hours long, Discovery Hikes cover a variety of terrain. Strenuous hikes might ascend an Outer Range peak or follow glacial streams far into the Alaska Range, while moderate hikes often meander across river bars or lowland tundra meadows. The hiking ratings should be taken seriously: even experienced, fit hikers may struggle to keep the pace while traveling off-trail on a "very strenuous" hike, while those rated moderate tend to be more leisurely.

Participants in a Discovery Hike cross the tundra near the Toklat River. Ranger-guided hikes help visitors learn more about Denali's history.

Besides teaching visitors to hike without a trail in this unfamiliar land, rangers open eyes, ears, and nose to mysteries of the landscape that might otherwise escape notice. Freshly turned tundra becomes the scene of a confrontation between grizzly and ground squirrel; a light whistle barely heard in the wind is the shriek of a marmot; translucent red berries on a woody bush are soapberries with a taste to match their name; a dangling purple flower called frigid shooting star smells like grape Kool-Aid—if you know to take a whiff. By hike's end, the unknown or imagined wilderness has become more real. Having been guided into the wilderness, some hikers are inevitably inspired to travel deeper into the backcountry on their own.

Backpacking

Total wilderness immersion is the chief advantage of overnight trips into Denali's backcountry wilderness. Spending days, not hours, in wild surroundings, backpackers are likely to encounter a greater variety of wildlife and every imaginable sort of weather. They also have increased opportunities to explore valleys and hills that no person has visited for weeks or perhaps years, if ever. Backpackers gain an intimate relationship with the landscape and a resounding sense of its scale, difficulties, and delights. There is no greater joy than to be camped in some distant, unnamed, hidden valley carved by ice, sprinkled with the rainbow colors of wildflowers, and inhabited by Denali's wild animals.

Unlike day hikers, backpackers cannot go anywhere they please. To ensure the solitude expected of a wilderness experience and to prevent the wear and tear that inevitably results from overcrowding, visitor use is dispersed throughout eighty-seven backcountry units; nearly half of those inside Denali's designated wilderness have limits on the total number of campers allowed each night. Before heading into the backcountry on overnight trips, backpackers must stop at the entrance area's Backcountry Information Center (BIC, adjacent to the Wilderness Access Center at mile 0.75) and obtain a permit for each night of their trip. Campers are limited to seven consecutive nights in a single unit and thirty nights total in the backcountry (the latter number applies from April 15 through September 30). Camper buses (otherwise regular shuttles, if camper buses are phased out in 2015) will drop backpackers at their chosen starting point. From there, they must determine their own routes and length of journey, returning to the road at trip's end for transportation back to the entrance area.

PREPARING FOR BACKCOUNTRY CHALLENGES

The Denali region's backcountry presents unique challenges for hikers who haven't previously explored subarctic landscapes or traveled deep into wilderness that has no maintained trails, no bridges over rivers, no boardwalks across bogs, no switchbacks up steep mountainsides, no signposts or campgrounds.

Hikers soon learn they can't travel nearly as far in a day off-trail trekking as when following a maintained path. Even experienced hikers may travel only a mile, or less, in an hour's time. Alder and willow branches reach out to grab legs and packs, and spongy tundra saps energy and demands more stamina than hard-packed surfaces. It's difficult, if not impossible, to keep feet dry when navigating wet lowland tundra, where tramping through swampy ground is almost inevitable. Stream crossings require careful scouting to find a safe route across icy glacial waters. And because this is grizzly country, backcountry travelers must always consider the presence of bears when choosing routes, making camp, and cooking and storing food.

While hiking the backcountry can be an intense exercise, both physically and mentally, the rewards are many: a sense of discovery, wilderness solitude, personal revelations, wildlife encounters, and a deepened appreciation of Denali's wild ecosystem.

Route Finding

The only paths beyond Denali National Park's entrance area, the Eielson Visitor Center, and the Wonder Lake area are those made by wildlife. Even where present, game trails are sporadic: well-defined in places, they fade out elsewhere.

Without developed and maintained human trails, visitors must find their own way across a landscape that may have patches of thick, waist- to head-high brush; long stretches of soggy, spongy tundra; and narrow, deeply incised tributary creeks. To complicate matters, distances in the open tundra can be deceiving: a hill that appears to be a mile away may in fact be several miles distant. And to the uninitiated, hills and valleys may have a confusing sameness that is disorienting.

Whether they're going on an hours-long day hike or week-long expedition, backcountry explorers should learn basic navigation skills before entering Denali's wilds and know how to read a topographic map, use a compass, and make route-finding decisions. This knowledge, in combination with research done at the park's BIC, allows hikers and backpackers to pick the most appropriate route for their group's abilities.

The best routes across Denali's subarctic wilderness are often river bottoms. Sand and gravel bars make for easy walking when compared to wet tundra, thick brush, or forest. For this reason, river valleys are also well traveled by wildlife. However, the valleys allow hikers to see longer distances, which diminishes the chances of surprise encounters.

Brushy areas should be avoided whenever possible, partly because visibility is limited, but also because bushwhacking is difficult, draining, and sometimes demoralizing work. Tundra travel, too, can prove disheartening. Wet tundra especially is difficult to cross, with its maze of sedge tussocks: mushroom-shaped grassy mounds. Narrow at the base and wide on top, tussocks are unstable to walk on; any step slightly off center makes them lean this way or that. High alpine tundra is easier to traverse, but mountain ridges often don't lead toward intended destinations. Traveling high, hikers may also face a steady diet of ups and downs as they meet one side creek after another. Those who cross hillsides must be careful of scree slopes, whose loose, rubbly rock may be unstable. Extra caution is necessary when traversing slopes above fast-moving glacial streams. Steep banks cut into a hillside may present an inviting shortcut, especially if they eliminate the need to cross a glacial stream, but a spill could prove disastrous.

Hikers or backpackers should regularly check their position, keep track of notable landmarks and distance traveled, and, if necessary, reassess their choice of route. Those who lose their way can use the region's major landscape features to reorient themselves. Most large rivers on the Alaska Range's northern side flow roughly from south to north—the McKinley and Thorofare rivers are notable exceptions—while the Alaska and Outer ranges and the park road run roughly east–west. Because most lands north of the range are tundra covered, hikers can usually climb a hill and, assisted by map and compass, get their bearings—unless low clouds reduce visibility.

A hiker replaces his socks after fording a swollen creek in Denali's backcountry.
Visitors are advised to use great caution while crossing streams.

NOTE: Several of Denali's broad northern valleys lead upstream to glaciers in the Alaska Range foothills. Hikers may be tempted to cross the ice, but such passages should be avoided by those without glacier-travel experience and specialized gear (such as crampons, ice axes, and climbing rope). Glacial surfaces can be extremely slick, and many of Denali's glaciers are crisscrossed with deep crevasses.

River Crossings

No bridges span the streams in Denali's backcountry. So while valley bottoms promise comparatively easy cross-country travel, they may also present great challenges if a chosen route requires a river crossing. This is especially true of the large glacial rivers that flow out of the Alaska Range. Fed by glacial meltwater, these streams can increase dramatically in volume on hot, sunny days as well as on rainy ones. It is therefore best to cross them in morning, before the day warms. If a destination can be reached by another, safer route, it is best not to attempt a crossing at all.

Besides being incredibly cold, Denali's glacial rivers are murky. Hikers and backpackers can't see where they're stepping, which means they're more likely to lose their balance and fall. Even if they make it to shore safely after plunging into a glacially fed river, hikers face the danger of hypothermia (see below). Before crossing a stream, make sure that extra clothes, stoves, and other gear are packed away in plastic bags or watertight stuff sacks so they are still usable if a fall does occur. Backpackers are also advised to unbuckle their packs, so they can be more easily removed if a fall occurs when crossing. Linking arms or using hiking poles can increase stability in fast-moving currents. And never should a stream be crossed in bare feet, despite the temptation to keep boots dry.

If a stream crossing is necessary, hikers must carefully choose their path. Along some stretches, the flow of braided rivers is captured in a single channel that may be chest-high or even deeper; elsewhere streams unravel into several loosely intertwined threads of water only inches deep. Hikers should look for places where the river has split into many branches. If uncertain about a river's depth, throw a large rock into the stream: a hollow ka-thump means deep water, while the clink of rock striking rock often indicates a shallow spot. (Hiking poles can also help to gauge a stream's depth.) Whatever route is finally chosen, hikers should always have a line of retreat in mind.

As evidence of the dangers that rivers pose, consider this: stream crossings, not grizzly bears, are the number one killer of Denali hikers and backpackers. At least four people have died since 1950 while attempting to cross streams; only one person has been killed by a bear inside Denali throughout the park's history, as described below.

Wildlife Encounters

Because much of Denali is prime grizzly country, backcountry travelers must always be on the lookout for bears. Park regulations prohibit visitors from intentionally approaching within 300 yards (275 meters) of grizzlies and black bears. If necessary, hikers and backpackers should change their routes rather than come too close to bears. A backpacker killed in 2012 had ventured too close to an adult male grizzly, taking photographs from as near as 60 yards. Though the exact circumstances remain uncertain, the bear eventually attacked and killed the man, the only such death documented since the park was established in 1917.

While grizzlies present the most obvious danger, hikers should also be wary of moose, especially females with calves. They are highly protective of their young and will attack humans who approach too closely. If a moose is encountered at close range, immediately retreat. Unlike grizzly encounters, running away from moose is advised, in order to quickly leave the moose's "personal space."

Humans actually present a greater danger to most Denali wildlife than vice versa. Park regulations prohibit any intentional harassment or feeding of wildlife, and hikers and backpackers (and other visitors) should also take care not to leave food where animals can find it. Visitors are also cautioned not to pursue animals, try to intercept their path, or approach within 25 yards (23 meters) of moose, caribou, sheep, wolves or other animals. Nor may they approach within 25 yards of animal dens or nests.

As a general rule, any distance that alters the behavior of an animal is too close.

Health Hazards

Besides the physical challenges and dangers that the landscape and wildlife pose to backcountry travelers, hikers and backpackers need to consider a variety of other wilderness hazards that range from annoying to life threatening.

Hypothermia

Denali's cold, wet weather is a potential killer, even in midsummer. Hikers and backpackers should come prepared for winter-like weather during any time of year and understand that conditions can change drastically even within a few hours' time, from warm sunshine to rainstorms or even subfreezing temperatures and snow. Even during a dry-weather day, a glacial river crossing that goes awry may cause a person to become deeply chilled.

Anyone who enters the backcountry should know how to prevent, recognize, and treat hypothermia, a cooling of the body's core temperature that can be disabling and even lead to death. Hikers can prevent hypothermia by staying dry—in part this means using high-quality raingear and tents—packing gear in waterproof bags, eating high-calorie foods, drinking plenty of fluids, and pacing themselves to prevent exhaustion. It's also wise to use a layering system when dressing.

Early signs of hypothermia are shivering and slurred speech. If unrecognized or untreated, these symptoms may be followed by clumsiness, drowsiness, muddled thinking, exhaustion, and ultimately, death. A person showing any of these signs should be put into warm, dry clothing; fed warm, nonalcoholic drinks; and, if possible, placed inside a shelter. No one showing signs of hypothermia should ever be left alone. The key is to stabilize and then slowly raise the body temperature; this requires protection from wet, cooling conditions.

Mosquitoes and Other Insect Pests

Alaska's mosquitoes usually appear in April, right after the thaw, and remain active through September. In the Denali region, early June to mid-July is considered the peak mosquito period. Mosquitoes inhabit virtually all landscapes, but are especially thick in wet areas.

A number of weapons have been created to help humans ward off mosquito attacks. Number one is DEET, a chemical that confuses mosquitoes' sensory systems. In high-enough concentrations, it is capable of "melting" plastic, so be sure to keep DEET away from any gear that contains plastic. Because of its effectiveness, DEET is the active ingredient in nearly all commercial insect repellents.

Notable exceptions include Avon's perfumed bath oil, Skin-So-Soft. Natural repellents have been used for generations, including raw or cooked garlic and pennyroyal, citronella, and other herbs.

Other insect pests include biting flies and gnats. In Alaska, two in particular can be troubling. No-see-ums are tiny, gray, silver-winged gnats whose prick-like bites produce small red itchy spots. White sox are small black flies with white legs that will often take a small chunk of flesh when biting and

Mosquito netting is the best way to keep the insects away. Mosquito numbers normally peak from late June through mid- to late July.

leave a large, inflamed, and itchy swelling that may remain for several days. Both white sox and no-see-ums have a talent for finding their way under loose clothing or into hair and ears. They too react to repellents, but seem less deterred than mosquitoes.

Giardia

Transmitted through the feces of many mammals, the intestinal parasite *Giardia lamblia* occurs in waters throughout the Denali region and may result in nausea, diarrhea, and intense cramping if it enters the body. The best precaution is to boil all stream or lake water for at least 1 minute, use a filter specifically designed to remove such microorganisms, or add iodine tablets to the water. If using a filter, avoid glacial water whenever possible, because the fine sediments in the water may clog your filter.

CHOOSING A BACKCOUNTRY DESTINATION

The descriptions that follow look at four basic regions of the national park that are roughly distinguished by the dominant terrain in each. These overviews should assist you in picking a general area in which to hike; as a next step, study maps and consider taking a bus ride to scout ahead of time. Remember: A part of the experience is exploration. Choose a route that appears to be within your ability, develop alternate plans in case the chosen route is too difficult or too easy, carry the equipment needed to meet Denali's backcountry challenges, and let your imagination and curiosity guide you from there to the top of the next ridge or around the next bend in the river.

Alaska Range Foothills

Low rounded hills and higher jagged peaks rise above wide U-shaped valley bottoms in this glacially sculpted terrain, where in summer small nodes of pale blue remnant glaciers and dark bare rock contrast sharply with flowering alpine meadows and vibrantly green tundra. Braided streams of icewater flow through north–south basins that act as natural avenues into these foothills, and side creeks lead to remote hidden valleys only rarely visited by humans.

Fringing the perennially ice- and snow-covered high peaks of the Alaska Range, this band of foothills stretches northeast–southwest through the heart of Denali National Park. Foothills of this description are found on both the south and north sides of the Alaska Range, but most are reached from the Denali Park Road on the north; only the hills between Cantwell and Anderson Pass are easily accessible on the south.

The broad valley floors that stretch north from the Alaska Range to the park road are 3000 to 4000 feet (915 to 1220 meters) in elevation, while the hills rarely rise above 7000 feet (2135 meters) and most lose their snow cover by mid-July.

The remnant glaciers that occur here are (with the notable exception of the Muldrow) much smaller than those that flow off Denali and other high peaks. Few are more than 5 miles long or 1 mile across.

While they don't attain the same great heights as the Alaska Range's core peaks, many foothills are rugged in their own right, with jagged, ice-carved ridges and steep mountain walls that require mountaineering skills. On the other hand, the tundra-topped or bare-rock summits of many peaks can be reached, with some exertion, by hill scramblers owning no special climbing expertise or gear. Even on the smallest of hills, hikers should use special caution when ascending talus slopes; though largely stable, these piles of rock debris may contain precariously balanced boulders.

Hikers and backpackers can most easily reach the Alaska Range foothills by following the large braided-river valleys that stretch from the park road into the mountains. Some stretches of the road (as in the Highway Pass–Stony Hill area) skirt the bases of low rounded hills, making them ideal for day hikers seeking higher ground. Hikers can also ascend gentle tundra saddles between stream valleys or, if highly ambitious, take a full day to ascend ridges rarely climbed except by sheep. Backpackers, meanwhile, can combine long valley-bottom treks with hill ascents, ridgeline traverses, and forays into remote alpine basins that offer glimpses back to the landscape of the Ice Age.

These lowland basins and their enclosing hills are inhabited by diverse open-ground wildlife: migrating caribou, chattering ground squirrels, root-digging grizzly bears, tundra-grazing Dall sheep, clucking willow ptarmigan, bushy-tailed red foxes, soaring golden eagles, and wolves hunting food for their family of pups.

Besides easy walking, the glacial valleys provide good campsites, lessening the impact on more fragile tundra. They do have one shortcoming, however: because the valleys are so broad and open, hikers and backpackers can't always quickly escape signs of the park road and its traffic. An alternative is to cross rolling tundra into the foothills, though this may require passage through thick brush or wet tundra so saturated with water that boots, socks, and feet become hopelessly soaked.

Those who travel far into the foothills may approach a glacier's terminal snout. This is a raw, mostly black, white, and gray world of rock, ice, and water with little green, only a few scattered patches of tundra. Here silvery, stepped waterfalls cascade down dark, sheer mountainsides, and rivers carry heavy loads of dirt and rock. Even these smaller rivers of ice may contain deep crevasses, and their surfaces, except where covered with morainal debris, are slick. Glacier travel demands specialized safety equipment such as ice axes, ropes, and crampons, plus the knowledge of how to use such gear. Those without previous experience should stay off glaciers, just as inexperienced climbers should avoid the Alaska Range's high peaks, with their huge rock walls and ice-covered slopes.

The Outer Range

Untouched by Ice Age glaciers, the Outer Range is a chain of low rocky hills north of the Alaska Range and the park road. The lower slopes of these hills are characteristically covered by thick brush that gives way at higher altitudes to a mix of open tundra meadows and bare-rock ridges. Unlike the wide glacial valleys flowing from the Alaska Range foothills, the Outer Range is penetrated by narrow, stream-cut drainages (the braided Toklat is a notable exception). Most streams are small clearwater creeks, but a half-dozen large glacial rivers arising in the Alaska Range also cut through the Outer Range.

Stretching from Denali's entrance area to the Eielson Visitor Center, the Outer Range rises several hundred to 3000 feet (915 meters) above adjacent lowlands. Only a few of its mountains attain heights of 6000 feet (1830 meters). Yet the tops of the Outer Range's highest peaks present staggering 360-degree views of the region's immense lowlands and waves of ridgelines.

Much of the Outer Range is prime habitat for both grizzlies and Dall sheep. Hundreds of sheep stay here year-round while occupying high ridges and alpine meadows of grass, low-lying shrubs, and wildflowers that are small and fragile looking, yet hardy enough to survive in the rocky soil of exposed, wind-buffeted ridges.

The range is easily reached from the park road, which skirts its southern flanks. Some of the Outer Range's south-facing slopes meet the road near or above brush line, and hikers can easily ascend directly to tundra, rocky ridges, and hilltops. Elsewhere, considerable bushwhacking through dense willow and alder thickets may be necessary to get uphill. In such places, the easiest way to get above brush line and into open tundra is to follow one of the many small clearwater creek channels that flow from the range and intercept the road. Creek beds may be a few feet to more than 100 feet wide and filled with gravel- to boulder-sized rocks. The creeks themselves tend to be small and shallow, so stream crossings are not usually a problem (except during spring runoff or after major rainstorms). Even with their abundant boulders and occasional clumps of willow, the creek channels make for easier walking than the thick brush that borders their lower sections.

More difficult and dangerous to cross are the large, swift-flowing glacial streams that flow north out of the Alaska Range and cut through the Outer Range, such as the Teklanika, East Fork, and Sanctuary rivers. Because these intimidating rivers are often in a single channel as they pass through the Outer Range, it is essential to plan routes that avoid having to ford them.

The Outer Range's road-accessible south-facing slopes normally lose their snow cover early in the summer, which makes them appealing destinations in June and early July. Above tree and brush line, the open alpine tundra provides good access to all sorts of high perches. Most can be ascended by non-climbers. The only requirements are good physical conditioning, a steady pace, and warm clothes. Even in summer, cool, blustery winds often blow across the higher, more exposed ridges to produce a wintry feel.

Though modestly sized when compared to their neighbors to the south, the range's tallest hills give far-reaching views in all directions. They present an especially breathtaking perspective of the neighboring Alaska Range, whose high mountains form a jagged wall of knife-edged peaks, most still unnamed. Far to the southwest, in a world too severe for either flowers or sheep, is the park's icy crown, which on clear days shimmers brightly above dark foothills.

Eielson to Wonder Lake and the Kantishna Hills

A place of subdued topography, this area has low rounded hills that gently give way to rolling tundra knolls and forested lowlands speckled with lakes and ponds. Whether made by glaciers or the work of beavers, these ponds and lakes—and their surrounding lands—provide important habitat for mammals, waterfowl, and shorebirds not found in the alpine areas of the Alaska and Outer ranges.

This region stretches 20 miles east–west along the park road from the Eielson Visitor Center to Wonder Lake and measures roughly 40 miles north–south, from the Kantishna Hills to the Clearwater Creek valley. Starting at the road, day hikers can walk the shores of Wonder Lake, traverse tundra-topped benches covered in late summer with succulent berries, or explore the Kantishna Hills' southernmost valleys and hillsides. Backpackers can follow the McKinley River as it flows west from the Muldrow Glacier, travel the backside of the Outer Range, or head into the Kantishna Hills, a 30-mile-long range whose highest summits approach 5000 feet (1515 meters) elevation.

South of the park road is the braided, glacially fed McKinley River and the lower, rubble-covered sections of the Muldrow Glacier. Like many of the park's other glacial streams, the McKinley can be dangerous to cross, especially in mid-summer when warm temperatures boost glacial runoff. Habitats beyond glacier and river's gravel bars range from lowland forest to wet tundra and swampland.

North of the road, to Wonder Lake, is undulating tundra, dissected by a clearwater stream named Moose Creek. Much of the tundra is wet and brushy, though some flattened ridgelines are covered by drier alpine tundra. Walking here can be difficult and sloshy. And in June and July, the mosquitoes can be maddening. There are some benefits, however: the views of Denali and other Alaska Range peaks are glorious when the sky is clear, and wildlife is abundant.

A view from Denali Park Road, between the Eielson Visitor Center and Wonder Lake, showing the heavily braided McKinley River and the Alaska Range beyond.

Hikers and backpackers may encounter moose, caribou, wolves, grizzlies, porcupines, beavers, and occasionally, even black bears. The many ponds provide nesting habitat for numerous species of waterfowl and shorebirds, while the brush protects a variety of songbirds.

In June and July the tundra is brightened by dozens of wildflower species, and in August and September it often produces a luscious crop of blueberries. Late summer is also a time of brilliant color as a mix of willows, berry plants, and dwarf birch turns the landscape aflame with yellows, purples, and reds.

North of Wonder Lake and separated from the Outer Range by several miles of lowland forest and wet tundra, the Kantishna Hills contrast with other parts of this area in a number of ways. The hills are located in Denali's "new park" and are outside the designated wilderness, so regulations are not as strict. Campfires are permissible, for example. Though the highest hills don't quite reach 5000 feet, they rise 3000 feet above the surrounding lowlands. Topped by dry, alpine tundra, the upper reaches of these hills look out upon both the Outer and Alaska ranges. Getting to hilltops can be challenging, however, because lower slopes are covered by thick brush or spruce forest.

Remote Denali

Comparing a map of Denali to the area descriptions above, readers will note that only a fraction of the national park is described. Even ignoring the snow-covered peaks of the Alaska Range, there are huge portions of the park to the north, west, and southwest which are generally ignored when planning trips in Denali. There is a reason: this is "Remote Denali," the national park lands distant from the park road, which are both very difficult to reach and nearly impossible to travel.

What is in remote Denali? To the north and west it is a mostly flat place of intimidating rivers, mixed forest and tundra lowlands, thick and nearly impenetrable brush, grizzly bears, and huge boggy areas that demand waterproof footgear. The country here is relentless, with no good routes. Even wildlife seems scarce, hidden in the immense spruce forest. In the park and preserve's southwest corner, there are high peaks, huge glaciers, and immense glacial streams, with no easy overland access. No wonder, then, that these areas in most years get almost no visitors at all.

Success in traveling throughout most of remote Denali depends on an ability to read the vegetation. In some places the tundra is firm and relatively dry. In other places, hikers and backpackers can't even touch the ground: the brush is so thick, they end up walking across the tops of willows. Rivers present an equal or even greater challenge. Depending on the weather, some may be uncrossable. The Herron and Foraker, for instance, are very large rivers with narrow, deep channels. Sometimes travelers have no choice but to follow streams high into the hills and cross glacial ice.

The bottom line: however tempting those vast, empty areas on the map may appear, remote Denali is no place to go for scenic splendors, wildlife watching, or backcountry fun. It's a landscape that's brutally hard on humans, one that demands wilderness travel expertise, careful attention to detail, and self-reliance. More than anything, it teaches humility.

The Grizzly Family

Mid-August in the Alaska Range foothills. I enter the backcountry with another Anchorage resident, Chip Dennerlein. The sky is thickly overcast, the air breezy and dry when we leave the park road. But any hopes that we'll stay dry are soon washed away. Within a couple hours, the first rain-drops fall. And rain will continue to fall the remainder of our trip.

Walking along a ridge top, we are blasted by chilling, windblown rain. Within minutes the tundra and my boots are soaked, and my raingear shows signs of leakage. The shower passes, becomes a drizzle. Rain falls lightly as we set up camp, then rebuilds in its intensity and taps against the tent all night and into the morning. As Chip says in his understated way, "This is serious rain." The rain is accompanied by thick, low-lying clouds and misty fog that hide our surroundings.

We spend most of our first two days cocooned in the tent or under a tarp we brought for shelter while cooking and eating. Located in a small swale near the top of a gentle rise, the tarp site proves to be an ideal wildlife viewing station. Much to our delight, the valley we've chosen has a lot of wildlife. While we eat dinner our first night, an adult fox with beautiful red fur and a large, bushy tail trots across a meadow within 100 yards of camp. On several occasions we spot a pair of northern harriers as they glide low along a ridgeline in search of rodents. One morning while Chip and I huddle under the tarp eating breakfast, twenty Dall sheep ewes and lambs descend out of the fog like ghostly apparitions and graze on a nearby tundra bench.

Then there's the bear family. Chip and I are hunkered down under the tarp, eating lunch, when something gets his attention. "Uh-oh," he says. "Did you hear that?"

"Hear what?" I ask.

"That growling noise."

Chip rises to his feet, peers down-valley, and turns back, his eyes wide with anxiety. "Three bears are below us," he whispers. "And they're coming our way."

Now I'm up on my feet too. Only 50 feet away are a mother grizzly and two one-and-a-half-year-old cubs, all of them chocolate brown. But they're no longer approaching us, nor are they looking in our direction. The sow, in fact, is leading the cubs away from our tent, tarp, and food cache. None of the bears appears agitated or curious, though the mother grizzly seems aware of our presence. When her family is 150 to 200 feet away, she stops and looks at us twice, then resumes her slow, ambling pace. A couple of other times she sniffs the air. I'm sure she's either seen or smelled us, but except for those two quick glances she totally ignores us. More surprising to me is the cubs' behavior: they don't seem to know we're around. Either that or they are well-disciplined kids.

We watch the grizzlies in silent awe. On her way uphill, the mother grizzly stops to dig in the ground, then begins to eat something; the root of a plant, I'd guess. One of the cubs mimics her behavior, digs a hole of its own. The other tries to horn in on her meal and gets rebuked with a loud, angry snort. It quickly backs off. The bears resume their ascent, both cubs close to their mother. We watch until they cross over a ridge, out of sight. It's been 10 to 15 minutes since Chip first heard them.

Later, we go to inspect the tent, which is downstream from our tarp-protected eating area, in the direction from which the bears approached. We find fresh diggings in the tundra, and only 20 feet from the tent there's a fresh bear track—but no signs that they approached more closely. Including bears that we spotted from a distance while hiking into this valley from the road, we've now seen ten grizzlies: two families of three, another of four. Bear country, indeed!

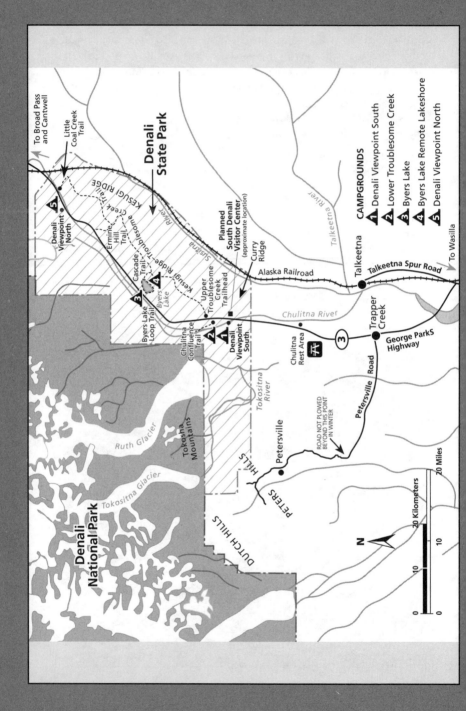

Denali State Park

To Broad Pass and Cantwell

Little Coal Creek Trail

KESUGI RIDGE

Denali Viewpoint North

5

Ermine Hill Trail

Little Coal Creek Trail

Cascade Trail

Kesugi Ridge–Troublesome Creek Trail

Byers Lake

Byers Lake Loop Trail

3

Chulitna Confluence Trail

Upper Troublesome Creek Trailhead

Planned South Denali Visitor Center (approximate location)

Curry Ridge

2

Denali Viewpoint South

Alaska Railroad

Susitna River

Talkeetna River

Talkeetna

Talkeetna Spur Road

To Wasilla

Chulitna River

Chulitna Rest Area

Trapper Creek

3

George Parks Highway

Petersville Road

ROAD NOT PLOWED BEYOND THIS POINT IN WINTER

Tokositna River

Petersville

PETERS HILLS

DUTCH HILLS

Ruth Glacier

Tokosha Mountains

Tokositna Glacier

Denali National Park

CAMPGROUNDS
1 Denali Viewpoint South
2 Lower Troublesome Creek
3 Byers Lake
4 Byers Lake Remote Lakeshore
5 Denali Viewpoint North

N

20 Miles

20 Kilometers

10

10

0

0

Chapter 7

SOUTH DENALI

South from the high pinnacles of the Alaska Range lies a young land that—by virtue of its location little more than 100 miles from the city of Anchorage— is often the first place visitors enter Denali. The land is young because it was entirely covered in glacial ice through the end of the most recent Ice Age, 9500 years ago. These great glaciers have mostly retreated from the lowlands into the ice-capped domain of the high Alaska Range peaks, but their snouts still reach into forested lowlands. The landscape abandoned by the ice has blossomed exuberantly. Encouraged by a climate warmer and moister than that north of the range, plant life grows large and dense with an accompanying profusion of moose, swans, eagles, salmon, bears, and other wildlife.

South Denali is not a single park, but a region defined by its proximity to The Mountain, vast tracts of public recreation land, and access from the George Parks Highway and Alaska Railroad (see "Getting There," below). The boundaries of this region are not officially specified but are roughly described by the crest of the Alaska Range to the north and west, the Susitna River and Talkeetna Mountains to the east, and a line through the towns of Talkeetna and Trapper Creek to the south. Denali National Park and Preserve reaches only as far as the termini of the great glaciers flowing out of the Alaska Range; the core of this region is occupied by Denali State Park. The remainder of the area comprises other state lands, some federal Bureau of Land Management holdings, borough lands, and considerable private lands held by Alaska Native corporations and others.

Unlike the north side of the range, where it is often possible to ramble across the open tundra in any direction, the dense vegetation of South Denali nudges explorers onto existing routes. To most easily experience South Denali, you must follow an established road, rail, trail, or river, or fly over it all. Many visitors use one of these established pathways to travel through the region on their way to the north side of the Alaska Range and the traditional entrance to Denali National Park; for others, South Denali is itself the destination. In fact, this region is the best Denali destination if your greatest desire is to catch a glimpse of the Denali and Alaska Range panorama, fish for salmon or trout, hike on a trail instead of cross-country, canoe peacefully across a lake, ride a historic railroad, or view glaciers and the enormous braided rivers that gush from their snouts. Wildlife

Denali State Park's Troublesome Creek–Kesugi Ridge Trail is one of Alaska's most popular backcountry trails and affords sweeping views of the Denali landscape.

is common, but seen less often than on the north side of the range because animals here are concealed in thick forest. Although the most accessible parts of South Denali are not within the national park, the landscape sometimes seems wilder because of the larger rivers, the unruly plant growth, and the relative dearth of interpretive information (with the notable exception of some state park facilities). There is little guidance for the visitor in a landscape where wilderness adventures beckon from all sides.

If possible, visitors are encouraged to begin a visit to South Denali at the Anchorage Museum of History and Art, where you can see the work of painter Sydney Laurence in the gallery of Alaska artists. Laurence was Alaska's foremost landscape artist, and his paintings of Denali's southern side are among his most famous. Several are displayed here, showing the many moods of the famous peak—sunlit and inspiring, somber and reflective. The most dramatic is an enormous horizontal canvas in an ornate frame, entitled simply *Mount McKinley*. The mountain rises with intimidating power over an equally ferocious rapid, the wildness of the scene evoking the wildness of the entire Alaska landscape with its rugged beauty, extremes of weather, violent geologic upheavals, life-and-death struggles of predator and prey, and an enormous scale that dwarfs the works of humankind. These paintings depict what a visitor is likely to find in South Denali.

SOUTH DENALI RESOURCES AND INFORMATION

With the exception of the historic train ride, South Denali is still young as a destination. This youthfulness is its allure as well as its challenge. There is relatively little information to guide visitors (though that is changing) and a lot of land to see for those who leave the highway/railroad corridor. However, this implies that there is also much to be discovered. South Denali offers visitors the allure of the unknown that is at the heart of our visions of Alaska.

For more information about Denali State Park, contact:

Alaska State Parks, Mat-Su/Copper Basin Area Superintendent
HC 32, Box 6706
Wasilla, AK 99654
907-745-3975
907-745-0938 (fax)
www.alaskastateparks.org

The Department of Natural Resources/Division of Parks Public Information Center
550 West Seventh Avenue, Suite 1260,
Anchorage, AK 99501
907-269-8400
907-269-8901 (fax)
http://dnr.alaska.gov

Visitor Services

Numerous campgrounds, recreational-vehicle parks, bed-and-breakfasts, hotels, rental cabins, cafés, and restaurants are scattered along the Parks Highway between Talkeetna and Denali National Park's entrance area. Lodging and restaurant information can be obtained from the following sources:

For businesses in the Talkeetna–Trapper Creek area, contact the Talkeetna Chamber of Commerce (907-733-2330; fax 907-733-2720; www.talkeetnachamber .org; Box 334, Talkeetna, AK 99676).

Denali Summer Times, a visitor-oriented newspaper published annually, provides information on visitor services from Cantwell to the Denali National Park entrance area and north to Healy. To order, 800-478-8300; ncountry@gci.net; www.denali101.com.

The Milepost, an annual mile-by-mile guide to highways in Alaska and west-ernmost Canada, contains information on businesses along the Parks Highway corridor as well as in the communities of Talkeetna, Trapper Creek, Cantwell, and Healy. To order, contact Morris Visitor Publications, *The Milepost* (907-272-6070; www.milepost.com; 301 Arctic Slope Avenue, Suite 300, Anchorage, AK 99518).

Information on lodging, restaurants, guiding services, and transportation is also available in the *Alaska State Vacation Planner*, published by the Alaska Travel Industry Association (907-929-2200 or 800-862-5275; info@alaskatia.org; www .travelalaska.com; 2600 Cordova Street, Suite 201, Anchorage, AK 99503).

Information on Denali Highway campgrounds and other public facilities is summarized in the Bureau of Land Management (BLM) Denali Highway brochure, available from BLM's Glennallen District Office (907-822-3217; fax 907-822-7335; www.blm.gov/ak; Box 147, Glennallen, AK 99588) or from the Alaska Public Lands Information Center (APLIC) in Anchorage (907-644-3361 or 866-869-6887; fax 907-271-2744; ANCH_Web_Mail@nps.gov; www.alaskacenters .gov; 605 West Fourth Avenue, Suite 105, 99501) or Fairbanks (907-459-3730; fax 907-459-3729; fair_interpretation@nps.gov; www.alaskacenters.gov; 101 Dunkle Street, Suite 110, 99701). *The Milepost* (see above) is also a good reference.

Getting There

Beginning in Anchorage (the usual starting point for trips to South Denali), most visitors reach this region one of two ways: via the Glenn and George Parks (or simply Parks) highways or by riding the rails.

Though it takes longer to reach Denali National Park by train, a railroad trip offers a strong connection to history, an equally scenic trip, and the chance to enjoy the passage through South Denali without having to worry about watch-ing the road instead of the mountains. (For more details, see "Riding the Alaska Railroad" at the end of this chapter.)

For information on the Alaska Railroad's passenger services, contact the Alaska Railroad Corporation, Passenger Services (800-544-0552 or 907-265-2494; reservations@akrr.com; www.alaskarailroad.com; P.O. Box 107500, Anchorage, AK 99510). The Anchorage depot is at 411 West First Avenue; the Fairbanks depot is at 280 North Cushman. At Denali National Park, the phone is 907-683-2233.

When to Go

Visitors can explore South Denali year-round, but most public facilities are closed from late September through early May (though Denali State Park's Byers Lake public-use cabins are available year-round). The prime time for hiking and backpacking is June through September; snowmobilers, mushers, and cross-country skiers come out to play when there's sufficient snow cover, usually from November through April.

DENALI STATE PARK CAMPGROUNDS AND CABINS

Five campgrounds are located within the park, four of them easily accessible by vehicle from the Parks Highway. All are first-come, first-served, with no reservations taken. In case of emergency, either the campground host (if present) or park staff should be contacted.

DENALI VIEWPOINT SOUTH CAMPGROUND

Location: Milepost 135.2 of the Parks Highway
Number of sites: 9 walk-in tent sites; RVs may use the large adjacent parking lot
Season: Late May through early October
Water: Yes
Facilities: Toilets, picnic tables, fire pits, bulletin board,s and interpretive displays
Fee: $10 per night

LOWER TROUBLESOME CREEK CAMPGROUND

Location: Milepost 137.2 of the Parks Highway
Number of sites: 10 walk-in tent sites; RVs can stay in adjacent parking area
Season: Late May through early October
Water: Yes
Facilities: Toilets, picnic tables, picnic shelter, fire pits, bulletin boards
Fee: $10 per night

BYERS LAKE CAMPGROUND

Location: Milepost 147 of the Parks Highway
Number of sites: 73, for both tents and RVs
Season: Late May through early October
Water: Yes
Facilities: Toilets, fire pits, picnic tables, bulletin boards and interpretive displays, nearby boat launch
Fee: $10 per night

BYERS LAKE REMOTE LAKESHORE CAMPGROUND

Location: Milepost 147 of the Parks Highway, on the far side of Byers Lake and accessible only by foot or boat
Number of sites: 6 walk-in or boat-in tent sites
Season: Late May through early October.
Water: Lake water, must be treated
Facilities: Toilet, picnic tables, bulletin boards
Fee: None

DENALI VIEWPOINT NORTH CAMPGROUND

Location: Milepost 162.7 of the Parks Highway
Number of sites: 20 walk-in tent sites, RV camping in large adjacent parking area
Season: Late May through early October
Water: Yes
Facilities: Toilets, fire pits, picnic tables, bulletin boards and interpretive displays
Fee: $10 per night

Byers Lake Public-Use Cabins

Three popular public-use cabins are located along the shores of Byers Lake. One is adjacent to the access road that leads to Byers Lake campground. The other two can be reached in summer by walking about 0.5 mile from a parking area, or by boat. In winter, visitors must park at the Alaska Veterans Memorial (milepost 147.1) and ski, snowshoe, mush, or snowmobile to the cabins, a distance of between 0.5 and 1 mile.

Location: Milepost 147 of the Parks Highway
Season: Year-round
Water: Lake water, must be treated
Facilities: Each of the cabins sleeps up to six people and is equipped with bunks, wood-burning stove, table, and benches. Cabin 3 is wired for electricity, so it's possible to hook up a generator. Visitors must bring their own firewood.
Fee: $60 per night during the summer "peak season" and $45 per night the rest of the year
Emergency: Contact the Byers Lake Campground host (summer only) or park staff
Reservations: Required. Cabins can be reserved no more than five consecutive nights, contact the Alaska State Parks Mat-Su office (907-745-3975; http://dnr.alaska.gov/parks/cabins).

SOUTH DENALI HIKING TRAILS

South Denali's most popular hiking destinations occur in Denali State Park. One of these is the Peters Hills, which has an unofficial and unmaintained network of footpaths, as well as excellent opportunities for off-trail hiking and backpacking adventures across tundra-topped hills and ridges. The primary developed and maintained trails are part of a network that connects Denali State Park's famed Kesugi Ridge with the Byers Lake Campground and three other trailheads located along the Parks Highway. The various trail segments and routes are described below.

Backpackers pass one of the many rock cairns that mark Denali State Park's Kesugi Ridge–Troublesome Creek Trail, helpful for navigating the ridge on foggy days like this one.

Recreation in South Denali

South Denali is best known for its views of Denali and other high Alaska Range mountains, and some of the viewpoints are within Denali State Park. Two popular spots are located along the Parks Highway, at mileposts 135.2 (Denali Viewpoint South) and 162.7 (Denali Viewpoint North). Each site includes scopes and interpretive displays. Hikers and backpackers can also get excellent views of Denali and other high Alaska Range peaks from Kesugi Ridge and the Peters Hills. Other recreational uses include camping, hiking, backpacking, berry picking, river floating, lake boating, wildlife watching, fishing, hunting, cross-country skiing, mushing, and snowmobiling. Several guides offer trips into Denali State Park. Information on businesses and nearby lodges can be obtained from the area superintendent's office (907-745-3975).

Denali State Park's managers rate trails easy, moderate, or difficult. Hikers and backpackers should note that the main Kesugi Ridge–Troublesome Creek Trail is 36 miles long and has a total elevation gain of about 5150 feet, including numerous ups and downs in the rolling terrain; above tree line the trail is marked by rock cairns, but map-reading and route-finding skills are recommended. Several other trail segments also have substantial gain and are rated moderate to difficult. The Troublesome Creek Trailhead is usually closed from mid-July through September 1 because of possible human–bear conflicts.

EASY

BYERS LAKE LOOP TRAIL

Route:	Begins and ends at Byers Lake Campground, accessible from milepost 147 of the Parks Highway. Footpath with rocks and roots in places, 1–3 feet wide.
Length:	4.8 miles one way (7.7 kilometers)
Elevation change:	Negligible (though there are some slight hilly sections)
Time:	2–4 hours
Highlights:	Views of Denali. Opportunities to see wildlife, including moose, bears, beavers, porcupines, squirrels, swans and other water birds, eagles, and songbirds. Spawning salmon can be seen in the shallows from late summer into fall (fishing for salmon is not allowed here). Berry picking in late summer and fall. Solitude and quiet. (See map, page 222.)

CHULITNA CONFLUENCE TRAIL

Route:	Begins at Lower Troublesome Creek Trailhead, milepost 137.2 of the Parks Highway. Footpath with rocks and roots in places, 1–3 feet wide.
Length:	1.2 miles round-trip (1.9 kilometers)
Elevation change:	Negligible
Time:	An hour or less round-trip
Highlights:	An easy walk through the woods to the Chulitna River, one of South Denali's largest streams. Opportunities to see forest wildlife and salmon that swim up Troublesome Creek (fishing is not allowed here). (See map, page 222.)

MODERATE

LITTLE COAL CREEK TRAIL

Route: Trailhead is at milepost 163.9 of the Parks Highway.
Footpath with rocks and roots in places, 1–3 feet wide.

Length: 3.3 miles one way (5.3 kilometers)

Elevation change: 715 feet to tundra, 1750 to trail's end (where it meets Kesugi Ridge Trail)

Time: 1–2 hours (or more) to reach the alpine tundra, another hour or two to the end

Highlights: Views of Denali and the surrounding landscape, including other high Alaska Range peaks, glaciers, foothills, and wooded lowlands. Opportunities to see wildlife, from moose to bears and smaller mammals, eagles, and songbirds. Wildflower meadows. Berry picking in late summer and fall. Solitude and quiet. (See map, page 222.)

ERMINE HILL TRAIL

Route: Trailhead is at milepost 156.5 of the Parks Highway.
Footpath with rocks and roots in places, 1–3 feet wide.

Length: 3.7 miles one way (6 kilometers) (ends in alpine tundra, at the Kesugi Ridge Trail)

Elevation change: 1300 feet

Time: 2–4 hours one way

Highlights: See Little Coal Creek Trail. (See map, page 222.)

Cumulus clouds and an azure sky are reflected in a tundra pond on a calm afternoon atop Denali State Park's Kesugi Ridge.

MODERATELY STRENUOUS

CASCADE TRAIL

Route: Accessible from the Byers Lake Loop Trail, which begins at the Byers Lake Campground. Footpath with rocks and roots in places, 1–3 feet wide.

Length: 2 miles one way (3.2 kilometers) (ends in alpine tundra, at the Kesugi Ridge Trail)

Elevation change: 1800 feet

Time: 2–3 hours one way

Highlights: See Little Coal Creek Trail.

NOTE: In 2012, park staff began rerouting the Cascade Trail. With more switchbacks and few tree roots to negotiate, the new path is more gradual and considerably easier to walk than the original one. It is also much safer, avoiding some steep stretches that bordered a canyon wall. Though unfinished as this book is being written, it may be completed by summer 2013. (See map, page 222.)

STRENUOUS

KESUGI RIDGE–TROUBLESOME CREEK TRAIL

Route: Hikers and backpackers can begin at either the Upper Troublesome Creek (milepost 137.6) or Little Coal Creek (milepost 163.9) trailhead. Footpath with rocks and roots in places, 1–3 feet wide; the trail is indistinct in places atop the ridge and marked with rock cairns.

Length: 36.2 miles (58.3 kilometers)

Elevation change: 5150 feet

Time: A few to several days to complete the entire route

Highlights: Spectacular views of Denali and other Alaska Range peaks from Kesugi Ridge when the sky is clear, as well as expansive views of the neighboring foothills, glaciers, rivers, and lowlands. Opportunities to see a variety of wildlife, from grizzlies and black bears to moose, porcupines, foxes, eagles, songbirds, and more. The route's tundra-topped ridgeline is also beautiful in itself, especially during the late summer and early fall color change. Berry picking in the fall. Solitude and natural quiet. (See map, page 222.)

NOTE: The Troublesome Creek Trailhead is seasonally closed when salmon are running and grizzlies come here to feed.

KESUGI RIDGE TRAIL:
LITTLE COAL CREEK TO ERMINE HILL

Route: Hikers and backpackers can begin at either the Little Coal Creek (Parks Highway milepost 163.9) or Ermine Hill (milepost 156.5) trailhead. Footpath with rocks and roots in places, 1–3 feet wide; the trail is indistinct in places atop the ridge and marked with rock cairns.

Length: 14.1 miles (22.7 kilometers)

Elevation change: 2650 feet

Time: One very long day to several days

Highlights: See Kesugi Ridge–Troublesome Creek Trail. (See map, page 222.)

KESUGI RIDGE TRAIL:
LITTLE COAL CREEK TO BYERS LAKE

Route: Hikers and backpackers can begin at either Little Coal Trailhead (Parks Highway, milepost 163.9) or Byers Lake Campground (milepost 147). Footpath with rocks and roots in places, 1–3 feet wide; the trail is indistinct in places atop the ridge and marked with rock cairns.

Length: 28.9 miles (46.5 kilometers)

Elevation change: 4650 feet

Time: A couple of very long days to several days

Highlights: See Kesugi Ridge–Troublesome Creek Trail. Also, beavers, swans, and other water birds at Byers Lake, and spawning salmon in the lake shallows from late summer into fall. (No salmon fishing is allowed in Byers Lake.) (See map, page 222.)

TROUBLESOME CREEK TO BYERS LAKE CAMPGROUND

Route: Hikers and backpackers can begin at either Byers Lake Campground (Parks Highway, milepost 147) or Upper Troublesome Creek Trailhead (milepost 137.6). Footpath with rocks and roots in places, 1–3 feet wide; the trail is indistinct in places atop the ridge and marked with rock cairns.

Length: 14.5 miles (23.3 kilometers)

Elevation change: 2500 feet

Time: One very long day to several days

Highlights: See Kesugi Ridge: Little Coal Creek to Byers Lake. Much of this trail segment passes through spruce-birch forest, beside Troublesome Creek and is seasonally closed when salmon are running and grizzlies come here to feed. (See map, page 222.)

SPORT FISHING

To obtain information on sport fishing opportunities within the Susitna River drainage, contact the Alaska Department of Fish and Game, Sport Fish Division (907-746-6300; fax 907-746-6305; www.adfg.alaska.gov; 1800 Glenn Highway, Suite 2, Palmer, AK 99645). The Sport Fish Division annually publishes a regulations summary for this area, which is part of the Cook Inlet management region. Information on fishing charters in South Denali can be obtained from the Talkeetna Chamber of Commerce (see above) and the Wasilla Chamber of Commerce (907-376-1299; fax 907-373-2560; contact@wasillachamber.org; www .visitwasilla.org/chamber).

WHITEWATER PADDLING ON THE CHULITNA RIVER

For independent river runners, Andy Embick's *Fast & Cold: A Guide to Alaska Whitewater* includes a detailed description of the Chulitna River and information on its difficulty, access, trip lengths, necessary maps, and put-in and take-out sites. The most popular put-in is at the Parks Highway bridge at the East Fork, milepost 185. The usual take-out is at milepost 133, at the Chulitna bridge near the southern boundary of Denali State Park. Length of this trip is 63 river miles.

The names of river-running companies permitted to operate in Denali State Park (which includes a portion of the Chulitna River) can be obtained from Alaska State Parks, Mat-Su/Copper Basin Area Superintendent (907-745-3975; www. alaskastateparks.org).

TRAVELING THE GEORGE PARKS HIGHWAY

Most visitors to South Denali drive the George Parks Highway (commonly called the Parks Highway) north from Anchorage or south from Fairbanks and the Denali National Park entrance. The 323-mile-long Parks Highway (Alaska Route 3) turns north from the Glenn Highway (Alaska Route 1) in Wasilla, 35 miles northeast of Anchorage. (Though the Parks Highway doesn't actually start in Anchorage, markers along the road give the mileage from Alaska's largest city.) The distance from Anchorage to Denali State Park's southern boundary is 132 miles; from Anchorage to Denali National Park's entrance area and the beginning of the Denali Park Road is 237.3 miles or about 4.5 hours' driving time. For those taking a northerly approach, the national park entrance area is 121 highway miles, or 2 to 2.5 hours' drive, from Fairbanks.

The Susitna River Valley (Mile 35 to Mile 115)

The Parks Highway passes through the Susitna Valley for most of its first 80 miles as it approaches South Denali. North of the city of Wasilla, the road briefly intersects the centers of two small communities, Houston and Willow, then winds through lowland forest. Much of the highway is bordered by thick spruce-birch

The Chulitna River

South Denali is traversed by a road, a railroad, and a river. The last of these pathways is the least traveled and most enchanting for those experienced river runners who thrive on the sound of rushing water and the bobbing of boats in a current. The Chulitna is never far from the Parks Highway, but it is usually a long way from the perception of the highway, which rarely intrudes either with sight or sound. Instead, the Chulitna offers up silty beaches covered in bear and moose tracks, salmon hovering at the base of clear-running side streams, bald eagles perched in spruce trees keeping an eye out for dinner, and occasional views of the Alaska Range peaks.

The Chulitna River has three forks at its headwaters. The highway and railroad cross the East and Middle forks, both of which arise in the Talkeetna Mountains and flow southward. These are clearwater streams fed by rain and melting snow. By contrast, the larger West Fork is a silty, glacier-fed river that quickly turns the clearwater streams to a muddy brown. As it flows farther south, the river is swollen with glacial runoff from the Fountain and Tokositna rivers.

The Chulitna is not a technically difficult river to raft or kayak, but successful navigation does require knowledge and skill in whitewater boating. After a put-in at the East Fork bridge of the Parks Highway (mile 185), the 63-mile journey to the Chulitna River bridge (mile 133, near the southern edge of Denali State Park) offers a constantly changing river landscape—from a bouncy clearwater stream, to a murky river filled with glacial silt spreading across several channels, to a swift-flowing river in a narrow canyon, to an enormous braided river stretching a mile or more across. Often the challenge for much of the trip is avoiding downed trees and grounding out on gravel bars, but after heavy rains the gravel bars disappear and the river becomes a veritable ocean.

The Chulitna River is a way for adventurers to travel through the dense vegetation of South Denali under their own power and in close contact with the elemental forces that both carve and incarnate the wild drama of the land.

woodlands, but north of mile 66 Denali appears off and on—weather permitting—as a distant white pyramid. The Alaska Range's second- and third-highest mountains, Mounts Foraker and Hunter, also show themselves occasionally as the road bends this way and that. Although the Susitna River is mostly hidden to drivers, the highway roughly follows its course, which is never far away.

This view from the Peters Hills shows two members of Denali's family: The High One rises on the right, while Begguya, or "Denali's Child," (officially known as Mount Hunter) is on the left.

Fed by Alaska Range glaciers, the Susitna flows southward more than 170 miles before crossing the Parks Highway at mile 104.3, where there are pull-outs allowing travelers to get out and explore the riverbank. South of here, the cold, silty, and intricately braided stream flows west of the highway as it rushes through wooded flatlands toward Cook Inlet. More than 50 miles wide in places, these Susitna lowlands are a mix of dense spruce-birch forest, thick alder-willow brush, and marshy wetlands dotted by thousands of ponds. In summer, these wetlands are nearly impossible to cross.

As it cuts north through the Susitna Valley, the highway between miles 71.4 and 96.6 crosses more than a dozen clearwater creeks—spawning grounds for all five of Alaska's salmon species. Kings, the largest, are the first to arrive, in June. They are followed by sockeyes, pinks, chums, and finally, in late July to August, silvers. These tributaries of the Susitna also have healthy populations of rainbow trout, grayling, and Dolly Varden. Road-accessible via the Parks Highway and side roads, they are among the state's most heavily fished streams.

Talkeetna (Mile 98.7)

First settled in the early 1900s by miners, trappers, and traders, Talkeetna today is an end-of-the-road community of rural homesteaders and tourism businesses that's best known as the "Gateway to Denali." But Talkeetna offers air and river, not overland, access to Denali's south side. Connected to the Parks Highway by the 14.5-mile Talkeetna Spur Road, the community's famed bush pilots take mountaineers and flightseers to the Alaska Range's biggest glaciers and tallest peaks. The town also is a staging point for fishing and float trips on nearby rivers. Besides its gateway reputation, Talkeetna boasts one of the premier roadside views of Denali and surrounding mountains at mile 13 of the Spur Road. Supplementing the grand sweep of landscape is a painted diorama that identifies many of the other landforms visible from this spot.

Lands surrounding modern Talkeetna were inhabited for thousands of years by semi-nomadic Dena'ina Athabascans called the Dghelay Teht'ana, or "Mountain People." Dependent on the region's fish and mammals, the Mountain People built seasonal camps near the junctions of three large rivers, calling the place Linghasdlent, "Where Streams Join." One river especially important for its salmon runs they called K'Dalkitnu, "River of Plenty" or "Fish Storage River." Over time, the name would evolve into its present form: Talkeetna.

The Mountain People were largely displaced in the early 1900s by growing numbers of white explorers, gold prospectors, trappers, and traders, who put down roots near the confluence of the renamed Talkeetna, Chulitna, and Susitna rivers. Talkeetna expanded significantly in 1915, when government railroad crews chose the settlement as a construction camp site.

Still mostly inhabited by miners, trappers, and homesteaders, Talkeetna in the late 1940s attracted its first bush pilots, including Don Sheldon. Sheldon established his reputation as a first-rate pilot while transporting the region's residents and their supplies, but he would attain his greatest fame as the first of Talkeetna's "Denali Flyers"—the daring pilots who fly mountaineers in and out of the Alaska Range.

Talkeetna became the main staging area for Denali climbing expeditions in the 1950s after mountaineer Bradford Washburn proved a southerly approach, the West Buttress Route, to be the easiest and safest path to the summit. Nowadays, with Denali attracting more than a thousand mountaineers annually, Talkeetna's air taxi operators busily shuttle expeditions from late April through early July. Since the mid-1990s, however, flightseeing has become an even bigger summertime business.

Flying small, ski-equipped single-engine planes, pilots take visitors on a variety of air tours into the Alaska Range. Even the shortest flights usually include a passage through the Great Gorge of the Ruth Glacier. Bordered by Yosemite-like gray granite walls and spires thousands of feet high, this spectacular chasm is North America's deepest gorge, measuring more than 9000 feet (2745 meters) from top to bottom; the lower 3800 feet, however, are hidden by glacial ice. Leaving the gorge, flightseers enter the immense, mountain-encircled glacial basins of the Don Sheldon Amphitheater (also known as the Ruth Amphitheater). Among the enclosing peaks are some of the range's most rugged and descriptively named peaks, including the Mooses Tooth and the Rooster Comb.

Most trips also include flights past Denali's southern flanks and present glimpses of several of its best-known and most challenging climbing routes: the East, West, and South buttresses; Cassin Ridge; and the West Rib. Longer tours completely encircle Denali and pass among the perennially snow- and ice-capped upper slopes, saw-toothed ridges, and vertical rock faces of other high Alaska Range peaks, many of them reaching above 10,000 feet (3050 meters).

Because Talkeetna is the main jumping-off spot for Denali climbers, the National Park Service has a ranger station here that serves as both its South District administrative headquarters and the center of the park's mountaineering operations. It's also used as a base for search-and-rescue missions and South Denali ranger patrols.

Talkeetna's downtown streets present a mix of older buildings from the pioneering past and modern businesses that cater to climbers, anglers, flightseers, and other South Denali visitors. Thirteen downtown buildings are on the National Register of Historic Places, and the Talkeetna Historical Society Museum displays artifacts and exhibits on mountaineering, mining, pioneering settlement, and the railroad; walking tours may also be arranged.

Petersville Road and the Peters Hills (Mile 114.9)

Built by miners in the 1920s, the Petersville Road intersects the Parks Highway at mile 114.9, within the sparsely populated community of Trapper Creek. Forty miles long (but unplowed beyond mile 14 in winter), the Petersville Road heads west and then north through forest and marshy flatlands toward the Dutch and Peters hills, giving access to the historic Cache Creek mining district and the far western corner of Denali State Park. A remote haven for adventurous hikers and backpackers, the foothills at road's end also present unmatched views of the Alaska Range's three highest mountains.

Two backcountry skiers roped together carefully follow a snow bridge across a crevasse in the Alaska Range's Don Sheldon Amphitheater.

An expanse of rolling tundra spreads into the distance from the Peters Hills along the far western edge of Denali State Park.

Cutting across a patchwork quilt of private, borough, and state-owned lands, this rutted, potholed, and sometimes water-pooled road can be intimidating even to those with high-clearance four-wheel-drive vehicles. However, for visitors who venture along its dirt and gravel track, Petersville Road provides a glimpse into the world of modern bush Alaska with its remote mining camps, roadhouses, homesteads, mushers' kennels, and historic mine buildings, most of them now abandoned. Few people go beyond mile 31.5, where there's a large pullout and trails into the Peters Hills. Beyond this point, the road drops steeply into a canyon.

The Peters Hills are gently rounded, tundra-topped knobs and ridgelines 15 miles long, 4 miles wide, and barely 4000 feet high. At their northern edge, they approach within a few miles of the Alaska Range. Both the Peters and nearby Dutch hills to the northwest are dissected by dozens of small, clear-water streams in which prospectors discovered gold in the early 1900s. Once ranked among Alaska's major placer-gold districts, the region now yields little ore. Today's adventurers come for the area's recreational opportunities: hiking and backpacking in summer; hunting in fall; snowmobiling, mushing, and skiing in winter. (See Chapter 8, "Denali in Winter," for more information on that season's recreational opportunities.)

From mile 31.5 of the Petersville Road, a system of unmarked and unmaintained but easy-to-follow footpaths leads north into alpine backcountry. Those who take these gentle uphill trails will come, after about an hour's walk, to a rolling bench with tundra meadows, small ponds, and unexpectedly marvelous views of the Alaska Range's ice-capped pinnacles; from here the continent's roof is less than 40 miles away. Beyond this bench, defined trails soon peter out, and the walking becomes more strenuous. Visitors who go beyond the trails should be experienced in backcountry travel and always alert for grizzly bears.

To reach the westernmost edge of Denali State Park, hikers and backpackers must travel 4 to 5 miles from Petersville Road—much of it uphill across untrailed tundra and through dense willow thickets. Those who make the effort are likely to find wonderful solitude, a wild and primeval landscape, and arguably the best views anywhere of Alaska's most famous mountain family. Denali (20,320 feet; 6200 meters), the family's patriarch, is joined along the northern skyline by Mount Foraker (17,400 feet; 5307 meters) and Mount Hunter (14,570 feet; 4444 meters).

Named in 1899 by military explorer Joseph Herron to honor Ohio senator Joseph Benson Foraker, the Alaska Range's second-highest peak also has two Athabascan names: Sultana ("The Woman") and Menlale ("Denali's Wife"). Standing between the soaring couple of Sultana and Denali is the region's third-highest mountain. Athabascans quite naturally called this peak Begguya, or "Denali's Child." But an explorer's desire to memorialize his aunt—Easterner Anna Falconett Hunter, who never visited Alaska—combined with a later surveying error, has instead left the peak misnamed as Mount Hunter.

Among the best places to enjoy this mountain panorama is 3929-foot (1198-meter) Long Point, 5 miles—as the raven flies—northeast of Petersville Road and a thousand feet above it. Hikers and backpackers who come here look upon the landscape that so inspired Alaska's preeminent landscape artist, Sydney Laurence. After learning to paint in New York and Europe, the Brooklyn native abandoned a promising career in 1904 to prospect for Alaska gold. Once in Alaska, Laurence hardly touched a paintbrush until 1912. A year later, given a grubstake and sled dog team, he headed north to paint Denali's portrait. By fall, Laurence had completed forty-three studies of the mountain, including those displayed at the Anchorage Museum of History and Art.

The Denali region opens up in every direction as hikers ascend to Long Point. Due south are lowlands that stretch to Cook Inlet, 100 miles away, while to the

South Denali Visitor Center

(NOTE: Construction has not yet begun on either the visitor center or access road, which is most likely to be placed between mileposts 132 and 135.)

For decades, tourism proponents, park officials, and politicians have pushed for the construction of a Denali visitor center south of the Alaska Range. Yet the first to do so was neither bureaucrat nor politician, but that visionary explorer and mountaineer, Bradford Washburn. As far back as the 1950s, and again in the '60s and '70s, Washburn proposed a simply built visitor center and lodge at Long Point, in the Peters Hills. Later suggestions included Senator Mike Gravel's "Denali City," a huge Teflon-domed structure in Denali State Park, just above the Tokositna River. That late-1970s idea collapsed under its own grandiosity, but in the 1990s visitor-center proponents began to once aggressively push for a tourism complex in "Little Denali" park. Initially they again targeted the Peters Hills, but a broad coalition of conservationists, hunters, homesteaders, and miners opposed that idea. So the target was moved to the Parks Highway corridor.

In 2006, representatives of the state, the Matanuska-Susitna Borough, and the National Park Service announced the new (and presumably final) location for a major South Denali visitor center: the slopes of Curry Ridge, a few miles from the highway inside Denali State Park—a location that still stirs controversy in some circles.

In 2012, plans for this visitor center were still being completed, with work to begin in 2013. At an elevation of between 1800 and 1900 feet (several hundred feet below the top of Curry Ridge), the completed visitor complex is naturally intended to provide "spectacular" views of Denali and neighboring Alaska Range peaks as well as the surrounding landscape, with designated viewpoints connected by a trail system providing 360-degree panoramas.

The "conceptual plan" shows that the center's main building would include an outdoor amphitheater and viewing decks, with visitors brought there from the highway via a shuttle bus system (though private vehicles might be allowed in the spring and fall shoulder seasons). The visitor center's interior would include a main gathering area, plus large exhibit hall, theater, multipurpose room for meetings and classes, bookstore, and restaurant. Besides the interpretive trail connecting the center and viewpoints, and a 3-mile nature-hiking loop, a more primitive wilderness trail would lead to the top of Curry Ridge, for those seeking greater solitude and a more remote experience.

As of this writing, the center's completion is still several years away.

northwest are the Dutch Hills, then several waves of unnamed hills, and finally the Alaska Range. Following the range's northerly sweep from west to east, visitors gaze upon the glaciers, valleys, and mountains that form Denali's south face. When clouds hide the Alaska Range's uppermost heights, eyes are drawn to the Tokositna Glacier. Fed by dozens of pale-blue fingers, it cuts through steep-sided peaks due south of Denali, then snakes between dark green forested foothills. The glacier, in turn, feeds the silt-laden Tokositna River, which bends around the Peters Hills' northeast flanks below Long Point, then meanders in wide arcs across marshy flatlands to join the Chulitna River.

Denali State Park (Mile 132.2 to Mile 169)

Beyond the edges of the Alaska Range's south-flowing glaciers is 325,240-acre Denali State Park, which nestles against the southeast side of the national park. Bisected by the Parks Highway between mileposts 132.2 and 169, and bordered on its eastern edge by the Alaska Railroad and the Susitna River, it is among Alaska's most accessible—and most scenic—parklands. The Alaska Range's high mountains, long glacial tongues, and ice-carved valleys are a looming presence from one end of the park to the other.

Denali State Park also gives highway travelers their best opportunities to leave the road corridor and explore South Denali's landscape. Several trailheads provide access to a trail along the rolling, alpine-topped Kesugi Ridge. Just east of the highway at mile 147 is Byers Lake, a serene woodland lake whose waters and shores are seasonal home to sockeye salmon, trumpeter swans, loons, beavers, moose, and bears. One of the region's outstanding recreational areas, Byers Lake has public-use cabins, campgrounds, a picnic area, and a lakeside trail. West of the highway, rafters float the braided Chulitna River as it meanders north–south through the park (see the Chilutna River sidebar). And in Denali State Park's far southwestern toe, hikers and backpackers roam gently rounded knobs in the Peters Hills. To get there, visitors must take the Petersville Road.

Denali Viewpoint South (Mile 135.2)

Driving north of Petersville Road, Parks Highway travelers get numerous glimpses of Denali—when clouds don't hide the mountain. But few visitors stop for gazing or photographs until mile 135.2. Three miles inside Denali State Park's southern boundary, Denali Viewpoint South has a large pullout with a lot of parking spaces plus interpretive displays, spotting scopes, and picnic sites. To the northwest are Denali and other great peaks with huge granite walls, craggy spires, and razor-edged ridges. Most are hidden by nearer foothills, but a handful of spectacular and famous mountains can be seen from this spot or others along the next 20 miles: Mount Huntington (12,240 feet; 3733 meters); Mount Dickey (9845 feet; 3003 meters); the Mooses Tooth (10,335 feet; 3158 meters); and

Mount Hunter. Out of these mountains pour several large glaciers covered by thick morainal debris: the Tokositna, the Ruth, the Buckskin, and the Eldridge. Adjacent to the viewing area is a small campground, with nine sites for tent campers. Both drinking water and toilets are available.

Troublesome Creek (Mile 137.2 and Mile 137.6)

Just north of the Denali Viewpoint South at mile 137.3 on the west side of the highway is a large pullout for Lower Troublesome Creek, while slightly farther north on the east side of the road is the Upper Troublesome Creek Trailhead—the southernmost trailhead for the Kesugi Ridge–Troublesome Creek Trail. The first or Lower Troublesome Creek Trailhead/parking area provides access to a short, half-mile trail that leads to the Chulitna River—the best opportunity to view up close this silty, glacially fed river that occupies the heart of South Denali. There is also a ten-site campground, a picnic area with shelter, drinking water, and toilets.

Troublesome Creek is a salmon stream, and when the fish are running during July it is possible to see them struggling upstream in the shallow, clear creek water. (Salmon fishing is prohibited here.) Because the abundant salmon attract bears, the Upper Troublesome Creek trailhead is closed from mid-July through early September to head off dangerous encounters between people and bears.

Hike Troublesome Creek

Visitors have a couple of options if they wish to explore Troublesome Creek. The first, and easier, option is Chulitna Confluence Trail, accessible from the Lower Troublesome Creek trailhead; the other is to follow the Upper Troublesome Creek Trail, which goes much farther and eventually intersects with the Kesugi Ridge Trail. The lower trail is easy, the upper one easy to moderately strenuous, depending on one's destination and ambition. See "South Denali Hiking Trails" earlier in this chapter for more details.

- Chulitna Confluence Trail, 1.2 miles round-trip
- Upper Troublesome Creek Trailhead, the southernmost access point for the 36.2-mile-long Kesugi Ridge–Troublesome Creek Trail system

Cottonball clouds are reflected in the calm waters of Byers Lake, one of the most popular visitor destinations in Denali State Park.

Byers Lake (MIle 147) and the Alaska Veterans Memorial (Mile 147.1)

Byers Lake is the recreational center of Denali State Park. Here, among spruce-birch forest, is the largest of the park's four road-accessible campgrounds (with seventy-three sites), its only three public-use cabins, a grassy picnic area, miles of woodland trails, and a small hike-in/boat-in lakeshore campground on the lake's far side, with a half-dozen tent-camping sites. Canoeists paddling the edges of this 2-mile-long lake share its waters with graceful trumpeter swans and loons that cry in eerie, haunting voices. Anglers fish from boats and shore, hopeful of catching lake trout or burbot. The surrounding forest is filled with the chatter of red squirrels and the songs of chickadees, warblers, and thrushes. Moose occasionally splash through the lake's shallows, beavers build lodges, and both black and grizzly bears feed on berries and salmon.

Hike Byers Lake

Depending on their timing, visitors may observe spawning salmon—and encounter fishing bears—while strolling the 4.8-mile forest trail that encircles Byers Lake. The trail also presents good opportunities to see or hear loons, swans, and other lake and forest wildlife and, in late summer and fall, pick berries. Mostly flat and easy to hike, this path is suitable for novice hikers and family outings, but those who walk it should be attentive.

For more ambitious hikers and backpackers, the lakeside trail connects with the Kesugi Ridge–Troublesome Creek Trail, via the Cascade Trail. The 2-mile ascent from Byers Lake to Kesugi Ridge is steep in places and strenuous, with 1800 feet of vertical gain, but at the top are open, rolling tundra, more gorgeous views of the Alaska Range, and remote wildness only a few miles from the highway. (As noted under the trail description, the Cascade Trail is being rerouted and improved, making the new path easier and safer to negotiate.) See "South Denali Hiking Trails" earlier in this chapter for more details.

Byers Lake is among the best places to observe the salmon that return to South Denali each summer. Sockeyes begin entering the lake in August. No longer silvery, their bodies are crimson, their heads olive green. Male-female pairs swim just offshore, guarding nests where muck has been cleared away to reveal the white, sandy lake bottom. The salmon circle relentlessly, aggressively attacking any fish that intrude upon their space. Soon eggs will be laid and fertilized and the salmon will die, adding nutrients to the lake system—and feeding bears that pull the salmon carcasses from the water.

On the Parks Highway just north of the Byers Lake entrance are two driveways for the Alaska Veterans Memorial, placed here to commemorate those Alaskans who served in the United States armed forces. Constructed in 1983, five large stone panels give a brief account of the history of each military service in Alaska. Here too there are picnic sites, interpretive displays, drinking water, and toilets.

Denali Viewpoint North (Mile 162.7)

From Byers Lake and the Veterans Memorial, the Parks Highway winds through Denali State Park another 22 miles. At mile 162.7 is the park's second major highway-corridor Denali viewpoint, complete with spotting scopes, interpretive displays, picnic area, recreational-vehicle camping, twenty walk-in tent campsites, drinking water, and toilets. Now almost due west, both the South and North peaks of Denali are clearly distinct, their shape suggesting the horned white head of some giant creature peering above the foothills.

Kesugi Ridge (Mile 137.6 to Mile 163.9)

Built from a mixture of volcanics, sediments, and granite, Kesugi Ridge is a 4–6-mile-wide, northeast-trending spine of rock that parallels the Parks Highway for 25 miles. Just east of the highway, Kesugi is easy to spot, but most road-bound travelers overlook it, because eyes are inevitably drawn to the west, where Alaska Range peaks leap into the sky. Kesugi and neighboring Curry Ridge to the south barely edge past 4500 feet (1370 meters) and have a gently rolling nature. Considered the upland "backbone" of Denali State Park, they're more tundra-topped plateau than mountain. Kesugi—a Dena'ina Athabascan word meaning "The Ancient One"—is nonetheless considered among Southcentral Alaska's premier hiking and backpacking routes. One reason is the view. The Alaska Range dominates the western horizon, topped off by the snow- and ice-capped throne of Denali. Many of these same great peaks can be seen from highway turnouts, but Kesugi shows the full panoramic sweep and connectedness of mountains, glaciers, tundra-draped foothills, wooded lowlands, and glacial rivers. A second reason is Kesugi's 36-mile-long trail system, which gives hikers and backpackers easy access to pristine alpine backcountry less than 5 miles from the highway.

The Kesugi Ridge–Troublesome Creek Trail is accessible from four trailheads and is the only trail on Denali's south side suitable for extended trips into the backcountry. Those who don't wish to do the entire route can take one of several shorter loops, ranging from 14.1. to 28.9 miles.

Kesugi's plateau-like top is most easily reached from Little Coal Creek (mile 163.9), where it's only 2 miles and 715 feet (218 meters) vertical gain from trailhead to tundra. Hikers and backpackers begin their journeys among spruce and birch trees, then emerge into the subalpine zone, where switchbacks pass between alders and willow thickets and meadows with lavender geraniums, purple monkshood, and delicate bluebells. The way finally emerges onto alpine tundra. Here the dirt path that serves as a trail is narrow and occasionally disappears, but the route is marked by rock cairns.

While crossing Kesugi Ridge, backpackers pass alpine ponds and sparkling, deliciously cold mountain brooks. This is a place to loll on luscious moss carpets, nap among purple lupine and magenta shooting stars, clamber up piles of volcanic boulders, watch bald eagles ride thermals, and walk where grizzlies and black bears walk.

A backpacker takes a rest break while exploring Kesugi Ridge in Denali State Park. Far to the west, 20,320-foot Denali rises above Alaska Range neighbors.

Hike Kesugi Ridge

Kesugi Ridge is the most popular hiking area in South Denali, with several different segments and loops to explore, depending on whether you're on a day hike or multiday camping expedition. Trail segments range from moderate to difficult. All mileages given are one way. For more details, see "South Denali Hiking Trails" earlier in this chapter.

Kesugi Ridge–Troublesome Creek Trail, 36.2 miles
Kesugi Ridge Trail: Little Coal Creek to Ermine Hill, 14.1 miles
Kesugi Ridge Trail: Little Coal Creek to Byers Lake, 28.9 miles
Ermine Hill Trail, 3.7 miles
Little Coal Creek Trail, 3.3 miles

Broad Pass and Cantwell (Mile 201.3 and Mile 209.9)

Thirty-two miles north of Denali State Park, the highway crosses the gentle summit of Broad Pass (2363 feet; 700 meters) in the midst of some of South Denali's most scenic terrain: enclosed by mountains, miles of gently rolling uplands are covered by tundra, taiga forest, and lens-shaped lakes. The crest of the pass is a major divide: it separates water flowing into the Susitna basin by way of the Chulitna River from water flowing into the Yukon River by way of the Nenana River. These large rivers in turn empty into Cook Inlet and the Bering Sea, respectively, their mouths separated by more than a thousand miles of coastline. Broad Pass is a cultural as well as a geographic divide: members of the Ahtna Athabascan tribe live to the north, while Dena'ina Athabascans dwell south of the pass. Caribou migrate back and forth across the pass on seasonal journeys, stopping now and then to feed on lichen and tundra greens. In fall, caribou share the tundra with human harvesters who come to pick blueberries. Bordering Broad Pass's upland basin to the west and northwest is a rugged wall of mountains belonging to the Alaska Range, while to the east and southeast are the Talkeetnas, with their own impressive collection of jagged spires and precipitous ridges.

North of Broad Pass is the town of Cantwell. Named after an army lieutenant who surveyed the area, Cantwell was established in the mid-1910s as a railroad construction camp and later became a flag stop for trains traveling between Anchorage and Fairbanks. Now home to 200 people, with several businesses that cater to travelers, the town is located at the intersection of the Parks and Denali highways. From 1957 to 1972, the Denali Highway provided the only road access into the region; connecting the Parks and Richardson highways, this still mostly unpaved roadway remains a scenic route popular with residents and visitors alike in summer and fall (see the Denali Highway sidebar).

The Alaska Range (Mile 215)

North of Cantwell, the Parks Highway enters the Alaska Range, which forms the mountainous wall separating Southcentral from Interior Alaska. Highway travelers are now less than 30 miles from Denali National Park's entrance area (mile 237.3). For much of this distance, the highway passes within a mile or two of Denali National Park's eastern boundary, which is defined by the Nenana River.

Highway travelers finish their passage through South Denali as they follow the Nenana River through the Alaska Range. Yet only since the completion of the Parks Highway in 1972 has such a road trip been possible. Before then, people rode the rails if they wanted the fastest, most direct route across the region.

RIDING THE ALASKA RAILROAD

For people who love the history and romance of railroads, there is no better way to travel through South Denali—or to reach the entrance to Denali National Park—than by train. The trip is longer than a straight drive by road, taking 7.5 hours to cover the 233 miles from Anchorage to the Denali National Park railroad depot (the trip between Fairbanks and the Denali depot is approximately 4 hours). However, the railroad trip offers a stronger connection to history, a similarly grand scenic trip, a deeper immersion in the pioneer Denali landscape that preceded modern roads, and a chance to just sit back and enjoy it, without having to worry about watching the road instead of the mountains.

It is difficult today to comprehend the importance of the first railroad in a region with no maintained overland transportation routes. Conceived as a way to access and transport coal, gold, and other minerals along the way, these tracks would be the first opportunity for the citizens of Fairbanks to ship goods overland to an ice-free, deepwater seaport. Previously, a rough track from Valdez along the route of today's Richardson Highway and summertime barges along the Yukon and Tanana rivers were the only means of moving goods in and out of the Interior. The railroad made such a huge improvement that even before completion, trains ran to the north and south construction termini and transferred passengers and goods to dog teams for travel through the remaining gap. The railroad spurred the development of many towns, including Talkeetna, Healy, and Anchorage, the latter founded as a construction camp. It also provided the first visitor access to the new Mount McKinley National Park, founded six years before the first tourists stepped off the train in 1923.

Construction of the railroad between 1915 and 1922 was an enormous engineering and logistical challenge. Crews worked from both the north and the south, so the section between Talkeetna and Healy was the last to be completed. This section encompassed the most rugged and isolated terrain, with the additional obstacle of the severe climate, which complicated the year-round construction project. An engineer on the project asserted that "the Pharaohs of Egypt, in building the pyramids, faced no greater difficulties and hardships" than the crews who completed the Alaska Railroad. When the Riley Creek trestle in Denali's main entrance area was finished in the spring of 1922 to make the railroad fully operational, the *New York Times* proclaimed it "the practical completion of one of the most difficult engineering projects undertaken by the United States Government."

Through train windows, passengers can see some of the challenges for themselves. The trestle over Hurricane Gulch at mile 284 (railroad mileposts begin at Seward; Anchorage is at mile 114 and Fairbanks is at mile 470) is by itself a marvel considering its isolation when under construction: 900 feet (275 meters) long with a drop of 384 feet (116 meters) to the creek bed below. Through the

A passenger train passes over the Riley Creek bridge in this undated photo. The Alaska Railroad has been bringing visitors to Denali National Park since 1923.

Nenana River canyon, the tracks cling to the sides of mountains and frequently cross deeply incised, treacherous-looking side streams. In fact, this stretch was truly treacherous in the early days, and tracks were torn down by washouts, avalanches, and landslides. Although the railroad became operational in 1922, construction continued for many years because of poor initial work that was easily sabotaged by the harsh natural elements of Alaska. However, those same natural elements make up the beauty and mystique that bring visitors onto the train today.

The railroad presents excellent views of Denali, although they are not as close or as frequent as those from the highway. If skies are clear, the mountain makes a strong appearance on either side of Talkeetna at miles 224 and 233, with some of the best views northwest of Chulitna Pass, around mile 274. The view is blocked in between, because the tracks pass behind Denali State Park's Curry and Kesugi ridges while crossing some of the most remote portions of the route, where rail

The Denali Highway

The 135-mile Denali Highway is a mostly gravel road that runs east from Cantwell to the town of Paxson on the Richardson Highway. Since completion of the George Parks Highway in 1972, the Denali Highway has been an off-the-beaten-path scenic route used by mountain bikers, anglers, hunters, campers, hikers, and sightseers. The Tangle Lakes–Delta River system attracts sport fishers and canoeists, while other ponds and lakes provide important nesting habitat for waterfowl and shorebirds.

Several spots along the road look north toward the Alaska Range's southern flanks. East of Denali National Park, this swath of mountainous terrain has several large glaciers and three peaks that rise above 12,000 feet (3660 meters). Travelers may see a variety of wildlife, including trumpeter swans, grizzlies, moose, fox, ptarmigan, and caribou.

Roadside facilities include Brushkana Creek and Tangle Lakes campgrounds and the Delta National Wild and Scenic River Wayside (with picnic area, campground, and boat launch), managed by the Bureau of Land Management. Lodges and inns are also scattered along the highway. Popular in both summer and fall (when fiery autumn colors lure sightseers), the Denali Highway is closed during the winter.

is the only access. Even today, homesteaders here are served by a "flag stop car," which they use to reach the road system. The dirt paths leading away from the tracks go to these homesteader cabins.

A more elaborate establishment was once found near mile 249, at a place named Curry. Now deserted, Curry started as a railroad construction camp, then became an overnight passenger stop in the 1920s, when train trips from Anchorage to Fairbanks took two days. A five-star hotel was built on the Susitna River's eastern bank, with a swimming pool and a three-hole golf course. Guests took a tram across the river and then hiked uphill to Curry Lookout, a hexagonal building atop Curry Ridge, for mountain views. Completion of the McKinley Park Hotel and faster train service doomed this resort hotel, which closed in 1939 and burned to the ground in 1957. Although Curry Lookout still stands (inside Denali State Park) and is designated a national historic landmark, getting there isn't as easy as it used to be because the passenger tram across the Susitna collapsed years ago. The easiest access now is from the Parks Highway, but it's a 6-mile uphill hike from Troublesome Creek, much of it through thick brush. (The hike will become considerably shorter and easier once the South Denali Visitor Center is completed.)

Many of the sights along the railroad route are similar to those along the highway. There is the same opportunity to spot large mammals, such as moose and black bear, to see salmon swimming up clearwater creeks, to watch swans floating slowly and gracefully across ponds and lakes, to look for faint signs of pioneering human habitation. But unlike traveling on the highway, there is a deep connection to the early history and spirit of Denali. When passengers pull up to the Denali National Park railroad depot and disembark to go to their campground or hotel, they are retracing the footsteps of the very first visitors who stepped off the train in 1923 to see the new Mount McKinley National Park.

Chapter 8

DENALI
IN WINTER

For most of the year, the Denali experience is defined by snow rather than mosquitoes, darkness rather than daylight, subzero cold rather than warm sunshine, mushing rather than wildlife viewing or hiking. Spanning more than seven months—from late September or early October into May—the subarctic winter is in most ways a more intimidating season to humans. But its possibilities and beauties are no less alluring: adventuresome dog sled travels, sparkling clear skies, luminous auroral displays, and vast expanses of white.

WINTER RESOURCES AND INFORMATION

Facilities and access are, not surprisingly, more limited in winter. But food and lodging can still be found in some Parks Highway corridor communities, and camping and recreational opportunities are possible in Denali National Park's entrance area.

Camping, Food, and Lodging

Vehicle-based camping is available only at Riley Creek Campground. No water is furnished in winter, but no campground fees are charged either; toilet facilities are available.

North of the Alaska Range, local hotel accommodations are available year-round in Healy, 12 miles north of the park entrance. For more information on Healy-area facilities, contact the Greater Healy–Denali Chamber of Commerce (907-683-4636; www.denalichamber.com). The nearest large grocery store is in Fairbanks, though Healy has a small convenience market. No rental equipment is available in the Denali area, though the park does lend visitors snowshoes for free.

Mountaineers approach the base of Mooses Tooth, a steep and jagged granite spire on the south side of the Alaska Range, accessible from the Ruth Glacier.

In the South Denali region, year-round lodging is available in both Talkeetna and Trapper Creek. In recent years there's been a steady growth in bed-
and-breakfasts. Both communities have small markets. Contact the Talkeetna
Chamber of Commerce for more information (907-733-2330; fax 907-733-2720;
www.talkeetnachamber.org; Box 334, Talkeetna, AK 99676).

Access and Trails

The Denali region has little developed access in winter. Denali National Park's
entrance area (mile 237.3 of the Parks Highway) is an access point for mushers,
skiers, snowshoers, and skijorers, as the park road remains open year-round to
at least park headquarters (mile 3.4). Using dog teams, Denali rangers annually establish an 85-mile winter route between headquarters and Wonder Lake,
although it is usually not complete until February. For those who don't own
their own kennels, local concessionaires provide guided dog sled trips.

Informal ski trails are also usually developed in the entrance area. A brochure showing entrance area trails is available at the Winter Visitor Center (the
Murie Science and Learning Center, mile 1.4) or on the Denali National Park
website, www.nps.gov/dena. The entire wilderness is open to quiet-sports winter use, although visitors planning overnight trips must still get a backcountry
permit and orientation (provided by a park ranger) at the Winter Visitor Center.
Recreational snowmobiling is possible on Denali's south side, and in preserve
and "new" park areas north of the Alaska Range. Winter visitors should contact
park staff for general information and current trail conditions.

Note that the park does collect entrance fees in winter, payable at the Winter Visitor Center. Information on entrance fees is summarized in Chapter 14,
"Exploring the National Park Entrance."

Winter visitors should contact park staff for general information and current
trail conditions, by calling 907-683-2294 or 907-683-9532. They may also email
the park at denali_info@nps.gov.

Winter Gear Essentials

Winter's harsh conditions require extra preparation. Below are recommended winter clothing and other gear.

Clothing

❑ Wind gear
❑ Cold-weather parka
❑ Wool/fleece pants and jacket
❑ Wool/fleece or other synthetic shirt (consider multiple layers)
❑ Wool/fleece hat
❑ Balaclava or other face mask
❑ Wool/fleece mittens and gloves
❑ Long johns
❑ Wool/synthetic socks (plus extras)
❑ Cold-weather boots, with extra liners if boot insulation is not waterproof
❑ Gaiters

Trail Items

❑ Ski gear, snowshoes, or other travel gear
❑ Pack with water-resistant cover
❑ Map and compass
❑ Pocketknife
❑ Headlamp (with extra batteries and bulb)
❑ Water bottles
❑ Chemical handwarmers
❑ Sunscreen and sunglasses
❑ Toilet paper and spade

Emergency Essentials

❑ Lighter, matches, other fire starter
❑ First-aid kit
❑ Repair kit
❑ Extra food, clothing
❑ Avalanche beacon and shovel if traveling in hilly or mountainous terrain
❑ Optional are GPS and satellite phone

Camping

❑ Four-season tent
❑ Winter sleeping bag
❑ Sleeping pad
❑ Sitting pad
❑ Drinking cup
❑ Cooking gear/utensils
❑ Stove and fuel
❑ Candle lantern
❑ Personal-care items

Winter Weather at Denali

Snow depth and temperature are for Denali National Park headquarters, at mile 3.4 of the park road; daylight hours are for the Denali Visitor Center, mile 1.5.

SNOW DEPTH		
MONTH	AVERAGE	EXTREME
October	3 in. (8 cm)	34 in. (86 cm)
November	7 in. (19 cm)	48 in. (122 cm)
December	12 in. (31 cm)	55 in. (140 cm)
January	16 in. (41 cm)	51 in. (130 cm)
February	19 in. (49 cm)	51 in. (130 cm)
March	20 in. (51 cm)	56 in. (142 cm)
April	16 in. (42 cm)	51 in. (130 cm)

TEMPERATURE							
	AVERAGE				EXTREME		
MONTH	HIGH		LOW		HIGH		LOW	
	°F	°C	°F	°C	°F	°C	°F	°C
October	33	1	15	−10	69	20	−24	−31
November	18	−8	1	−17	56	13	−37	−38
December	12	−11	−5	−20	48	9	−52	−47
January	11	−12	−6	−21	51	11	−51	−46
February	17	−8	−3	−19	52	12	−54	−48
March	25	−4	1	−17	56	13	−47	−44
April	39	4	16	−9	67	19	−25	−32

HOURS OF DAYLIGHT			
DATE	SUNRISE	SUNSET	DAYLIGHT HOURS
October 21	9:03 AM	6:18 PM	9 hours, 15 minutes
November 21	9:39 AM	3:44 PM	6 hours, 5 minutes
December 21	10:43 AM	3:04 PM	4 hours, 21 minutes
January 21	10:06 AM	4:07 PM	6 hours, 1 minute
February 21	8:33 AM	5:46 PM	9 hours, 13 minutes
March 21	7:53 AM	8:13 PM	12 hours, 20 minutes
April 21	6:04 AM	9:44 PM	15 hours, 40 minutes

THE DENALI WINTER EXPERIENCE

Winter's arrival in the Denali region is signaled by subfreezing temperatures (see weather tables), snowfall, avian and human migrations, and the shutdown of most facilities. In the national park, buses stop running, campgrounds close (except for Riley Creek), businesses outside the park entrance are boarded up, and visitors and seasonal workers head south. The park road stays open to the Teklanika rest stop (mile 30.2) until closed by snow—usually in late September. After the first heavy snows, the road is plowed only to park headquarters (mile 3.4), which is open year-round. Winter reaches Denali's south side one to two weeks later; state campgrounds and other park facilities along the Parks Highway normally shut down by mid-October (though the Alaska Veterans Memorial just beyond milepost 147 remains open and serves as a parking area for visitors who reserve the Byers Lake public-use cabins, which can be used year-round).

Although in early October Denali National Park's entrance area has the feel of a ghost town, there's actually lots going on: Chattering red squirrels stockpile scores of spruce cones while flocks of boreal chickadees devour seeds within the forest canopy. Moose browse on bushes along the park road, and at partly frozen Horseshoe Lake beavers busily cut and cache willows while there's still open water.

Getting Around in Winter

One continuing center of human activity is the Denali National Park sled-dog kennels (see Chapter 4), where rangers and sled dogs prepare for winter expeditions. Kennels staff take dogs on training runs as soon as there's enough snow. By December they are ready for overnight patrols. Driving seven or eight dogs, mushers often take the main winter trail, an 85-mile route that roughly parallels the park road from headquarters to Wonder Lake. Historically, rangers used dog teams to patrol for poachers, back in the 1920s when illegal hunting was rampant.

Winterfest

To celebrate the winter season, since 2001 residents of the Denali region have organized a party they call the Winterfest, with events both within the park and in neighboring communities. Festivities include a community potluck (visitors are welcome) and square dance, snow-sculpting contest, nature scavenger hunt, indoor board games, children's craft activities, Alaskan storytelling, dog sled rides, ranger-led snowshoe hikes, chili feed, and 5K family run/ski/walk/bike/skijor/snowshoe event, among other things. Information about Winterfest can be found at www.nps.gov/dena /planyourvisit/winterfest.htm.

Today the patrols assist winter park visitors, monitor backcountry conditions, and ensure that park rules are respected. By winter's end, the dog teams may have traveled close to 3000 miles (4800 kilometers). Only one thing besides insufficient snow stops the sled-dog patrols: extreme cold. When temperatures drop below –40°F (–40°C), mushers stay indoors.

Park patrollers aren't the only ones mushing into Denali's wilderness. Until recent decades, when snowmobile use increased dramatically, dog teams were the primary form of winter transportation in most of Alaska, including the Denali region. Even in today's mechanized world, recreational mushers find their sport a rewarding way to explore Alaska's wildlands. Many Alaska residents own dog kennels, and some regularly run teams into the backcountry of Denali state and national parks.

Mushers—as well as skiers, skijorers (skiers pulled by sled dogs), and snowshoers—find Denali National Park a particularly appealing destination because its wilderness core north of the Alaska Range remains one of the few places in Alaska still closed to snowmobile use. In the quiet of Denali's backcountry, the only human-related sounds likely to be heard are the occasional barking of dogs and the scraping of sled runners or skis across the snow.

Winter Days and Nights

In deepest winter—the two or three weeks before and after solstice—much of the entrance area, including park headquarters, receives no direct sunlight; the gentle ridge to the south is high enough to block the sun as it carves a brief, shallow arc through the subarctic sky. Still, the sky is often crystal clear—so clear, in fact, that skiers and mushers can travel by the light of the full moon, with snow crystals sparkling in the soft lunar glow.

On moonless nights, Denali holds other attractions. The ink-black sky grows vibrantly alive with uncountable numbers of sparkling stars and the shimmering light of the aurora borealis (see sidebar).

By mid-February the harshest part of winter has passed, though another three months remain until green-up. Lengthening days and warming temperatures draw mushers, snowmobilers, and skiers to the Peters Hills and the Tokositna River Valley, heavily used recreation areas in Denali State Park. The Alaska Range's southern side is generally much wetter than the northern foothills, but at this time of year the air is often crystal clear and cold, and the sun floats in a cerulean sky, bathing the frozen landscape in a golden glow that's deceptively warm: temperatures are likely to drop below 0°F (–18°C) when darkness returns.

Even now, few animals are likely to be seen, but tracks are bountiful in forested hills and open valleys: moose, river otter, ptarmigan, red squirrel, hare, lynx, marten. Other tracks have been left by snowmobiles; they crisscross the lowlands and lower hillsides, signs of the area's ever-increasing popularity.

The Northern Lights

Denali isn't widely known for its beautiful night skies—simply because most people visit in summer, when the sky never fully darkens. But residents know that for eight months of every year, one of the region's greatest spectacles is to be found overhead: the aurora borealis, or northern lights.

A pale, luminous band arching across the heavens, the aurora wavers slowly, almost imperceptibly, sometimes for minutes, sometimes for hours, before fading from sight. Or it may suddenly explode into bright curtains of green light rippling wildly over the hills and peaks of the Alaska Range. Growing ever more intense, now tinged with red or purple, the lights shimmer, flicker, pulsate, undulate. At times they are the flickering embers of a heavenly fire. Other times they are like leaping flames, exploding fireworks, or shimmering waves that appear at the horizon and move upward across an oceanic sky.

Scientists have determined that these auroral apparitions are atmospheric phenomena, produced when streams of charged particles from the sun, known as solar winds, intersect the Earth's magnetic field. Although most solar particles are deflected, some filter into the planet's upper atmosphere and collide with molecules of gases such as nitrogen and oxygen. The resulting reactions produce glowing colors. The aurora most commonly is pale green, but at times its borders are tinged with pink, purple, or red. Especially rare is the all-red aurora, formed when charged solar particles collide with high-altitude oxygen. The science may be complex, but the results are pure beauty, especially when viewed in the Denali wilderness.

The main ingredients for prime auroral viewing are a clear and dark night sky and a high level of solar activity. In Denali's perpetual midsummer light, the sky is too bright to observe the northern lights. By late August, the night sky becomes dark enough to sometimes see these luminous lights. But winter, with its long hours of darkness, presents the best opportunities. Even then, the aurora is not visible every night, nor is it visible throughout the night, because the solar activity that produces the northern lights occurs sporadically. Only in recent years have scientists been able to predict, with increasing accuracy, when auroral displays will be visible and their strength. Those who'd like more information on the aurora borealis, as well as aurora forecasts, can visit the University of Alaska Fairbanks Geophysical Institute's aurora information website: www.gi.alaska.edu/AuroraForecast.

When the machines leave, there is only natural quiet, broken by the rush of wind, the squawk of a raven, the *sic-sic-sic* of a squirrel, the chirping of redpolls. As daylight fades, the surrounding mountain landscape takes on a surreal appearance. Nearby are the Tokositna Glacier and Valley, the Dutch Hills and Tokosha Mountains, all suffused in shades of rose and pink. Beyond them, the high-mountain family of Denali, Sultana, and Begguya stretch upward into deep blueness. This, too, is one of the joys the winter season brings: more opportunities to savor The High One rising from wild surroundings.

Winter Recreation

Almost no one goes very far into the park in the dead of winter. Winter recreation demands an entirely different frame of mind: it's a mental as well as physical adventure. Depending on the weather, there may be no dependable trail, and backcountry travelers can get stopped for days by storms. More than ever, visitors are confronted with the idea of being on their own, and the need to be self-reliant. Those who get into trouble will likely have to rescue themselves.

The few who do venture into Denali's backcountry find a transformed landscape: water in its many forms is now the dominant feature as ice, river overflow, and almost limitless varieties of snow. Although it's easy to imagine this winter landscape as one that's frozen in time, it is constantly shifting shape as water becomes snow becomes ice becomes water again, on and on. It's also a world in which temperatures may drop to –40°F (–40°C) or colder for days at a time, a world that daily receives 6 hours or less of sunlight between late November and late January. Curiously, some areas are easier to explore in winter than in summer, as snow-buried brush and frozen rivers increase access to places otherwise difficult to reach.

Winter travel conditions vary enormously. Soft, wet snow can slow dog teams and skiers to a crawl. At other times strong, persistent winds harden deep snowpack and sweep frozen rivers clean, making it possible to mush, ski, or snowshoe just about anywhere.

Winter trips deep into the wilderness require considerable commitment, preparation, and expertise (and a backcountry permit, available from the Murie Science and Learning Center, which serves as the park's Winter Visitor Center, mile 1.4 of the park road). But visitors don't have to go far into the backcountry to experience the trials—and glories—of winter travel. Several places provide access to Denali's perimeter parklands: Petersville Road and Cantwell on Denali's south side and the Stampede Trail near Healy on the north side are entryways used by mushers, skiers, and snowmobilers. But the prime access spot for those who wish to escape motorized traffic is Denali National Park's entrance area. Here there's a campground, a small, informal system of ski and snowshoe

Few people venture deep into Denali's backcountry during the long winter season; those who do must be prepared for extreme conditions.

trails, park staff to answer questions, and best of all, miles and miles of wild country to explore in silence.

Because few winter trails are maintained within the entrance area, many visitors chart their own course. Even the established ski and snowshoe trails can provide a challenge, because route selection is often based on the trailbreaker's experience level, without regard for those who might follow. Unplanned routes may lead to unwanted encounters with trees at the bottoms of steep drops—or to steep, difficult ascents on soft, "punchy" snow or slick ice. High winds or heavy snowfall may quickly erase trails, so winter travelers need to pay attention to where they're going, and where they've come from.

Denali's wilderness seems to press more closely against the entrance area in winter. It doesn't take long to reach places that are perfectly quiet and still, where visitors can feel completely detached from their usually busy lives. On day trips from park headquarters, it's possible to explore the Outer Range foothills above tree line; descend into the beautiful valleys of Hines, Rock, and Riley creeks; or ski leisurely along the sled-dog patrol trail or the snow-covered park road. Moose, wolves, foxes, hares, and other wildlife sometimes use these packed trails, but skiers and mushers are more likely to see their tracks than the animals themselves. They may also hear the howls of wolves and the answering yips and howls of the park's sled dogs—Denali's winter song.

WINTER WILDLIFE

At first glance, Denali's midwinter landscape seems empty of wildlife. Gone are many of the park's most visible animals: grizzlies and ground squirrels, marmots and beavers, golden eagles and gulls. Most of Denali's birds have migrated to warmer climes. Bears and some rodents wait out the cold in hibernation, insulated in dens and holes beneath the snow. Many of Denali's animals, however, remain active throughout the long and challenging winter, eking out a living with the help of special adaptations to the cold and snow.

A dominant presence in summer, grizzly bears enter dens in September and October and remain there until April or May. Pregnant females are the first to den and, in the company of their newborn cubs, the last to leave their shelters in spring; adult males den last and emerge first. Often, the time of den building is tied to the first heavy snowfalls of autumn or winter: Denali grizzlies have excavated dens as early as August, in response to 6-inch snowfalls. Built to size for the most efficient use of body heat, occasionally with nests of grass, willow, or other vegetation, dens are usually dug into the tundra on moderate to steep slopes. Some border riverbeds, in cut banks, while others are high in the mountains.

Grizzlies don't need to defecate, urinate, eat, or drink during their months-long dormancy, and their body temperature and metabolic rate drop only

The white coats of Dall sheep provide excellent camouflage in winter. Here, a ewe hunts for food after an early winter snowfall.

slightly. By winter's end, grizzlies lose 25 to 50 percent of their body fat, but for healthy bears, the loss is all, or nearly all, fat. Most extraordinary is the fact that pregnant bears give birth during this cycle of extended fasting, then nurse their cubs for several months while still in hibernation.

The hibernation mechanisms of rodents are vastly different from those of bears. Arctic ground squirrels, for example, enter a death-like torpor in which body temperature drops to near freezing (or even below) and bodily functions slow dramatically. Periodically throughout the winter, the ground squirrel rouses itself, bringing body temperature and heart rate back to normal. Exactly why this happens isn't clear. One reason, apparently, is to eliminate body wastes.

Marmots too go into a deep dormancy that is periodically broken. Beavers, though hidden, remain active through the winter inside mud-smeared "winterized" lodges, surviving on willows harvested in fall and now safely stored beneath pond ice.

While the absence of bears, ground squirrels, and other animals is striking, this apparent dearth of wildlife is deceiving. Closer inspection reveals an
abundance of animal tracks: ptarmigan, moose, caribou, wolverines, foxes,
hares, wolves, lynx, and many smaller mammals all leave their signs in the
snow. Voles, lemmings, and shrews inhabit a world of tunnels and chambers
beneath the snow, while ptarmigan, snowshoe hares, and weasels put on a
winter camouflage of white that protects them from larger predators.

Another species blending well with winter's white is the Dall sheep. Like
many northern animals, the sheep's coat thickens in winter. The fleece, 2 to 3
inches deep, with coarse, hollow hairs that help to trap warmth, is ideally suited
for extreme cold and high winds and enables sheep to survive on the high,
windswept ridges where low-growing tundra plants stay exposed.

Denali's wildlife has adapted to winter in numerous other ways as well. The
long back feet of the snowshoe hare work like snowshoes—hence the name—by
spreading the animal's weight and increasing its mobility on snow. Lynx, which
dine almost exclusively on hares in winter, have a similar adaptation; their out-
sized feet (3.5 to 4 inches wide and 4 inches long) and lightweight bodies help
keep these northern cats from sinking deeply into the snow, and long legs provide extra power to chase prey through the snowpack. The large hooves of caribou also act something like snowshoes and are used as shovels when the caribou
dig through snow for food.

Among birds, ptarmigan grow dense feathers on the tops and bottoms of
their feet, which then function as snowshoes. Their claws also grow longer,
for a better grip on ice or crusted snow. Chickadees enter a kind of regulated
hypothermia to survive the 19–20-hour midwinter nights, dropping their body
temperature 10° to 12°F (5° to 6°C) below normal. They also shiver to increase
warmth, and have dense plumage. Another seed-eating songbird to inhabit
Denali in winter is the redpoll, a sparrow-like finch easily identified by the red
splotch on its head and a small black neck bib. Among the tiniest of Alaska's
birds, redpolls are also among the hardiest. Like chickadees, they have dense
winter plumage. They also have the ability to store seeds in a pocket-like pouch
within their esophagus. Settled in a sheltered perch for the night, they eat and
digest surplus seeds gradually. Ravens, too, are wonderfully adapted to northern winters. Solid black feathers absorb whatever solar heat is available, and
thick, overlapping outer feathers make ravens virtually windproof while an
insulating layer of down holds the heat in.

Several birds—ravens, chickadees, gray jays, and magpies among them—
cache food to survive the winter months. (Many mammals do this, too—for
instance, red squirrels, beavers, pikas, wolverines, and foxes.) But the large
majority of birds escape winter's hardships by heading south. Of the 166 species
identified at Denali, only about two dozen regularly stay the winter.

A cow moose and her calf cross the Park Road in Denali's entrance area follow-ing a September snowfall that hints at the long winter to come.

ESSENTIAL DENALI

On the surface, the winter landscape of Denali appears very different from that of summer because of the absence of migratory birds and hibernating wildlife, the submersion of the tundra's green beneath a layer of white, the replacement of endless daylight with long darkness. But winter is the dominant season, and it provides deep insights into the essence of Denali—into what makes the Denali region unique and worth protecting for future generations.

There are the animals—moose, caribou, sheep, bear, wolves, and others—which in winter demonstrate why they and not others are perfectly adapted to inhabit this northern region. There is the intact natural ecosystem, the intimate workings of which can easily be discerned in the snow, where the tracks of a snowshoe hare are topped by those of a lynx, or where the prints of many wolves radiate from the carcass of a dead moose. There are the mushers with their dog teams, who reenact the journeys of Denali's earliest rangers and Alaska's earliest inhabitants and so preserve an authentic connection with the past. There is the wilderness, which in winter challenges people to be even more self-reliant and self-sufficient than in summer, but which offers even greater rewards of solitude, inspiration, and peace.

Finally, there is The Mountain, which is seen more often in winter than in summer, but is otherwise unchanging, providing a sense of stability and strength to the land. The Mountain reminds us that the essence of Denali does not change with the seasons, only its manifestations. Whatever the season, Denali is truly unique in the experience it offers the traveler, and in the importance of what it protects for the world.

A rock ptarmigan still cloaked in winter's white
moves among remnant snow patches high on
Primrose Ridge in early spring.

APPENDIX A:

DENALI WILDLIFE AND PLANT CHECKLISTS

The checklists below have been compiled and provided by park staff.

MAMMALS OF DENALI

The following is a list of the thirty-nine mammals known to inhabit Denali National Park and Preserve. Some, like the Dall sheep and arctic ground squirrel, are easily visible from Denali Park Road. Others, like the little brown bat, pygmy shrew, and singing vole, are seldom, if ever, observed by the casual visitor, but all have their roles to play in Denali's subarctic ecosystem.

Bat
☐ Little brown bat   (*Myotis lucifugus*)

Carnivores
☐ Black bear   (*Ursus americanus*)
☐ Grizzly bear   (*Ursus arctos*)
☐ Coyote   (*Canis latrans*)
☐ Red fox   (*Vulpes vulpes*)
☐ Lynx   (*Lynx canadensis*)
☐ American marten   (*Martes americana*)
☐ American mink   (*Mustela vison*)
☐ Northern river otter   (*Lontra canadensis*)
☐ Least weasel   (*Mustela nivalis*)
☐ Short-tailed weasel (ermine)   (*Mustela erminea*)
☐ Wolf   (*Canis lupus*)
☐ Wolverine   (*Gulo gulo*)

Hooved Mammals/Ungulates
❐ Caribou   (*Rangifer tarandus*)
❐ Dall sheep   (*Ovis dalli*)
❐ Moose   (*Alces alces gigas*)

Insectivores
❐ Cinereus shrew   (*Sorex cinereus*)
❐ Montane shrew   (*Sorex monticolus*)
❐ Pygmy shrew   (*Sorex hoyi*)
❐ Tiny shrew   (*Sorex yukonicus*)
❐ Tundra shrew   (*Sorex tundrensis*)
❐ Water shrew   (*Sorex palustris*)

Pika, Hare
❐ Collared pika   (*Ochotona collaris*)
❐ Snowshoe hare   (*Lepus americanus*)

Rodents
❐ Arctic ground squirrel   (*Spermophilus parryii*)
❐ American beaver   (*Castor canadensis*)
❐ Brown lemming   (*Lemmus trimucronatus*)
❐ Northern bog lemming   (*Synaptomys borealis*)
❐ Hoary marmot   (*Marmota caligata*)
❐ Meadow jumping mouse   (*Zapus hudsonius*)
❐ Muskrat   (*Ondatra zibethicus*)
❐ North American porcupine   (*Erethizon dorsatum*)
❐ Northern flying squirrel   (*Glaucomys sabrinus*)
❐ Red squirrel   (*Tamiasciurus hudsonicus*)
❐ Meadow vole   (*Microtus pennsylvanicus*)
❐ Northern red-backed vole   (*Clethrionomys rutilus*)
❐ Singing vole   (*Microtus miurus*)
❐ Taiga vole   (*Microtus xanthognathus*)
❐ Tundra vole   (*Microtus oeconomus*)

BIRDS OF DENALI

The following birdwatching checklist includes the relative seasonal abundance and habitat requirements of more than 160 bird species identified at Denali National Park. Because of the cyclical occurrence of some species, their abundance may vary from year to year. The names and sequence follow the American Ornithologists' Union *Checklist of North American Birds*, Seventh Edition. Keys to using the checklists are below.

KEYS TO THE BIRDING CHECKLISTS		
ABUNDANCE		
A	Abundant	Species observed repeatedly in expected habitats
C	Common	Species observed frequently in expected habitats
FC	Fairly Common	Species occurs regularly in most expected habitats
U	Uncommon	Species occurs regularly, but is observed infrequently even in most expected habitats
R	Rare	Species occurs regularly but in small numbers
O	Occasional	Species has been recorded no more than a few times and is beyond the periphery of normal annual range
X	Accidental	Species has been recorded only a time or two; it is so far beyond its normal annual range that further observations are considered unlikely
n/a	No applicable information	
HABITAT		
At	Alpine tundra	
Lp	Lakes and ponds	
Lpw	Lake, ponds & wetlands	
Mt	Moist tundra	
R	Rivers & streams	
Rb	River bars	
Rc	Riparian corridors	
Rr	Rocky ridges	
S	Shrubs	
Tf	Taiga forest	
W	Wetlands	
SEASONAL AND BREEDING STATUS		
Sp	Spring	Spring migration period occurring from late March through early June
Su	Summer	Mid-June through July
B	Breeding	Early April to mid-June
F	Fall	Fall migration, occurring from late July through mid-October
W	Winter	Late October through March

MIGRATION STATUS CODE	
Resident	Overwinters regularly in area
Occasional Resident	Some members of the species may overwinter in years of very high food supplies
Young Disperse	Adults are resident, but young usually move out of the general area
Complete Migrant	Virtually all members of the species leaving the breeding range and Alaska during non-breeding season
Partial Migrant	Seasonal movements away from a breeding range by some, but not all, members of a species with overlap between breeding and non-breeding ranges
Irruptive Migrant	Irruptions may occur in one year but not again for many years; distances and numbers of individuals involved are less predictable than for partial or complete migrants

	SPRING	SUMMER	BREEDING	FALL	WINTER	HABITAT	MIGRATION STATUS
LOONS							
Red-throated loon (*Gavia stellata*)	U	U	R	U	n/a	Lp	Complete Migrant
Pacific loon (*Gavia pacifica*)	R	R	R	R	n/a	Lp	Complete Migrant
Common loon (*Gavia immer*)	U	U	U	U	n/a	Lp	Complete Migrant
Yellow-billed loon (*Gavia adamsii*)	X	n/a	n/a	X	n/a	Lp	Complete Migrant
GREBES							
Horned grebe (*Podiceps auritus*)	FC	FC	FC	FC	n/a	Lp	Complete Migrant
Red-necked grebe (*Podiceps grisegena*)	U	U	U	U	n/a	Lp	Complete Migrant
WATERFOWL							
Greater white-fronted goose (*Anser albifrons*)	U	U	R	FC	n/a	Lpw	Complete Migrant
Snow goose (*Chen caerulescens*)	R	R	n/a	U	n/a	Lpw	Complete Migrant
Canada goose (*Branta canadensis*)	R	R	n/a	R	n/a	Lpw	Complete Migrant
Brant (*Branta bernicla*)	X	n/a	n/a	n/a	n/a	Lpw	Complete Migrant
Trumpeter swan (*Cygnus buccinator*)	C	C	C	C	n/a	Lpw	Complete Migrant
Tundra swan (*Cygnus columbianus*)	U	U	n/a	U	n/a	Lpw	Complete Migrant
Gadwall (*Anas strepera*)	O	n/a	n/a	n/a	n/a	Lpw	Complete Migrant
Eurasian wigeon (*Anas penelope*)	O	n/a	n/a	n/a	n/a	Lpw	Complete Migrant
American wigeon (*Anas americana*)	C	C	C	C	n/a	Lpw	Complete Migrant
Mallard (*Anas platyrhynchos*)	FC	FC	U	FC	n/a	Lpw	Complete Migrant
Blue-winged teal (*Anas discors*)	R	R	n/a	R	n/a	Lpw	Complete Migrant
Northern shoveler (*Anas clypeata*)	FC	U	U	U	n/a	Lpw	Complete Migrant
Northern pintail (*Anas acuta*)	C	C	C	C	n/a	Lpw	Complete Migrant
Green-winged teal (*Anas crecca*)	C	C	C	C	n/a	Lpw	Complete Migrant
Canvasback (*Aythya valisineria*)	R	R	n/a	R	n/a	Lpw	Complete Migrant
Redhead (*Aythya americana*)	R	R	n/a	R	n/a	Lpw	Complete Migrant
Ring-necked duck (*Aythya collaris*)	U	R	n/a	U	n/a	Lpw	Complete Migrant
Greater scaup (*Aythya marila*)	FC	FC	FC	FC	n/a	Lpw	Complete Migrant
Lesser scaup (*Aythya affinis*)	C	C	C	C	n/a	Lpw	Complete Migrant
Harlequin duck (*Histrionicus histrionicus*)	FC	FC	FC	U	n/a	R	Complete Migrant
Surf scoter (*Melanitta perspicillata*)	FC	FC	U	FC	n/a	Lpw	Complete Migrant
White-winged scoter (*Melanitta fusca*)	FC	FC	U	FC	n/a	Lpw	Complete Migrant
Black scoter (*Melanitta nigra*)	U	U	R	U	n/a	Lpw	Complete Migrant
Oldsquaw (*Clangula hyemlais*)	U	U	U	U	n/a	Lpw	Complete Migrant
Bufflehead (*Bucephala albeola*)	FC	FC	FC	FC	n/a	Lpw	Complete Migrant

	SPRING	SUMMER	BREEDING	FALL	WINTER	HABITAT	MIGRATION STATUS
WATERFOWL (CONTINUED)							
Common goldeneye (*Bucephala clangula*)	U	R	n/a	U	n/a	Lpw	Complete Migrant
Barrow's goldeneye (*Bucephala islandica*)	C	C	U	C	n/a	Lpw	Complete Migrant
Red-breasted merganser (*Mergus serrator*)	U	U	U	U	n/a	Lpw, R	Complete Migrant
Common merganser (*Mergus merganser*)	R	R	n/a	R	n/a	Lpw	Complete Migrant
EAGLES, HAWKS, AND FALCONS							
Osprey (*Pandion haliaetus*)	O	n/a	U	O	n/a	Lp, R	Complete Migrant
Bald eagle (*Haliaeetus leucocephalus*)	U	U	U	U	O	Lp, R	Partial Migrant
Northern harrier (*Circus cyaneus*)	C	C	C	C	n/a	At, Mt	Complete Migrant
Sharp-shinned hawk (*Accipiter striatus*)	U	U	U	U	n/a	Tf	Complete Migrant
Northern goshawk (*Accipiter gentilis*)	U	U	U	U	R	Tf	Resident, Irruptive Migrant
Swainson's hawk (*Buteo swainsoni*)	O	O	n/a	O	n/a	n/a	Complete Migrant
Red-tailed hawk (*Buteo jamaicensis*)	U	R	R	U	n/a	Tf	Complete Migrant
Rough-legged hawk (*Buteo lagopus*)	R	R	n/a	U	n/a	At, Rr	Complete Migrant
Golden eagle (*Aquila chrysaetos*)	C	C	C	C	R	At, Rr	Complete Migrant, Occasional Resident
American kestrel (*Falco sparverius*)	FC	FC	FC	FC	n/a	Tf	Complete Migrant
Merlin (*Falco columbarius*)	FC	FC	FC	FC	n/a	Tf	Complete Migrant
Peregrine falcon (*Falco peregrinus*)	O	O	R	O	n/a	Rr, Rc	Complete Migrant
Gyrfalcon (*Falco rusticolus*)	U	U	U	U	R	At, Rr	Resident, young disperse
GROUSE, PTARMIGAN							
Ruffed grouse (*Bonasa umbellus*)	R	R	R	R	R	Tf	Resident
Spruce grouse (*Falcipennis canadensis*)	FC	FC	FC	FC	FC	Tf	Resident
Willow ptarmigan (*Lagopus lagopus*)	A	A	A	A	A	S, Mt	Resident
Rock ptarmigan (*Lagopus mutus*)	FC	FC	FC	FC	FC	At	Resident
White-tailed ptarmigan (*Lagopus leucurus*)	U	U	U	U	U	At, Rr	Resident
CRANES							
Sandhill crane (*Grus canadensis*)	U	U	U	C	n/a	W	Complete Migrant

	SPRING	SUMMER	BREEDING	FALL	WINTER	HABITAT	MIGRATION STATUS
PLOVERS							
Black-bellied plover (*Pluvialis squatarola*)	O	O	n/a	n/a	n/a	Lp	Complete Migrant
American golden-plover (*Pluvialus dominica*)	U	U	U	U	n/a	At	Complete Migrant
Semipalmated plover (*Charadrius semipalmatus*)	FC	FC	FC	FC	n/a	Rb	Complete Migrant
Killdeer (*Charadrius vociferus*)	O	n/a	n/a	n/a	n/a	n/a	Complete Migrant
SANDPIPERS							
Greater yellowlegs (*Tringa melanoleuca*)	U	R	R	R	n/a	Lpw	Complete Migrant
Lesser yellowlegs (*Tringa flavipes*)	C	C	C	C	n/a	Lpw	Complete Migrant
Solitary sandpiper (*Tringa solitara*)	U	U	U	U	n/a	Lp, R	Complete Migrant
Wandering tattler (*Heteroscelus incanus*)	U	U	U	U	n/a	Rb, R	Complete Migrant
Spotted sandpiper (*Actitis macularia*)	FC	U	U	FC	n/a	R, Lpw	Complete Migrant
Upland sandpiper (*Bartramia longicauda*)	U	U	U	U	n/a	At	Complete Migrant
Whimbrel (*Numenius phaeopus*)	U	U	U	U	n/a	Mt	Complete Migrant
Hudsonian godwit (*Limosa haemastica*)	X	n/a	n/a	n/a	n/a	Lp	Complete Migrant
Ruddy turnstone (*Arenaria interpres*)	X	n/a	n/a	n/a	n/a	n/a	Complete Migrant
Black turnstone (*Arenaria melanocephala*)	n/a	X	n/a	n/a	n/a	n/a	Complete Migrant
Surfbird (*Aphriza virgata*)	U	U	U	U	n/a	At	Complete Migrant
Sanderling (*Calidris alba*)	n/a	n/a	n/a	X	n/a	Lp	Complete Migrant
Semipalmated sandpiper (*Calidris pusilla*)	U	R	n/a	R	n/a	W	Complete Migrant
Western sandpiper (*Calidris mauri*)	R	O	n/a	O	n/a	W	Complete Migrant
Least sandpiper (*Calidris minutilla*)	C	C	FC	C	n/a	Mt, At	Complete Migrant
Baird's sandpiper (*Calidris bairdii*)	U	U	U	U	n/a	At	Complete Migrant
Pectoral sandpiper (*Calidris melantos*)	U	R	n/a	R	n/a	Lpw	Complete Migrant
Dunlin (*Calidris alpina*)	R	O	n/a	n/a	n/a	Lpw	Complete Migrant
Long-billed dowitcher (*Limnodromus scolopaceus*)	U	U	R	U	n/a	Lpw	Complete Migrant
Common snipe (*Gallinago gallinago*)	C	C	C	C	n/a	Lpw	Complete Migrant
Red-necked phalarope (*Phalaropus lobatus*)	C	FC	U	FC	n/a	Lp	Complete Migrant
Red phalarope (*Phalaropus fulicaria*)	X	X	n/a	n/a	n/a	Lp	Complete Migrant

	SPRING	SUMMER	BREEDING	FALL	WINTER	HABITAT	MIGRATION STATUS
JAEGERS, GULLS, TERNS							
Pomarine jaeger (*Stercorarius pomarinus*)	n/a	X	n/a	n/a	n/a	n/a	Complete Migrant
Long-tailed jaeger (*Stercorarius longicaudus*)	FC	FC	FC	FC	n/a	At	Complete Migrant
Bonaparte's gull (*Larus philadelphia*)	FC	U	U	U	n/a	Lpw	Complete Migrant
Mew gull (*Larus canus*)	A	A	A	A	n/a	Rb, Lpw	Complete Migrant
Herring gull (*Lanus argentatus*)	R	R	n/a	R	n/a	Rb, Lpw	Complete Migrant
Glaucous-winged gull (*Larus glaucescens*)	R	R	n/a	R	n/a	Rb, Lpw	Complete Migrant
Arctic tern (*Sterna paradisaea*)	FC	U	U	U	n/a	Lp	Complete Migrant
MURRELETS							
Long-billed murrelet (*Brachyramphus perdix*)	n/a	n/a	n/a	X	n/a	n/a	Complete Migrant
OWLS							
Great-horned owl (*Bubo virginianus*)	FC	FC	FC	FC	FC	Tf	Resident
Snowy owl (*Nyctea scandiaca*)	O	n/a	n/a	O	O	Mt	Partial Migrant
Northern hawk owl (*Surnia ulula*)	U	U	U	U	U	Tf	Irruptive Migrant
Great gray owl (*Strix nebulosa*)	O	O	O	O	O	Tf	Irruptive Migrant
Short-eared owl (*Asui flammeus*)	U	U	U	U	n/a	Mt, At	Complete Migrant
Boreal owl (*Aegolius funereus*)	U	U	U	U	U	Tf	Resident
HUMMINGBIRDS							
Rufous hummingbird (*Selasphorus rufus*)	n/a	X	n/a	n/a	n/a	n/a	Complete Migrant
KINGFISHERS							
Belted kingfisher (*Ceryle alcyon*)	U	U	U	U	n/a	Rc, Lp	Complete Migrant
WOODPECKERS							
Downy woodpecker (*Picoides pubescens*)	R	R	R	R	R	Tf	Resident
Hairy woodpecker (*Picoides villosus*)	R	n/a	R	R	R	Tf	Resident
Three-toed woodpecker (*Picoides tridactylus*)	U	U	U	U	U	Tf	Resident
Black-backed woodpecker (*Picoides arcticus*)	R	R	R	R	R	Tf	Resident
Northern flicker (*Colaptes auratus*)	FC	FC	FC	FC	n/a	Tf	Resident

	SPRING	SUMMER	BREEDING	FALL	WINTER	HABITAT	MIGRATION STATUS
FLYCATCHERS							
Olive-sided flycatcher (*Contopus cooperi*)	U	U	U	U	n/a	Tf	Complete Migrant
Yellow-bellied flycatcher (*Empidonaz flaviventris*)	n/a	O	n/a	n/a	n/a	S, Tf	Complete Migrant
Western wood-pewee (*Contopus sordidulus*)	U	U	U	U	n/a	Tf	Complete Migrant
Alder flycatcher (*Empidonax alnorum*)	U	U	U	U	n/a	S, Tf	Complete Migrant
Hammond's flycatcher (*Empidonax hammondii*)	R	R	R	n/a	n/a	Tf	Complete Migrant
Black phoebe (*Sayornis nigricans*)	n/a	X	n/a	n/a	n/a	n/a	Complete Migrant
Say's phoebe (*Sayornis saya*)	FC	FC	FC	FC	n/a	Rr	Complete Migrant
SHRIKES							
Northern shrike (*Lanius excubitor*)	U	U	U	U	O	S, Tf	Resident, Partial Migrant
JAYS, CROWS							
Gray jay (*Perisoreus canadensis*)	A	A	A	A	A	S, Tf	Resident
Steller's jay (*Cyanocitta stelleri*)	n/a	X	n/a	n/a	n/a	Tf	Complete Migrant
Black-billed magpie (*Pica pica*)	C	C	C	C	C	S, Tf	Resident
Common raven (*Corvus corax*)	FC	FC	FC	FC	U	Tf, Rr	Resident
LARKS							
Horned lark (*Eremophilia alpestris*)	C	C	C	C	n/a	At	Complete Migrant
SWALLOWS							
Tree swallow (*Tachycineta bicolor*)	U	U	U	U	n/a	Tf	Complete Migrant
Violet-green swallow (*Tachycineta thalassina*)	C	C	C	C	n/a	Rc, Tf	Complete Migrant
Bank swallow (*Riparia riparia*)	FC	FC	FC	FC	n/a	Rc, R	Complete Migrant
Barn swallow (*Hirundo rustica*)	R	R	O	R	n/a	n/a	Complete Migrant
Cliff swallow (*Petrochelidon pyrrhonota*)	FC	FC	FC	FC	n/a	Rc, Rr	Complete Migrant
CHICKADEES							
Black-capped chickadee (*Poecile atricapillus*)	FC	U	U	FC	FC	S, Tf	Resident
Boreal chickadee (*Poecile hudsonicus*)	C	C	C	C	C	S, Tf	Resident
NUTHATCHES, CREEPERS							
Red-breasted nuthatch (*Sitta canadensis*)	n/a	n/a	O	O	O	Tf	Irruptive Migrant
Brown creeper (*Certhia americana*)	n/a	O	n/a	O	n/a	Tf	Complete Migrant

	SPRING	SUMMER	BREEDING	FALL	WINTER	HABITAT	MIGRATION STATUS
DIPPERS							
American dipper (*Cinclus mexicanus*)	R	R	R	R	R	Rb, R	Resident
KINGLETS							
Golden-crowned kinglet (*Regulus satrapa*)	n/a	O	n/a	O	n/a	S, Tf	Complete Migrant
Ruby-crowned kinglet (*Regulus calendula*)	C	C	C	FC	n/a	Sf	Complete Migrant
OLD WORLD WARBLERS							
Arctic warbler (*Phylloscopus borealis*)	U	C	C	C	n/a	S	Complete Migrant
THRUSHES, ROBINS							
Northern wheatear (*Oenanthe oenanthe*)	FC	FC	FC	FC	n/a	Rr, At	Complete Migrant
Townsend's solitaire (*Myadestes townsendi*)	U	U	U	U	n/a	Rr, At	Complete Migrant
Gray-cheeked thrush (*Catharus minimus*)	FC	FC	FC	FC	n/a	S, Tf	Complete Migrant
Swainson's thrush (*Catharus ustulatus*)	C	C	C	C	n/a	S, Tf	Complete Migrant
Hermit thrush (*Catharus guttatus*)	U	U	U	U	n/a	S, Tf	Complete Migrant
Varied thrush (*Ixoreus naevius*)	C	C	C	C	n/a	Tf	Complete Migrant
American robin (*Turdus migratorius*)	A	A	A	A	n/a	S, Tf	Complete Migrant
WAXWINGS							
Bohemian waxwing (*Bombycilla garrulus*)	U	U	U	U	n/a	Tf	Complete Migrant
STARLINGS							
European starling (*Sturnus vulgaris*)	X	X	n/a	n/a	n/a	n/a	Complete Migrant
PIPITS							
American pipit (*Anhus rubescens*)	A	A	A	A	n/a	At	Complete Migrant
WOOD WARBLERS							
Orange-crowned warbler (*Vermivora celata*)	C	C	C	C	n/a	S, Tf	Complete Migrant
Yellow warbler (*Dendroica petechia*)	U	U	U	FC	n/a	S, Tf	Complete Migrant
Yellow-rumped warbler (*Dendroica coronata*)	A	A	A	A	n/a	S, Tf	Complete Migrant
Townsend's warbler (*Dendroica townsendi*)	O	n/a	n/a	n/a	n/a	Tf	Complete Migrant

	SPRING	SUMMER	BREEDING	FALL	WINTER	HABITAT	MIGRATION STATUS
WOOD WARBLERS (CONTINUED)							
Blackpoll warbler (*Dendroica striata*)	U	U	U	U	n/a	Tf, Rc	Complete Migrant
American redstart (*Setophaga ruticilla*)	X	X	n/a	n/a	n/a	n/a	Complete Migrant
Northern waterthrush (*Seiurus noveboracensis*)	U	R	U	U	n/a	S, Rc	Complete Migrant
Wilson's warbler (*Wilsonia pusilla*)	C	C	C	C	n/a	S	Complete Migrant
TANAGERS							
Western tanager (*Piranga ludoviciana*)	n/a	X	n/a	n/a	n/a	n/a	Complete Migrant
SPARROWS, LONGSPURS, BUNTINGS							
American tree sparrow (*Spizella arborea*)	A	A	A	A	n/a	S, At	Complete Migrant
Savannah sparrow (*Passerculus sandwichensis*)	C	C	C	C	n/a	Mt, At	Complete Migrant
Fox sparrow (*Passerella iliaca*)	C	C	C	C	n/a	S	Complete Migrant
Lincoln's sparrow (*Melospiza lincolnii*)	U	FC	FC	U	n/a	S	Complete Migrant
White-crowned sparrow (*Zonotrichia leucophrys*)	A	A	A	A	n/a	S	Complete Migrant
Golden-crowned sparrow (*Zonotrichia atricapilla*)	U	U	U	U	n/a	S	Complete Migrant
Dark-eyed junco (*Junco hyemalis*)	A	A	A	A	n/a	S, Tf	Complete Migrant
Lapland longspur (*Calcarius lapponicus*)	C	C	C	C	n/a	At	Complete Migrant
Smith's longspur (*Calcarius pictus*)	n/a	O	n/a	n/a	n/a	Mt	Complete Migrant
Snow bunting (*Plectrophenax nivalis*)	FC	FC	FC	FC	n/a	At, Rr	Complete Migrant
BLACKBIRDS							
Red-winged blackbird (*Agelaius phoeniceus*)	n/a	O	n/a	O	n/a	Lpw	Complete Migrant
Rusty blackbird (*Euphagus carolinus*)	U	R	R	U	n/a	Lpw	Complete Migrant
Brown-headed cowbird (*Molothrus ater*)	X	X	n/a	n/a	n/a	n/a	Complete Migrant

	SPRING	SUMMER	BREEDING	FALL	WINTER	HABITAT	MIGRATION STATUS
FINCHES							
Gray-crowned rosy finch (*Leucosticte tephrocotis*)	FC	FC	FC	FC	n/a	At, Rr	Complete Migrant
Pine grosbeak (*Pinicola enucleator*)	U	U	U	U	U	Tf	Irruptive Migrant
White-winged crossbill (*Loxia leucoptera*)	U	U	U	U	U	Tf	Irruptive Migrant
Common redpoll (*Carduelis flammea*)	C	C	C	C	C	S, Tf	Resident
Hoary redpoll (*Carduelis hornemanni*)	R	n/a	n/a	R	R	S, Tf	Irruptive Migrant
Pine siskin (*Carduelis pinus*)	U	U	n/a	U	n/a	Tf	Irruptive Migrant

PLANTS OF DENALI

Denali National Park's subarctic environment limits the number of species that can survive in this northern region. The park's 6 million acres are home to only about 650 species of flowering plants; the number of species jumps to more than 1500 if mosses, lichens, and liverworts are included. A similar-sized area in the tropical locale of Costa Rica supports more than 9000 plant species. Trees, shrubs, wildflowers, and berry plants belonging to Denali's taiga forest and alpine tundra communities are summarized below. Valuable references are listed under "Recommended Reading."

Common Plants of the Taiga Forest Community
Trees and Shrubs
Pine Family
❏ White spruce   (*Picea glauca*)
❏ Black spruce   (*Picea mariana*)
❏ Common juniper   (*Juniperus communis*)

Willow Family
❏ Willow   (*Salix* sp.)
❏ Quaking aspen   (*Populus tremuloides*)
❏ Balsam poplar   (*Populus balsamifera*)

Birch Family
❏ Dwarf birch   (*Betula nana*)
❏ Alaska paper birch   (*Betula papyrifera*)
❏ American green alder   (*Alnus crispa*)

Saxifrage Family
❏ Northern red currant   (*Ribes triste*)

Rose Family
❏ Shrubby cinquefoil   (*Potentilla fruiticosa*)
❏ Prickly rose   (*Rosa acicularis*)

Oleaster Family
❏ Soapberry   (*Shepherdia canadensis*)

Crowberry Family
❏ Crowberry   (*Empetrum nigrum*)

Heath Family
- ❏ Labrador tea   (*Sedum palustre*)
- ❏ Kinnikinnik   (*Arctostaphylos uva-ursi*)
- ❏ Red bearberry   (*Arctostaphylos rubra*)
- ❏ Blueberry   (*Vaccinium uliginosum*)
- ❏ Lingonberry   (*Vaccinium vitis-idaea*)

Honeysuckle Family
- ❏ Highbush cranberry   (*Viburnum edule*)

Wildflowers
Lily Family
- ❏ Death camas   (*Zygadenus elegans*)

Orchid Family
- ❏ Northern green orchid   (*Platanthera hyperborea*)

Sandalwood Family
- ❏ Bastard toadflax   (*Comandra umbellata*)

Crowfoot Family
- ❏ Pasque flower   (*Pulsatilla patens*)
- ❏ Larkspur   (*Delphinium glaucum*)
- ❏ Monkshood   (*Aconitum delphinifolium*)

Saxifrage Family
- ❏ Grass-of-parnassus   (*Parnassa palustris*)
- ❏ Three-toothed saxifrage   (*Saxifraga tricuspidata*)

Pea Family
- ❏ Milk vetch   (*Astragalus frigidus*)
- ❏ Lupine   (*Lupinus nootkatensis*)
- ❏ Pea vine   (*Hedysarum mackenzii*)

Evening Primrose Family
- ❏ Tall fireweed   (*Epilobium angustifolium*)

Dogwood Family
- ❏ Dwarf dogwood   (*Cornius canadensis*)

Wintergreen Family
☐ Shy maiden   (*Moneses uniflora*)
☐ Large-flowered wintergreen   (*Pyrola grandiflora*)

Gentian Family
☐ Four-parted gentian   (*Gentiana propingua*)

Phlox Family
☐ Tall Jacob's ladder   (*Polemonium acutiflorum*)

Borage Family
☐ Bluebells   (*Campanula rotundifolia*)

Honeysuckle Family
☐ Twinflower   (*Linnea borealis*)

Valerian Family
☐ Valerian   (*Valeriana capitata*)

Composite Family
☐ Yarrow   (*Achillea borealis*)
☐ Arnica   (*Arnica latifolia*)
☐ Siberian aster   (*Aster sibiricus*)
☐ Arrowleaf sweet coltsfoot   (*Petasites sagittatus*)
☐ Black-tipped groundsel   (*Senecio lugens*)
☐ Goldenrod   (*Solidago multiradiata*)

Common Plants of Alpine Meadows and Mountaintops
Clubmoss Family
☐ Fir clubmoss   (*Lycopodium selago*)

Grapefern Family
☐ Moonwort   (*Botrichium lunaria*)

Cypress Family
☐ Mountain juniper   (*Juniperus communis*)

Lily Family
☐ Death camas   (*Zygadenus elegans*)
☐ Alp lily   (*Lloydia serotina*)

Orchid Family
☐ Frog orchid   (*Coeloglossum viride*)

Willow Family
☐ Net-veined willow *(Salix reticulata)*

Buckwheat Family
☐ Pink plume *(Polygonum bistorta)*

Pink Family
☐ Arctic sandwort *(Minuartia arctica)*
☐ Moss campion *(Silene acaulis)*

Buttercup Family
☐ Windflower *(Anemone parviflora)*
☐ Narcissus-flowered anemone *(Anemone narcissiflora)*
☐ Snow buttercup *(Ranunculus nivalis)*
☐ Alpine meadow rue *(Thalictrum alpinum)*

Poppy Family
☐ Macoun's poppy *(Papaver macounii)*

Mustard Family
☐ Purple cress *(Cardamine purpurea)*
☐ Parry's wallflower *(Parrya nudicaulis)*

Stonecrop Family
☐ Roseroot *(Sedum rosea)*

Saxifrage Family
☐ Purple mountain saxifrage *(Saxifraga oppositifolia)*
☐ Spiderplant *(Saxifraga flagellaris)*
☐ Prickly saxifrage *(Saxifraga tricuspidata)*
☐ Kotzebue grass of parnassus *(Parnassia kotzebuei)*

Rose Family
☐ Tundra rose *(Potentilla fruticosa)*
☐ One-flowered cinquefoil *(Potentilla uniflora)*
☐ Mountain avens *(Dryas octopetala)*
☐ Prickly rose *(Rosa acicularis)*

Pea Family
☐ Arctic lupine *(Lupinus articus)*
☐ Alpine milk vetch *(Astragalus alpinus)*
☐ Blackish oxytrope *(Oxytropis nigrescens)*

Geranium Family
☐ Wild geranium *(Geranium erianthum)*

Violet Family
☐ Yellow violet   (*Viola biflora*)

Evening Primrose Family
☐ Tall fireweed   (*Epilobium angustifolium*)

Dogwood Family
☐ Dwarf dogwood   (*Cornus canadensis*)

Crowberry Family
☐ Crowberry   (*Empetrum nigrum* ssp.
                                          hermaphroditum)

Heath Family
☐ Lapland rosebay   (*Rhododendron lapponicum*)
☐ Alpine azalea   (*Loiseleuria procumbens*)
☐ Bell heather   (*Cassiope tetragona*)
☐ Lowbush cranberry   (*Vaccinium vitis-idaea*)
☐ Bog blueberry   (*Vaccinium uliginosum*)

Primrose Family
☐ Pixie eyes   (*Primula cuneifolia*)
☐ Rock jasmine   (*Androsace chamaejasme*)
☐ Shooting star   (*Dodecatheon frigidum*)

Gentian Family
☐ Moss gentian   (*Gentiana prostrata*)

Borage Family
☐ Alpine forget-me-not   (*Myosotis alpestris*)

Figwort Family
☐ Kittentails   (*Synthyris borealis*)
☐ Elegant paintbrush   (*Castilleja elegans*)
☐ Capitate lousewort   (*Pedicularis capitata*)
☐ Wooly lousewort   (*Pedicularis lanata*)

Composite Family
☐ Siberian aster   (*Aster sibiricus*)
☐ Arctic goldenrod   (*Solidago multiradiata*)

RECOMMENDED READING

GENERAL NATURAL HISTORY

Armstrong, Robert H., and Marge Hermans. *Alaska's Natural Wonders: A Guide to the Phenomena of the Far North.* Portland, OR: Alaska Northwest Books, 2000.

Ewing, Susan. *The Great Alaska Nature Factbook: A Guide to the State's Remarkable Animals, Plants, and Natural Features,* rev. ed. Portland, OR: Alaska Northwest Books, 2011.

Follows, Don. *Denali: The Story Behind the Scenery.* Wickenburg, AZ: KC Publications, 1997.

Heacox, Kim. *In Denali: A Photographic Essay of Denali National Park and Preserve, Alaska.* Santa Barbara: Companion Press, 1992.

Kavanagh, James. *The Nature of Alaska: An Introduction to Familiar Plants, Animals, and Outstanding Natural Attractions.* Phoenix: Waterford Press, 2005.

Murie, Adolph. *A Naturalist in Alaska.* Tucson: University of Arizona Press, 1990.

National Park Service. *Alaska Park Science: Scientific Studies in Denali.* Anchorage: Alaska Geographic, 2006.

Pielou, E. C. *After the Ice Age: The Return of Life to Glaciated North America.* Chicago: The University of Chicago Press, 1992.

———. *A Naturalist's Guide to the Arctic.* Chicago: The University of Chicago Press, 1995.

Rennick, Penny, ed. *Denali.* Anchorage: Alaska Geographic Society, 1988.

———. *Prehistoric Alaska.* Anchorage: Alaska Geographic Society, 1994.

Sherwonit, Bill. *Denali: A Literary Anthology.* Seattle: The Mountaineers Books, 2000.

Walker, Tom. *Denali Journal,* 20th anniversary edition. Denali: Raven Ridge Press, 2010.

GEOLOGY

Collier, Michael. *Geology of Denali National Park and Preserve*, rev. ed. Anchorage: Alaska Geographic, 2007.

BIRDS

Armstrong, Robert. *Alaska's Birds: A Guide to Selected Species*, 5th ed. Portland, OR: Alaska Northwest Books, 2008.

———. *Guide to the Birds of Alaska*, rev. ed. Portland, OR: Alaska Northwest Books, 2003.

Kertell, Kenneth, and Alan Seegert, with revisions and updates by Carol McIntyre and Alan Seegert. *Bird Checklist of Denali National and Preserve*. (Pamphlet). Anchorage: Alaska Geographic, 2006.

McIntyre, Carol, Nan Eagleson, and Alan Seegert. *Birds of Denali: An Introduction to Selected Species*. Anchorage: Alaska Geographic, 2002.

MAMMALS

McIntyre, Rick. *Grizzly Cub: Five Years in the Life of a Bear*. Portland, OR: Alaska Northwest Books, 1990.

Mech, L. David, et al. *The Wolves of Denali*. Minneapolis: University of Minnesota Press, 1998.

Murie, Adolph. *The Grizzlies of Mount McKinley*. 1981. Reprint. Seattle: University of Washington Press, 2000.

———. *The Wolves of Mount McKinley*. 1944. Reprint. Seattle: University of Washington Press, 2001.

———. *Mammals of Denali*. 1962. Reprint. Anchorage: Alaska Geographic, 1999.

Rawson, Timothy. *Changing Tracks: Predators and Politics in Mt. McKinley National Park*. Fairbanks: University of Alaska Press, 2001.

Sherwonit, Bill. *Alaska's Bears*. Portland, OR: Alaska Northwest Books, 1998.

Smith, Dave. *Alaska's Mammals: A Guide to Selected Species*. Portland, OR: Alaska Northwest Books, 1995.

Van Ballenberghe, Victor. *In the Company of Moose*. Mechanicsburg, PA: Stackpole Books, 2004.

PLANTS

Pratt, Verna E. *Wildflowers of Denali National Park*. Anchorage: Alaskakrafts, 1993.

Schofield, Janice J. *Discovering Wild Plants: Alaska, Western Canada, The Northwest*, rev. ed. Portland, OR: Alaska Northwest Books, 2003.

———. *Alaska's Wild Plants: A Guide to Alaska's Edible Harvest*, rev. ed. Portland, OR: Alaska Northwest Books, 2003.

Viereck, Les. *Alaska Trees and Shrubs*, 2nd ed. Fairbanks: University of Alaska Press, 2007.

HUMAN HISTORY

Brown, William. *Denali, Symbol of the Alaskan Wild: An Illustrated History of the Denali-Mount McKinley Region, Alaska*. Anchorage: Alaska Geographic, 1993.

Haigh, Jane. *Searching for Fannie Quigley: A Wilderness Life in the Shadow of Mount McKinley*. Chicago: Swallow Press, 2007.

Pearson, Grant. *My Life of High Adventure*. Englewood Cliffs, NJ: Prentice-Hall, 1962. Original is out of print. New edition with contributions by Philip Newill published by Literary Licensing, 2011.

Sheldon, Charles. *The Wilderness of Denali*. Lanham, MD: Derrydale Press, 2000.

Sherwonit, Bill. *Denali: A Literary Anthology*. Seattle: The Mountaineers Books, 2000.

Walker, Tom. *Kantishna Mushers, Miners, Mountaineers: The Pioneer Story Behind Mount McKinley National Park*. Missoula, MT: Pictorial Histories Publishing Company, 2005.

———. *McKinley Station: People of the Pioneer Park*. Missoula, MT: Pictorial Histories Publishing, 2009.

Wickersham, James. *Old Yukon: Tales, Trails, and Trials*. Fairbanks: University of Alaska Press, 2009.

MOUNTAINEERING

Expedition Planning

Coombs, Colby. *Denali's West Buttress: A Climber's Guide to Mount McKinley's Classic Route*. Seattle: The Mountaineers Books, 1997.

Roper, Steve, and Allen Steck. *Fifty Classic Climbs of North America*. San Francisco: Sierra Club Books, 1979.

Secor, R. J. *Denali Climbing Guide*. Mechanicsburg, PA: Stackpole Books, 1998.

Waterman, Jonathan. *Surviving Denali: A Study of Accidents on Mount McKinley 1910–1990*. New York: The American Alpine Club, 1991.

———. *High Alaska: A Historical Guide to Denali, Mount Foraker & Mount Hunter*. New York: The American Alpine Club, 1988.

Mountaineering History and Adventure

Beckey, Fred. *Mount McKinley: Icy Crown of North America*. Seattle: The Mountaineers Books, 1999.

Davidson, Art. *Minus 148°: First Winter Ascent of Mount McKinley*. Seattle: The Mountaineers Books, 2013.

Moore, Terris. *Mt. McKinley: The Pioneer Climbs*. Seattle: The Mountaineers Books, 1981.

Roberts, David. *The Mountain of My Fear and Deborah: Two Mountaineering Classics*. Seattle: The Mountaineers Books, 2012.

Sherwonit, Bill. *To the Top of Denali: Climbing Adventures on North America's Highest Peak*, rev. ed. Portland, OR: Alaska Northwest Books, 2012.

———. *Alaska Ascents: World Class Mountaineers Tell Their Stories*. Portland, OR: Alaska Northwest Books, 1996.

Stuck, Hudson. *The Ascent of Denali: A Narrative of the First Complete Ascent of the Highest Peak in North America*. New York: Charles Scribner's Sons, 1914. Now reprinted by several presses.

Tabor, James. *Forever on the Mountain: The Truth Behind One of Mountaineering's Most Controversial and Mysterious Disasters*. New York: W. W. Norton & Co., 2008.

Walker, Tom. *The Seventymile Kid: The Lost Legacy of Harry Karstens and the First Ascent of Mount McKinley*. Seattle: The Mountaineers Books, 2013.

Washburn, Barbara, Bradford Washburn, and Lew Freedman. *The Accidental Adventurer: Memoir of the First Woman to Climb Mount McKinley*. Kenmore, WA: Epicenter Press Inc., 2001.

Washburn, Bradford, and David Roberts. *Mount McKinley: The Conquest of Denali*. New York: Harry N. Abrams, Inc., 1991.

Waterman, Jon. *In the Shadow of Denali: Life and Death on Alaska's Mount McKinley*. Guilford, CT: Lyons Press, 2009.

ENTRANCE AREA
Hiking, Natural History

Capps, Kris. *Denali Walks*. Anchorage: Alaska Geographic, 2007.

River Running

Embick, Andy. *Fast & Cold: A Guide to Alaska Whitewater*. Valdez: Valdez Alpine Books, 1994.

Jettmar, Karen. *The Alaska River Guide: Canoeing, Kayaking, and Rafting in the Last Frontier*, 3rd ed. Birmingham, AL: Menasha Ridge Press, 2008.

DRIVING THE DENALI PARK ROAD

Capps, Kris. *Denali Road Guide*. Anchorage: Alaska Geographic, 2005.

BACKCOUNTRY
Hiking and Backcountry Navigation

Littlepage, Dean. *Hiking Alaska*, 2nd ed. Helena, MT: Falcon Press, 2006.

Nierenberg, Jon. *Backcountry Companion: Denali National Park and Preserve*. Denali National Park: Alaska Natural History Association, 2001.

Waits, Ike. *Denali National Park, Alaska: Guide to Hiking, Photography, and Camping in Denali National Park, Alaska*, 3rd ed. Anchorage: Wild Rose Guidebooks, 2010.

Safe Behavior in Bear Country

Herrero, Stephen. *Bear Attacks: Their Causes and Avoidance*, 2nd ed. Guilford, CT: Lyons Press, 2002.

Smith, Dave. *Backcountry Bear Basics: The Definitive Guide to Avoiding Unpleasant Encounters*, 2nd ed. Seattle: The Mountaineers Books, 2006.

Maps

Denali National Park and Preserve (1:225,000 scale). Anchorage: Alaska Geographic, 2007.

Alaska Atlas & Gazetteer (1:300,000 scale). Yarmouth, ME: DeLorme Mapping, 2010.

SOUTH DENALI

History, General Interest

Brown, William. *Denali, Symbol of the Alaskan Wild: An Illustrated History of the Denali–Mount McKinley Region, Alaska*. Anchorage: Alaska Geographic, 1993.

Greiner, James. *Wager with the Wind: The Don Sheldon Story*. 1974. Reprint. New York: St. Martin's Press, 1982.

Leo, Richard. *Way Out Here: Modern Life in Ice-Age Alaska*. Seattle: Sasquatch Books, 1996.

Rennick, Penny, ed. *Alaska's Railroads*. Anchorage: Alaska Geographic Society, 1992.

Sheldon, Roberta. *The Heritage of Talkeetna*, rev. ed. Talkeetna: Talkeetna Editions, 2008.

Guides

Embick, Andy. *Fast & Cold: A Guide to Alaska Whitewater*. Valdez: Valdez Alpine Books, 1994.

Jettmar, Karen. *The Alaska River Guide: Canoeing, Kayaking, and Rafting in the Last Frontier*, 3rd ed. Birmingham, AL: Menasha Ridge Press, 2008.

Limeres, Rene, and Gunnar Pedersen. *The Complete Guide to Alaska Fishing*. San Francisco: Foghorn Press, 1995.

Littlepage, Dean. *Hiking Alaska*, 2nd ed. Helena, MT: Falcon Press, 2006.

Nienhueser, Helen, and John Wolfe. *55 Ways to the Wilderness in Southcentral Alaska*, 5th ed. Seattle: The Mountaineers Books, 2002.

Sherwonit, Bill. *Alaska's Accessible Wilderness: A Traveler's Guide to Alaska's State Parks*. Portland, OR: Alaska Northwest Books, 1996.

WINTER IN DENALI
Mushing
Fortier, Karen. *Sled Dogs of Denali National Park*. Anchorage: Alaska Geographic, 2002.

Natural History
Armstrong, Robert H., and Marge Hermans. *Alaska's Natural Wonders: A Guide to the Phenomena of the Far North*. Portland, OR: Alaska Northwest Books, 2000.

Forrest, Louise R. *Field Guide to Tracking Animals in Snow*. Harrisburg, PA: Stackpole Books, 1988.

Hall, Calvin, Daryl Pederson, and George Bryson. *Northern Lights: The Science, Myth, and Wonder of Aurora Borealis*. Seattle: Sasquatch Books, 2001.

Winter Adventures
Collins, Julie, and Miki Collins. *Riding the Wild Side of Denali*. Kenmore, WA: Epicenter Press, 1998.

Miller, Daryl. "The Alaskan Mile." *The American Alpine Journal* 38 no. 70 (1996): 79–87. Golden, CO: American Alpine Club, 1996.

INDEX

Bold page numbers indicate maps; italic page numbers indicate photographs.

293

ABOUT THE AUTHOR

Born in Bridgeport, Connecticut, in 1950, author Bill Sherwonit fell in love with the Denali region soon after settling in Alaska in the early 1980s. Denali's wild riches and wilderness spirit have pulled him back almost every year since then. In 1987 he reached The High One's summit, but more typically he explores Denali National and State Parks' lower hills and valleys.

Sherwonit has contributed to a wide range of magazines, journals, newspapers, and anthologies. He is also the author of thirteen books about Alaska; his most recent books include *Living with Wildness: An Alaskan Odyssey* and *Changing Paths: Travels and Meditations in Alaska's Arctic Wilderness*. He's also the author of two other books about the Denali experience: *To the Top of Denali: Climbing Adventures on North America's Highest Peak* (a newly revised and updated edition was published in 2012) and *Denali: A Literary Anthology*.

A resident of Anchorage since 1982, Sherwonit continues to explore and write about the wild nature to be found throughout Alaska, from remote backcountry wilderness to his adopted hometown. For more information about his writing, visit his website at www.billsherwonit.alaskawriters.com.

THE MOUNTAINEERS, founded in 1906, is a nonprofit outdoor activity and conservation organization whose mission is "to explore, study, preserve, and enjoy the natural beauty of the outdoors..." Based in Seattle, Washington, it is now one of the largest such organizations in the United States, with seven branches throughout Washington State.

The Mountaineers sponsors both classes and year-round outdoor activities in the Pacific Northwest, which include hiking, mountain climbing, ski-touring, snowshoeing, bicycling, camping, canoeing and kayaking, nature study, sailing, and adventure travel. The Mountaineers' conservation division supports environmental causes through educational activities, sponsoring legislation, and presenting informational programs.

All activities are led by skilled, experienced volunteers, who are dedicated to promoting safe and responsible enjoyment and preservation of the outdoors.

If you would like to participate in these organized outdoor activities or programs, consider a membership in The Mountaineers. For information and an application, write or call The Mountaineers Program Center, 7700 Sand Point Way NE, Seattle, WA 98115-3996; phone 206-521-6001; visit www.mountaineers .org; or email info@mountaineers.org.

The Mountaineers Books, an active, nonprofit publishing program of The Mountaineers, produces guidebooks, instructional texts, historical works, natural history guides, and works on environmental conservation. All books produced by The Mountaineers Books fulfill the mission of The Mountaineers. Visit www.mountaineersbooks.org to find details about all our titles and the latest author events, as well as videos, web clips, links, and more!

The Mountaineers Books
1001 SW Klickitat Way, Suite 201
Seattle, WA 98134
800-553-4453
mbooks@mountaineersbooks.org

The Mountaineers Books is proud to be a corporate sponsor of The Leave No Trace Center for Outdoor Ethics, whose mission is to promote and inspire responsible outdoor recreation through education, research, and partnerships. The Leave No Trace program is focused specifically on human-powered (nonmotorized) recreation.

Leave No Trace strives to educate visitors about the nature of their recreational impacts and offers techniques to prevent and minimize such impacts. Leave No Trace is best understood as an educational and ethical program, not as a set of rules and regulations.

For more information, visit www.lnt.org, or call 800-332-4100.

OTHER TITLES YOU MIGHT ENJOY FROM
THE MOUNTAINEERS BOOKS

Denali: A Literary Anthology
Bill Sherwonit
A collection of 23 essays on Denali from well-known writings to undiscovered gems

**The Seventymile Kid:
The Lost Legacy of Harry
Karstens and the First Ascent
of Mount McKinley**
Tom Walker
A retelling of the 1913
Hudson Stuck Expedition,
the first team to stand atop
Mount McKinley, North America's
highest peak

**Minus 148 Degrees: First Winter
Ascent of Mount McKinley**
Art Davidson
A gripping mountaineering classic of
the first winter ascent of Mt. McKinley

**Mac's Field Guide:
Denali National Park**

**Mac's Field Guide:
Alaskan Wildlife**
Craig McGowan
Two-sided, color nature identification
guide with detailed illustrations on a
laminated, waterproof card